J.
KRishNAMURTi
AT About
85 to 90
YRS.

KRISHNAMURTI
THE OPEN DOOR

KRISHNAMURTI
The Open Door

MARY LUTYENS

FARRAR STRAUS GIROUX
NEW YORK

Copyright © 1988 by Mary Lutyens

All rights reserved

First published in 1988 by John Murray Ltd, London

First American printing, 1988

Printed in Great Britain

Library of Congress Cataloging-in-Publication Data
Card Number: 87–046406

With this volume of my biography I complete the task entrusted to me by Krishnamurti who died on February 17, 1986.

Contents

Illustrations

Acknowledgements

It is impossible adequately to thank Mary Zimbalist who copied out for me extracts from her diaries covering the last six years of Krishnamurti's life. Since Krishnamurti asked her several times to write a book about him, what it was like to be with him, what he said etc., I have unreservedly quoted many of his utterances to her. I am also deeply grateful to Dr T. Parchure and Scott Forbes for allowing me to use their invaluable records of Krishnamurti's last illness and death.

The following have sent me written accounts of their recollections of Krishnamurti which have been a great help: Mary Cadogan, Anita Desai, Mark Edwards, Friedrich Grohe, P. Krishna, Jean-Michel Maroger and Stephen Smith.

I also want to thank those who have so patiently helped me by sending newspaper cuttings, cassettes and transcripts of Krishnamurti's talks and discussions or given me permission to quote from their own works or answered my letters of enquiry: David Bohm, Radha Burnier, Asit Chandmal, Jane Hammond, Radhika Herzberger, Mark Lee, Ray McCoy, Sunanda Patwardhan and Bill Taylor.

Copyright in all Krishnamurti's work from 1968 is held by the Krishnamurti Foundation England who have granted permission for all quotations.

Introduction

The bare facts of Krishnamurti's early life are too well known to warrant more than the briefest outline here. Born on May 11, 1895, in the small town of Madanapalle, 180 miles west of Madras, he was the eighth child of strictly vegetarian Brahmin parents. His father, Jiddu Naraniah, was a minor government official. Krishnamurti's mother died when he was ten, and early in 1909 his father retired and moved with his four surviving sons to the international Headquarters of the Theosophical Society at Adyar, Madras, where he was given a secretarial job.

At this time, the majority of Theosophists believed in the near coming of the Lord Maitreya, the World Teacher, and the leaders of the Society had for some years been looking for a body whom the Lord might occupy when he came, as he was said to have occupied the body of Jesus and, two thousand years earlier, that of Sri Krishna.

Soon after Naraniah came to Adyar, Krishnamurti was picked out by Charles Webster Leadbeater, one of the chief lecturers for the Society, who claimed clairvoyance. Leadbeater saw Krishnamurti on the beach at Adyar and declared that his aura was without a trace of selfishness. Leadbeater wrote to his colleague, Mrs Annie Besant, President of the Society, who was then in Europe, to tell her that he believed he had found the 'vehicle' for the Lord. When Mrs Besant returned to India later in the year she endorsed Leadbeater's 'discovery', and not long afterwards obtained Naraniah's consent to adopt Krishnamurti and his younger brother Nitya, from whom he refused to be parted.

In 1911 an organisation was founded by Mrs Besant and Leadbeater called the Order of the Star in the East, of which Krishnamurti was made the Head. This was to prepare the members of the Society for the coming of the Lord Maitreya. In 1912 Mrs Besant took the boys to England and left them there to be educated by Theosophical tutors. They remained in Europe until the end of

1921 when Mrs Besant summoned them back to India for Krishnamurti to begin his mission as a lecturer for Theosophy and the Order of the Star in the East. Krishnamurti returned reluctantly. By that time Nitya, who earlier in the year had contracted tuberculosis, was said by a specialist in Switzerland to be cured. After two months in India the brothers went on to Sydney where Leadbeater had been living as the head of a Theosophical community since 1917. On the voyage to Australia Nitya had a recurrence of his illness so, after a few weeks' stay in Sydney, it was decided that the brothers should return to Switzerland via America.

While breaking their journey at San Francisco, they accepted the loan of a cottage in the Ojai Valley, 1,500 feet above sea level and some eighty miles north of Los Angeles—a valley that was recommended as being particularly beneficial to consumptives.

The brothers remained there at Pine Cottage, as it was called, for the next eleven months. In August 1922, not long after they arrived at the cottage, Krishnamurti underwent a spiritual experience that completely transformed his life. This experience was followed by excruciating pain in his head and spine, which came to be known as 'the process' and which continued on and off for many years when he was not travelling or giving talks. In October 1922 the cottage and six acres of land and a larger house, which they called Arya Vihara, were bought for the brothers by a trust set up by Mrs Besant. In June 1923, when the brothers at last returned to Europe, Nitya was again pronounced cured, but he was to have a relapse the following year and to die in November 1925—an overwhelming grief for Krishnamurti.

Nevertheless, Krishnamurti continued to pursue his mission—with enthusiasm now since his transforming experience—travelling, giving talks in Europe, India, Australia and America, and holding gatherings at Castle Eerde at Ommen in Holland, an eighteenth-century castle and large estate given for his work by Baron Philip van Pallandt. All the while he was gradually evolving his own philosophy. In April 1927 Mrs Besant declared to the press: 'The World Teacher is here.'

It was a great shock to all the leaders of Theosophy and to most of Krishnamurti's followers when in August 1929 at the Ommen Gathering, Krishnamurti, in the presence of Mrs Besant and 3,000

Star members, dissolved the Order of the Star*. He never actually denied being the World Teacher; he said, 'I do not care if you believe I am the World Teacher or not. That is of very little importance. . . . I do not want you to follow me. . . . You have been accustomed to being told . . . what your spiritual status is. How childish! Who but yourself can tell you if you are beautiful or ugly inside?'¹

*   *   *   *

Krishnamurti told me, when I was writing the second volume of his biography, 'If I was writing the life I would begin with the vacant mind.' Is 'the vacant mind' the clue to the understanding of K (as I shall call him hereafter), both as a man and as a teacher? This vacancy and lack of memory in K has proved a great drawback in recording his life. When writing of a living person there is the handicap of criticism from his friends and contemporaries who all have their own vision of him, but there is usually the counterbalance of his own recollections, whereas in K's case, when he did come out with some memory, one could never be sure whether it was his own or merely something somebody had told him. On the other hand, can any religious or philosophical teacher ever have had his public utterances made so abundantly available in books and on audio and video tapes?

In one of the two books K wrote himself (in contrast to his other books which are edited versions of his talks or discussions or were dictated, as were his *Letters to the Schools*), he gave two memories of his boyhood and childhood that seem utterly authentic: 'He [he almost invariably spoke of himself in the third person, usually as K] was standing there [by the river] with no one around, alone, unattached and far away. He was about fourteen. They had found his brother and himself quite recently and all the fuss and sudden importance given to him was around him. Standing there alone, lost and strangely aloof, was his first and lasting remembrance of those days and events. He doesn't remember his childhood, the schools and the caning.'

And again: 'As a young boy he used to sit by himself under a

---

* The annual report of the Order of the Star in the East for 1926 gave the total number of members as 43,000 in forty countries. Only about two-thirds of these were also members of the Theosophical Society.

large tree near a pond in which lotuses grew; they were pink and had a strong smell. From the shade of that spacious tree he would watch the green snakes and the chameleons, the frogs and the water snakes.'

In the same book he wrote about himself: 'He has never been hurt, though many things happened to him, flattery and insult, threat and security. It was not that he was insensitive, unaware: he had no image of himself, no conclusion, no ideology.'[2]

There is, however, another and more important source of personal memories. In the summer of 1913 in Normandy he was set to write an essay by one of his tutors on 'Fifty Years of my Life'. He made it autobiographical, intending to add to it year by year. All that was actually written was some 3,500 words giving a sketch of his life up till 1911. This firsthand account is very valuable since it shows that at eighteen his memory seems to have been as clear as anyone else's. It also shows that at the time of his mother's death in 1905 he was clairvoyant. This was confirmed by his father.[3]

The death of his mother when he was ten must have caused K bewildered grief for he was particularly close to her, having been so often prevented from going to school by recurrent bouts of malaria. The move to Adyar might not have affected him much since his father's job as a rent collector had necessitated several moves from one place to another. But the change in his life when Leadbeater took him up was dramatic. It has often been emphasised that Leadbeater 'discovered' him from the beauty of his aura and not from his appearance because with Leadbeater's homosexual predilections (he had been involved in a homosexual scandal in 1906) the 'discovery' of a beautiful young boy would not have been remarkable. According to contemporary accounts K was undernourished and scrawny, with lice even in his eyebrows, mosquitobites all over him and crooked teeth. (His teeth were still being straightened after he went to England in 1912.) With his head shaved in front to the crown and falling to his knees in a pigtail at the back, he could not have been a prepossessing figure in spite of his wonderful eyes. A slatternly aunt looked after the household. K had had two sisters but one had died before his mother and the other was married and lived with her husband's family. K himself said that if he had not been taken up by Leadbeater he would almost certainly have died. If K was indeed the eighth child of his parents, four other children must have died as well as his sister, for he had only his married sister and one older brother living. His other two brothers were younger.

A photograph of K taken in January 1910 shows what an extraordinary change must have taken place in his appearance in the eleven months since he was 'discovered'. It is the picture of a boy of perfect beauty. But by then his hair had grown and his physical strength had been built up by very long bicycle rides, swimming, tennis, exercises on parallel bars and what was considered to be nourishing food, with a great deal of milk, most unsuitable for an Indian body accustomed to milk only in the form of curd. (In consequence of having so much milk and porridge forced down him, K suffered agonies of indigestion right up to 1916.)

Mrs Besant was on a seven-month tour of America and Europe at the time K was 'discovered'. It was not until November 27, 1909 that she arrived back in Madras and met K for the first time. By then he and his brother Nitya, three years younger, on whom K was deeply dependent, had been taken away from school, where K was beaten almost every day because of his inability to learn, and were being taught by two Englishmen, an Indian and an Italian as well as by Leadbeater himself. (Later on another Indian, B. Shiva Rao, became an extra tutor.) The emphasis was on English in the hope that K would be able to speak to Mrs Besant in that language when she arrived. Although it was necessary for K to learn English if he was to become the World Teacher, it seems a great pity that he was allowed to forget his native Telegu and taught no other Indian language beyond a smattering of Sanscrit. When Mrs Besant read aloud to the two boys it was English books. *The Jungle Books* and *The Scarlet Pimpernel* were two K remembered in his essay and 'enjoyed very much'. The Shakespeare plays she also read to them were not commented on.

From the moment Mrs Besant, then aged sixty-two, first saw K on the station platform at Madras she loved him and continued to love him until her death, a feeling that was reciprocated. She was the only person he never forgot throughout his life, even though she died in 1934; he always spoke of her with reverence and devotion. (He referred to her always as Dr Besant although she had only an honorary degree conferred on her by the Hindu University at Benares in 1921.)

Introduction

The statement in Pupul Jayakar's recent memoir of Krishnamurti that Leadbeater 'certainly demanded a Brahmin body' for the 'vehicle' is not borne out by the facts.[4] Mrs Besant in a public lecture in Chicago in 1909 on her favourite subject, 'The Coming Teacher', had announced, 'We look for him to come in the Western World this time—not in the East as did Christ two thousand years ago.' Indeed, the Western vehicle had already been chosen by Leadbeater. This was a good-looking American boy, Hubert van Hook, son of Dr Weller van Hook of Chicago. Leadbeater had picked him out while on a lecture tour of America a few years before and had brought him to Europe where Mrs Besant had met him. When Mrs Besant saw him again in Chicago in 1909 she was so struck by him that she persuaded his mother to leave her husband and take him to Adyar to be trained by Leadbeater for his stupendous role. At the very time K was 'discovered', Mrs van Hook and Hubert were on their way to Madras, never dreaming that Hubert had been supplanted.

What poor Hubert's feelings were can be imagined. Nevertheless, he and his mother remained at Adyar for five years. He was allowed to share K's lessons and play tennis with him but forbidden by Leadbeater to touch K's tennis racquet or bicycle for fear of contamination. When interviewed in later life Hubert expressed great bitterness.[5] It is doubtful whether K was aware at the time that there had been a prior choice. Hubert was a very clever boy and it is possible that Leadbeater considered that K's 'vacant mind' would be more malleable than Hubert's

*   *   *   *

In the first volume of my biography of K, I gave a detailed account of his life up to 1929 when at the age of thirty-four he dissolved the Order of the Star and resigned from the Theosophical Society. The story was told largely in his very personal letters to my mother who, during the years of his education in England, was the person he loved most and the only one he wanted to be with. The second volume, which brought his life up to 1980, was concerned with the flowering of his teaching, the new friendships and relationships he formed and his travels practically all over the world, giving public talks in order to pass on to others the solution he had found for the ending of sorrow and the conflict of mankind.

6

Introduction

K saw the outer conflict in the world as being inseparable from the inner conflict in man. Society was the result of the individual and the individual the result of society; therefore we are, each one of us, responsible for all the horror and sorrow in the world and, because every human being on earth suffers from the world's suffering, we share a consciousness with the rest of humanity and are not really individuals at all except superficially. No ideologies, no religions, no authorities, no social reforms can ever end conflict and sorrow; the only thing that can is a complete mutation of each human psyche, a stepping out of the river of human consciousness, a change in the very brain cells themselves. And the mutation has to be instantaneous; it is useless *trying* to change, for what we are today we will inevitably be tomorrow.

It was to discover how this mutation could be brought about that people came to K's talks year after year, read his books, listened to his audio tapes and watched him on video. What he had to say was sometimes so difficult to express in words that he could only attempt to say what it was by saying what it was not. For instance, in trying to come upon what love is, he wrote:

> . . . fear is not love, dependence is not love, jealousy is not love, possessiveness and domination are not love, responsibility and duty are not love, self-pity is not love, love is not the opposite of hate any more than humility is the opposite of vanity. So if you can eliminate all these, not by forcing them but by washing them away as the rain washes the dust of many days from a leaf, then perhaps you will come upon this strange flower which man always hungers after.[6]

However, he had no difficulty in finding words for the nature of *in-loveness*. Someone confessed to him, 'I have fallen in love, but I know there is no future in this relationship. It is a situation I have experienced many times before, yet I am desperately unhappy without this person. How can I get myself out of this state?' K's response was:

> The loneliness, the bleakness, wretchedness you feel without this person existed before you fell in love. What you call love is mere stimulation, the temporary covering-up of your own emptiness. You escaped from loneliness through a person, used this person to cover it up. Your problem is not this relationship but rather it is the problem of your own emptiness. . . . It is because you have no love in you that you continually look for love to fill you from the outside.[7]

Introduction

The nearest one will probably ever come to K's consciousness is in the extraordinary document he wrote in 1960–62. One or two of the people close to him were opposed to the publication of this manuscript, fearing that it would dishearten his followers since it showed that he was not like other men; he seemed to live in a different dimension, so how could ordinary people hope to become like him, hope to bring about a transformation in themselves? He answered this question when he said, 'We do not all have to be Edisons to turn on the electric light' and 'Christopher Columbus went to America in a sailing ship; we can go by jet.'[8]

What we gather from this manuscript, published under the title *Krishnamurti's Notebook*, is that what K called 'the benediction', 'the immensity', 'the sacredness', 'the vastness' and, most often, 'the otherness' or 'the other', was with him almost continuously. What was 'the other'? He always had a sense of being protected. Was it 'the other' that protected him? Did he come to 'the other' or did 'the other' come to him? In the same way it had been asked in 1927: did K's consciousness blend with that of the Lord Maitreya or did the Lord's consciousness blend with K's? At any rate, 'the other' was not personalised. Was it a power from a source from which all genius is drawn?

As for 'the vacant mind', already referred to, it was not difficult to believe in as I first remember him in about 1914. At times he was so vague and dreamy that he would start violently if suddenly spoken to; he seemed miles away just standing there; he hardly ever sat down except at meals. Yet in some moods he and Nitya would laugh and joke and generally play the fool, moods in which we children delighted. He would sometimes read P. G. Wodehouse or Stephen Leacock aloud to us, laughing so much that he could hardly get his words out. I can recall him so clearly, standing leaning against the bookcase in our drawing-room reading aloud 'Gertrude the Governess' (a particular favourite from *Nonsense Novels*), most of the story lost in his gales of laughter.

His love of laughing never left him, but the extreme vagueness did not last after his experience at Ojai in 1922 except in the sense that he never carried over from one day to another the burden of the past, and that often immediately before addressing an audience he had not the least idea what he was going to say. In the summer of 1924, when he first started talking privately to four girls of whom I, just sixteen, was the youngest, he was tinglingly alive and enthusiastic, telling us that we must change radically, what *'fun'* it was to change. The motive for change was different in those days; it was in order to become a pupil of the Master* so that we would be better fitted to serve the World Teacher when he came, whereas in later years it was in order to save the world from sorrow and self-destruction; but the need for a total transformation was just as urgent. We were staying with Nitya, my mother and a few other friends of K's in a castle-hotel on the top of a mountain at Pergine near Trento. K was twenty-nine then and Nitya twenty-six. K would talk to us all in the mornings in a field below the castle after we had played a game of rounders or volley-ball, but he spoke privately to the four girls in the afternoons because it was these four who were to go to Sydney in a few months' time, at K's wish, to be 'brought on' along the Path of Discipleship by Leadbeater.

K spoke of the need for passionate feeling. An intellectual concept merely of the World Teacher was useless. It was 'the power to fall in love, to give oneself completely' that he found so lacking, especially in older people. We must not suppress feeling but sublimate it. 'Say to yourself', he told us, 'that I have every feeling in the world but they are all subservient to my will.' We must put aside all personal desires. Cleanliness, both physical and mental, was essential if we were to become pupils of the Master, but above all 'greatness in thought and feeling'. The worst thing was to be mediocre. You could rise to the highest position in the land and still be mediocre—it was a matter of *being*, not accomplishment. This horror of mediocrity ran through K's teaching all his life. (A month before his death he was telling the children at Rishi Valley, the oldest of his Indian schools, what the world mediocre meant and explaining to them that even if they became Prime Minister they could still be mediocre.)

It was much harder for the young people around K in those early days than it was for his young devotees later on. He told us that

---

* Most Theosophists at that time believed in the Masters, the Mahatmas, who had chosen to remain in human incarnation in order to help humanity along the path to perfection instead of passing into Nirvana. They were said to live in a valley in Tibet and could be visited in one's astral form on the astral plane. Two of these Masters, Kuthumi and Morya, held the Theosophical Society under their special protection and were willing to accept pupils if of sufficient spiritual development. Only Leadbeater could tell one when one had been accepted by a Master.

although it was only human nature to want an ordinary life with a husband, children and a home of our own we could not have any of those things and serve the Lord Maitreya too. These young girls were being urged to lead a celibate life outside a nunnery.

K's attitude to sex changed as time went on. In 1969 he was writing:

Why have you made sex a problem? Really it doesn't matter at all whether you go to bed with someone or whether you don't. Get on with it or drop it but don't make a problem of it. The problem comes from this constant preoccupation. The really interesting thing is not whether we do or don't go to bed with someone but why we have all these fragments in our lives. In one restless corner there is sex with all its preoccupations; in another corner there is some other kind of turmoil; in another a striving after this or that, and in each corner there is the continual chattering of the mind. There are so many ways in which energy is wasted.[9]

And three years later he was saying to a group of his followers: 'They used to tell me in my youth, you must be a perfect instrument, in what you do, what you say and how you write. Then only can the teacher use it [the body]. And you are saying exactly the same thing in a different way: "You must show that you lead a perfect life" . . . You're prejudiced, you're conditioned. You say, "He must not sleep with somebody. He must not tell a lie. He must be vegetarian. He must be etc. etc." That's your conditioning. Concern yourself with your own conditioning.' It was the teaching that K was concerned with, not the personality of the teacher. 'Why do you bother whether the teacher is this, that, blue-eyed, purple-eyed or long-haired? When the house is burning you don't enquire into the colour of the man that set it on fire.'[10]

Given below are some extracts copied verbatim from the diary I kept at Pergine; they show what the pressure from K was like on young people in those early years:

September 1 [*1924*]. Today I went over to rest at the Square Tower and there had over an hour's conversation with Krishna. He began as he always does, 'Well, Mary,' repeated at intervals while I remain inarticulate and look stupid. He wanted then to know why I wished to become a pupil of the Master. He wanted to make quite sure that it was not because everyone around was trying to become one and I wanted to have a shot at it. I tried to convince him that this was not so. I must say he seemed to understand wonderfully—and he has the great power of making things appear almost

Introduction

ludicrously simple. He said that one of the first things was to have an open mind—which I had not got—for it was almost disgraceful that I had so many prejudices and fixed opinions which formed terrible barriers. He said I had an over-developed mentality but that I had altogether left behind my emotional development. He then asked me a blank question: I desired something, knew what was in the way, was positive of my power to get over the obstacles—so why didn't I get there? A question I have aksed myself many times. In the end he answered it himself—because I had not yet decided it was worth while giving up my whole life. That I did not feel it sufficiently. He said that I had never yet discovered anything strong enough to take me out of myself. He said that I must feel so acutely that I should be able to jump out of the window. He said I was too damned calculating—and like an iceberg.

He said many more things that I cannot remember—but nothing can portray the enthusiasm with which he brought out his similes—the fire which lit up his eyes. I could see the effort he was making to drum his own eagerness into me—I know quite well, as he said, he would give his very life to help ('to make you happy for the rest of your life in whatever you do—I would honestly—I'm not joking—give my life') and yet it was quite impossible for me to respond.

September 5. This afternoon I had another long talk with Krishna and I am going to do my best to put it into words. He was delighted to hear I was feeling beastly—and took it as a good omen. He began as always by saying, 'Well, how's the iceberg getting on?' He pointed out the disadvantages of being unfeeling—and all the selfishness of it. He said I must get rid of the layers of brick I had plumped on the top of my natural instincts—that it was disgraceful to be so lethargic—especially at my age—that I had a heavy body that was in the way—that I gave myself away at every movement—when I played games, walked or talked. The reason for this state of affairs was quite evident. I had seen Betty* getting into tempers etc. and instinctively I had said, 'Well, I shan't let myself be like that.' And now he could see every day I had a feeling of irritation, of affection which was gone in a minute. That this 'self recollectedness' could be of marvellous utility if used in the right way. He said that if I once made up my mind to change—and I must change at once—that I could beat them all—get along with great strides—that he felt this in his bones. He said—'supposing someone comes to you and says they are in love with you, ready to go to the other end of the earth for you—to worship you, what would you do? You'd take it quite calmly and say, "Alright—go on then".' He said that from morning to night he was thinking of me—that even two years ago when he had

* Elisabeth, the sister next to me in age who became a composer. She was one of the four girls at Pergine. The other two were Ruth Roberts and Helen Knothe, an American, who was K's favourite at that time.

woken up to all this, he had thought—will Mary come to it? He said that if only it was assured that we could all be together working in the future that he would be happy—that if I turned from it like Barbie and Robert* it would drive him mad—that he had been fond of me ever since I was a baby but I must, must, must change. He sat there drumming his enthusiasm into me. None of us realise how truly great he is—how that every minute he is sacrificing himself, working, working, working.

September 25. I have had more wonderful talks with Krishna—in one of which he made me weep—urging on me the need for immediate effort in case the vision of the mountain top should fade away. In the last talk it was I who nearly made him weep—and he finished by saying that no one will ever love me as much as he does—that none of us know what real love, real devotion is. That he wanted to see me great, happy and beautiful—and if his had been an ordinary life he would have asked me to marry him long ago.

K was mistaken in thinking I was unfeeling. I was in truth devoured by a secret, very human love for Nitya. From 1926 to 1929 I was very close to K. We had been drawn together by Nitya's death. While I was with him I could live in an ecstasy of sublimated love. My devotion, however, was not able after three years to withstand the temptations of the world during his long absences in India and America, although he wrote frequently, very beautiful letters. When I became engaged to be married in 1929 he was hurt— maybe for a day or two and then for my sake more than for his own—whereas I inflicted on myself a deep injury that lasted for sixteen years. I never, however, lost touch with K; I saw him whenever he came to London and never stopped loving and revering him. It was to be forty years, though, from the time of my first marriage before I started working for him again.

* My only brother and my eldest sister whom Nitya had loved. They had reacted against Theosophy in 1914.

I

Changing the Brain Cells

By the time K dissolved the Order of the Star in 1929 he had experienced many of the feelings of ordinary humanity. He was to forget these completely; nevertheless they must have remained somewhere in his being for him to have been able to help others by such deep understanding of their problems. He had known homesickness and loneliness when he first came to England; he had known disappointment at failing his matriculation examination three times; he had known the misery which other people's jealousy can cause, not only to themselves; he had known loss of faith and disillusionment; he had been in love at twenty-six and known the misery of being separated from his love by duty when Mrs Besant sent for him to return to India in 1921; he had known the acute embarrassment of being openly worshipped and also of being laughed at; he had known adverse publicity; he had known intense physical agony; he had known months of grave anxiety over the health of his beloved brother Nitya; he had known the pain of everything he held most sacred being made ridiculous and vulgar; above all he had known devastating grief at Nitya's death. But no experience had to be repeated for him to learn its full lesson.

When he heard of Nitya's death in 1925 while on board ship bound for Colombo it seemed for ten days that he was shattered. In the words of Shiva Rao, who was sharing a cabin with him, 'At night he would sob and moan and cry out for Nitya, sometimes in his native Telegu which in his waking consciousness he could not speak,' yet when he arrived at Madras twelve days later, another friend recalled that 'his face was radiant; there was not a shadow on it to show what he had been through.'

Before the end of the voyage K had written: 'I have wept but I do not want others to weep but if they do I know now what it means.

13

. . . I know now with greater certainty than ever before that there is real beauty in life, real happiness that cannot be shattered by any physical happening, a great strength which cannot be weakened by passing events, and a great love which is permanent, imperishable and unconquerable.'¹¹

Throughout the war years K remained at Ojai, giving no talks and seeing hardly anyone except the Rajagopals, who lived with him, and Aldous Huxley and his wife who became great friends. Most days K would go for very long walks by himself. These quiet years were, I believe, of supreme importance to him—a period of gestation which resulted in the flowering of his teaching and the writing which, encouraged by Aldous Huxley, was later published as *Commentaries on Living*

*   *   *   *

By himself at Ojai in 1931 K was writing to my mother, 'My being alone like this has given me something tremendous and it's just what I need. Everything has come so far in my life at the right time.'

Everything in his life continued, it seemed, to come just at the right time, at any rate where people were concerned. When he returned to India after the war in 1947, having been away for nine years, he made a new group of friends who were to help incalculably in his work; in the early fifties he made an important new Italian friend, and in 1964 Mary Zimbalist, the widow of Sam Zimbalist the film producer, was to come into his life and be his closest companion and confidante until his death. She was a gentle, elegant, Europeanised American from a well-established New York family. Her father had lived in Paris for some years and she spoke fluent French and seemed at ease in all worlds.

Mary Zibalist is the only person mentioned by name at this stage because it was with her at Ojai in February 1980 that the second volume of my book ended. K was to be eighty-five in May that year and was to live another six fruitful years. He was vigorous in mind and body and had recently undergone a psychic experience in India of which he dictated an account to Mary. He had had 'peculiar meditations' which were 'unpremeditated and grew with intensity', and one night he 'woke up to find something totally different and new. The movement had reached the source of all energy. . . . Desire cannot possibly reach it, words cannot fathom it, nor can the string of thought wind itself round it. One may ask with what assurance do you state that it is the source of all energy? One can only reply with complete humility that it is so.' On returning to Ojai, 'after the body had somewhat rested, there was the perception that there was nothing beyond this.'[12]

At thirty-five K had been the most beautiful human being I could imagine, not only in face but in carriage, suppleness and general air of sparkling inner well-being. In old age he can best be described in the words of a man who was for a few years very close to him:

When one meets him what does one see? Truly, to a superlative degree there is nobility, power, grace and elegance. There is an exquisite breeding, a heightened aesthetic sense, enormous sensitivity and penetrating insight into any problems that one might bring to him. Nowhere in Krishnamurti is there the slightest trace of anything vulgar, mean or commonplace. One may understand his teaching or not understand it; one may perhaps criticize this or that in his actions or his words. But it is not conceivable that anybody could deny the enormous nobility and grace that flow from his person. One could perhaps say that he has a style or a class quite above, quite beyond, the common run of man. No doubt these words would embarrass him. But there you are. His dress, bearing, manners, movement and speech are in the highest sense of the word, princely. When he enters a room someone quite extraordinary is there.

K always felt a dissociation between himself and his body. He had a very special responsibility for his body and looked after it as a cavalry officer might have looked after his horse—a simile that appealed to him. He drove it hard, rarely letting it off its yoga exercises (physical ones only) and long afternoon walks, however tired he was. For many years he did Dr Bates's eye exercises regularly with the result that he never had to wear glasses. He was also extremely strict with his diet. A lifelong vegetarian, though not a vegan, he indulged in no stimulants, not even tea or coffee. The care he took with his clothes was again akin to a cavalry officer's concern with the grooming of a horse. Wherever he went he wore the appropriate clothes for the country or place he was in so as to fade as much as possible into the background. It was not his fault that because of a natural elegance, a natural good taste in clothes and the figure of a young man he stood out wherever he went.

*　　　　*　　　　*　　　　*

In his last years K was deeply concerned with how his work was to be carried on after his death. He was insistent that there should be no interpreters of his teaching, that no one should have authority to speak in his name, that no temple or dogma should be built up around his teaching. 'Truth is not yours or mine,' he said. 'It has no country, no race, it has no people, it has no belief, no dogma. I have repeated this ad nauseam.' But discussion was not interpretation, he averred. 'Discuss, criticise, go into it. Read K's books and intellectually tear it to pieces. Or intellectually go with it. Discuss. That's not interpretation.'[13]

K was particularly anxious that the Foundations he had set up to administer his work should act as one and that the schools he had started in India, England and America should continue to flourish. In his last two years he had become greatly interested in the building of a Krishnamurti adult centre on land belonging to his English school, Brockwood Park, in Hampshire. He wanted it to be quite apart from the school, a quiet place where people seriously concerned with his teaching could go and study it. He also wanted similar centres to be built at Rishi Valley and Rajghat in India.

As K saw violence increasing everywhere in the world, the need for a radical change in the human psyche became ever more urgent before mankind destroyed itself. He was well aware that after all the years he had been speaking to huge audiences in many parts of the world, not one person, certainly not one of those closest to him, had undergone a mutation. Yet if this mutation could take place in only one person, his teaching could go on flowering. He had the idea that the more the members of his Foundations could be brought together and the more they could be with him, the more chance there would be of them working together in harmony as one body.

At the same time during his last six years he wished through discussion to dig deeper and deeper into the significance of life. He welcomed the chance to talk publicly or privately to any man or woman deeply concerned with the problems of living, though he knew it was no good talking to anyone with a didactic or closed mind. Enquiry had to be tentative. For several years he had been holding discussions with scientists and psychologists in the West and with pandits and scholars in the East, both individually and in groups and seminars. He had given newspaper interviews and radio and television broadcasts in several countries but in these it was

impossible to touch more than the surface of his teaching. In so
many of his interviews it was apparent how anxious the interviewers
were to pigeon-hole him, to compare him with some other religious
teacher or philosopher. Raymond Mortimer, who never met him,
once said to me that he could not be a great religious teacher because
he had never read the Gospels!

*   *   *   *

Since 1966 K had not lived at Ojai pending the result of a lawsuit
with Rajagopal who, from the time of Nitya's death, had managed
all his financial affairs, edited his books and arranged for their
publication as the President of a Trust, Krishnamurti Writings
Inc. (KWINC). In the years while the lawsuit dragged on K, when in
California, had stayed with Mary Zimbalist in her beautiful house at
Malibu and had given his annual talks at Santa Monica. He had
dissociated himself from KWINC and set up Krishnamurti Foundations in England, America and India in 1968, '69, and '70
respectively. In 1974 the lawsuit was at last settled out of Court;
KWINC was dissolved and another organisation, K & R Foundation,
of which Rajagopal had control, was formed. This organisation was
to retain the copyright in K's works prior to July 1968.* A hundred
and sixty acres of land at the western end of the valley, including the
Oak Grove where K had held annual gatherings since 1928, and
eleven acres at the upper end, including Pine Cottage where K had
had his mystical experience in 1922, and the larger house close by, Arya
Vihara, were conveyed to the Krishnamurti Foundation of America.

Mary Zimbalist, in accordance with K's wishes (which were
always her own too), sold her house at Malibu and built a house at
Ojai incorporating Pine Cottage. She was not required to pay for
the land but the house would at her death revert to the American
Foundation. It was not until March 1978 that the new house was
ready for her and K to move into, though K had resumed speaking
in the Oak Grove in 1975. At the same time as the house was going
up, a primary day school, the Oak Grove School, adjoining the Oak
Grove, was started. This was the only Krishnamurti school in the
United States.

*   *   *   *

* The copyright in this early work has now reverted to the American Foundation.

On returning from India to Ojai in February 1980, K with his tremendous new energy felt that he was not being 'used enough'. 'What am I to do here for two months?' he asked Mary Zimbalist. 'I am being wasted.' He felt at times that something was calling him from far away. This was a great worry to Mary.

The Secretary of the American Foundation was Erna Lilliefelt. She and her husband, Theodor, were two others who had come into K's life at just the right moment. Without them he would hardly have been able to set up the American Foundation in 1969 or start the Oak Grove School. Erna was the linchpin of the Foundation.

K found much to do, as it happened, in connection with the new Oak Grove School, talking to the staff and parents. Mark Lee, an American who had an Indian wife, a paediatrician, was the first Director of the school. He had previously been Head of the junior school at Rishi Valley and had taught at other schools in California, England and Switzerland. Many parents had moved to the Ojai Valley so that their children might attend the school and they played a much greater part in the running of it than if it had been a boarding school, often causing difficulties.

K was certainly not wasted when in March David Bohm went to stay at Ojai with his wife and started holding discussions with him. David Bohm was Professor of Theoretical Physics at Birkbeck College, London University. He had been a friend of Einstein and had written books on the quantum theory and relativity. His latest book, *Wholeness and the Implicate Order*, published in the summer of 1980, propounding a revolutionary theory of physics in accordance with K's teaching of the wholeness of life, was to be widely recognised for its scientific discoveries. He had attended nearly all K's talks in Europe and California since 1961 and they had already had many discussions together, but during this 1980 visit eight dialogues took place between them in April. These, together with five others which took place at Brockwood Park in June, were published under the title *The Ending of Time*.[14] This has proved to be one of K's most successful publications. The dialogues were edited anonymously, by Mary Cadogan, the Secretary of the English Foundation, who had worked for K since 1958.

Mary Cadogan is herself a successful author,[15] but this was the first book she had edited for Krishnamurti and she was certainly thrown in the deep end. To some people this book reads like a thriller; others find it hard going. It is a conversation with quick questions and responses and does not, therefore, lend itself to quotation. It deals with the ending of thought as well as the ending of time—that is, psychological time and thought which are the past. All that we have learnt, all that we are, the whole content of our consciousness, is the past stored in our memory as thought, and the cluttering up of the brain with the past means that there is no true insight because everything is seen through a cloud of thought which must always be limited by the self. The past as thought, memory, must go for the new to be. 'That emptying of the past, which is anger, jealousy, beliefs, dogmas, attachments etc. must be done,' K says. 'If that is not emptied, if any part of that exists, it will inevitably lead to illusion brought by desire, by hope, by wanting security.'

'Is it really possible', K asks, 'for time to end—the whole idea of time as the past—chronologically, so that there is no tomorrow at all? There is the feeling, the actual reality, psychologically, of having no tomorrow. I think that is the healthiest way of living—which doesn't mean that I become irresponsible! That would be too childish.' In going into this question K and David Bohm speak of the ground of all being, which is the beginning and ending of everything, and of the necessity for mankind to touch this ground if life is to have real significance.

If the brain remains in self-created darkness it wears itself out with the resulting conflict. Can such a brain ever renew itself? Can the deterioration of the brain cells and senility be prevented? K suggests that through insight it is possible for the brain to change physically and act in an orderly way which leads to a healing of the damage caused by all the years of wrong-functioning.

In the Foreword to a booklet of two dialogues between K and David Bohm of a later date, Bohm illuminates this:

. . . it is worth remarking that modern research into the brain and nervous system actually gives considerable support to Krishnamurti's statement that insight may change the brain cells. Thus, for example, it is now well known that there are important substances in the body, the hormones and the neurotransmitters, that fundamentally affect the entire functioning of the brain and the nervous system. These substances respond, from moment to moment, to what a person knows, to what he thinks, and to what all this means to him. It is by now fairly well established that in this way the brain cells and their functioning are profoundly affected by knowledge and passions. It is thus quite plausible that insight, which must arise in a state of mental energy and passion, could change the brain cells in an even more profound way.[16]

*　　*　　*　　*

In May K gave six talks in the Oak Grove at Ojai to a large gathering and held two Question and Answer meetings. Because he was always speaking to different audiences (though many of the same people turned up to listen to him year after year) his talks varied very little, though in some he seemed more inspired and expressed himself more clearly or more forcibly than in others. He usually started every talk now by telling his audience, 'This is not an entertainment nor is it a sermon', and emphasising that he and the audience were investigating *together* certain aspects of living. He was not telling them anything or forcing anything on them. He was not their guru. 'The speaker is not making any kind of propaganda,' he said in one of these Ojai talks. 'We are not instituting one belief against another belief, one dependence on another. There is nothing to prove. We are all of us thinking over together, giving our attention to the fact, that we are conditioned, and out of this conditioning we are creating more and more havoc in the world, more and more misery and confusion. . . . And we are asking whether this conditioning can be totally eradicated.'

Later on in the talk he was saying, 'If we observe, according to some psychologist, some philosopher, some guru, then we are observing according to their knowledge, and with that knowledge in our mind we try to look at ourselves. Therefore we are not looking at ourselves, we are looking through the eyes of another. And this is the tyranny that human beings have put up with for a million years or more.'

In answer to the question: 'Is it possible ever to be free of self-centred activity?' K replied in part: 'To be free from your own experience, from your own knowledge . . . does not take time. That is one of our excuses; we must have time to be free. When you see that one of the major factors of the self is attachment and you see what it does to the world, and what it does in your relationship with another . . . your own perception sets you free.'[17]

K maintained that there could be a complete ending to sorrow,

K (right) with Hubert van Hook and Nitya, Adyar 1909

K at Ommen, 1927

and that where there was suffering there was no love. All possessive relationships led to sorrow whether they were inside or outside marriage. He had said earlier:

I am not against sex, but see what is involved in it. What sex gives you momentarily is the total abandonment of yourself, so you want a repetition over and over again of that state in which there is no worry, no problem, no self. You say you love your wife. In that love is involved sexual pleasure, the pleasure of having someone in the house to look after your children, to cook. You depend on her; she has given you her body, her emotions, her encouragement, a certain feeling of security and well-being. Then she turns away from you; she gets bored or goes off with someone else, and your whole emotional balance is destroyed, and this disturbance which you don't like, is called jealousy. There is pain in it, anxiety, hate and violence. So what you are really saying is, 'As long as you belong to me I love you but the moment you don't I begin to hate you. As long as I can rely on you to satisfy my demands, sexual and otherwise, I love you, but the moment you cease to supply what I want I don't like you.' So there is antagonism between you, there is separation, and when you feel separate from another there is no love.[18]

Why Does the Flower Grow?

On May 22, K and Mary Zimbalist flew to England where they stayed for a month at Brockwood Park. This was the Krishnamurti school in Hampshire, between Petersfield and Winchester, which had been founded in 1969—a large, white-stuccoed late eighteenth-century house set in thirty-six acres of park and garden with beautiful trees, beeches, limes and sweet chestnuts. There were about sixty students at Brockwood of many different nationalities, an equal number of girls and boys, ranging in age from fourteen to twenty. The Krishnamurti schools, as well as following the ordinary school curriculum with preparation in England for Ordinary and Advanced level examinations, aimed at freeing the student from the conditioning of racial, national and ideological prejudice. K wrote that the schools were 'to be concerned with the cultivation of the total human being. These centres of education must help the student and the educator to flower naturally. The flowering is really very important, otherwise the education becomes merely a mechanical process orientated to a career. . . . It is the concern of these schools to bring about a new generation of human beings who are free from self-centred action. No other educational centres are concerned with this and it is our responsibility, as educators, to bring about a mind that has no conflict within itself and so end the struggle and conflict in the world about us.'[19]

The Principal of the Brockwood School was Dorothy Simmons who, with her husband Montague, had built up the school from the beginning. When K first met Dorothy Simmons in 1967 her husband had just retired after twenty years from running a State school. She was a professional sculptor who had never done any teaching but had become deeply interested in K's ideas. Montague had been a teacher of English and would be responsible for the academic side of the school.

Dorothy was yet another of those who came into K's life just at the right moment. He was told by his then financial adviser, Gérard Blitz, founder of the Club Méditerranée, that there was not enough money to start a school. At the lawyer's office in London in August 1968, when the English Foundation was legally set up in the presence of all those who were to become trustees, the school project was discussed. Monsieur Blitz said, 'As you know, Krishnaji, we would do anything for you—even jump out of the window—but to start a school, that is impossible.' Monsieur Blitz then left by taxi for Heathrow to catch his flight back to Paris. He had hardly closed the door before K and Dorothy Simmons were in a corner discussing the starting of a school. K never considered money; he would say, 'Act, and if it's right the money will come in', and it always did. K had no money of his own apart from £500 a year for life settled on him by Miss Mary Dodge. Financial support for his work came from donations, legacies and royalties from his books. But £40,000 had been offered to him by a generous follower to buy a house somewhere in France for his retirement and, since he had no intention of ever retiring, he asked if he might spend the money on a school. The request was willingly granted and Brockwood Park was the result.

*   *   *   *

K and Mary Zimbalist stayed in what was called the West Wing when they were at Brockwood, connected to the school though not a part of it, beautifully furnished and decorated by Mary. K had breakfast and supper in the West Wing but lunched with the school. The school food, strictly vegetarian, was excellent.

Dr T. K. Parchure was awaiting K at Brockwood. A doctor from the hospital in the compound of the Krishnamurti school at Rajghat, Varanasi (Benares), he had frequently attended K in India and Europe since 1974. As well as advising on his diet and general care, he supervised his morning exercises and gave him a daily massage. His presence was a great help to Mary also, for one of her chief concerns was for K's health.

K and Mary came to London once a week when they were at Brockwood. Joe Links, whom I had married in 1945, and I always met them in our car at Waterloo and drove them to Savile Row where K visited his tailor, Huntsman. Joe would leave us there and

K, Mary and I would invariably lunch at Fortnum & Mason, in the fourth-floor restaurant, always at the same table. Although the choice on the menu for vegetarians was limited to cheese flan, vegetables and sweets (K was very fond of crême caramel), the place suited us well. It was quiet and airy and a pleasant walk away from Huntsman through the Burlington Arcade. Moreover, it was almost next door to Hatchard's bookshop where K would usually go after lunch to replenish his stock of thrillers.

When we met, K would plunge straight into telling me about what had been happening to him since he last saw me. Even if what he had to say was private, our table in a corner was too far away from the next table for us to be overheard. He never had to waste time in asking me about myself. I rarely mentioned my own life to him. I knew, anyway, what he would say and since I was unwilling or unable to change my course why waste his time in consulting him? I liked to feel that he could be perfectly relaxed with me. He fortunately had a very good relationship with Joe who was personally very fond of him and respectful of him, though not always agreeing with what he said in his talks. K, for his part, seemed to value Joe's advice in practical matters as an unbiased man of the world whom he trusted for the very reason that he was an outsider as far as the Foundation was concerned. But Joe always dressed particularly carefully when we were going to meet K and had the car cleaned inside and out.

*   *   *   *

On June 12 I went to Brockwood for a publications committee meeting. In 1968, at the time of the break with KWINC, K had set up a publishing committee in England under the chairmanship of George Wingfield Digby, Keeper of the Department of Textiles at the Victoria and Albert Museum, an expert on oriental porcelain and author, among other books, of a life of Blake. His wife Nelly, Ian Hammond, retired from a successful architectural practice, and his wife Jane, an expert in transcribing K's talks and discussions, Mary Cadogan, Sybil Dobinson and I were all members of the Committee. Our job was to edit K's talks and writings and see them through the press and bring out a quarterly Bulletin. The copyright of all K's works after 1968 had been legally vested in the English Foundation. America had no publishing committee and therefore an

American, Alan Kishbaugh, the representative in California of Farrar, Straus & Giroux, was a member of our Committee. The Indian Foundation had their own Publications Committee which took care of the editing and publishing of K's talks and discussions in India for the Indian Market.

The Indian Foundation had never been happy with this arrangement, and for eight years there had been some friction between the English and Indian Commitees. The Indians naturally wanted to bring out an international book of the Indian talks but we were not confident as to the quality of their editing, nor was K. The two chief representatives of the Indian Committee were Sunanda Patwardhan, who had a Ph.D. in Sociology, and her husband, Pama, who had been Vice-Chairman of the publishers Orient Longman before his retirement in 1975. They were now at Brockwood for the meeting and we hoped very much to reach a satisfactory settlement. But there was one great difference between the Indian Committee and ours: whereas we were empowered to make decisions, they had to refer everything back to the Trustees of the Indian Foundation for approval, which was the reason why these difficulties had been going on for so long. The decisions we had so far come to had been vetoed by the Indian Trustees.

This time we worked out with the Patwardhans the terms of a settlement which we hoped the Indian Foundation would agree to: in future the international books, published first by Gollancz in England and then by Harper & Row in America, should follow a three-year cycle. In the first year, an English-edited book would be published for which England would receive all the royalties; in the second year there would be an English-edited book for which India would have the Indian rights; and in the third year there would be a book compiled and edited in India with world rights for India, but for which the English Committee would have editorial responsibility. India would also have the right in perpetuity to edit and publish for the Indian market any of K's talks and discussions given in India. A legal document setting out these terms was drawn up and, in due course, signed by the Indian Trustees. We hoped that we were to have no more publication difficulties between the two Foundations.

*   *   *   *

In late June K went with Mary Zimbalist to the Janker Clinic at Bonn for the third year running. Dr Scheef, the head of the Clinic, X-rayed K and carried out other tests. The results were that the lump he felt under his diaphragm and the occasional pain he felt there were due to a hernia and were of no consequence.

After three days in Geneva, shopping and resting, they arrived at Gstaad on July 1. For the past twenty years K had spent part of every summer at Chalet Tannegg, a rented villa at Gstaad, in order to hold an international gathering at the nearby little town of Saanen which attracted huge crowds. Every year when he arrived Vanda Scaravelli, who rented the villa for him, had been there to greet him with a former cook of hers, Fosca, who, although as old at K, enjoyed working the few weeks at Tannegg.

K had first come to know Vanda in 1937, three years before her marriage to the Marchese Luigi Scaravelli, Professor of Philosophy at the University of Rome. Vanda's father had been Alberto Passigli, an aristocratic Florentine landowner, founder of the *Maggio Musicale* and the *Amici della Musica* in Florence. Vanda herself was a pianist of professional standard and altogether a most gifted woman. K had frequently stayed with her at the beautiful house above Fiesole, Il Leccio, which she and her brother had inherited from their father, and she introduced K to many prominent figures in the artistic world in Rome. Her husband died in 1957. She had a daughter married to a Canadian living in Toronto and a son who managed her estate. After Mary Zimbalist became close to K, Vanda gradually withdrew. She continued to open up Tannegg for him every year but would go back to Florence for part of the Gathering, to return shortly before he left.

A close friend of K's, Radha Burnier, came to Saanen that year and shared a villa with the Patwardhans who were also there for the Gathering. She was the daughter of Sri Ram who had been President of the Theosophical Society at Adyar before John Coates. She was already the Head of the Esoteric Section of the Society and now, following Coates's retirement, she and her aunt, Rukmini Arundale, were contesting for the Presidency of the Society. While she was at Saanen the news came that she had been elected with 9,300 votes to Mrs Arundale's 5,400. K was delighted.

K gave seven talks at Saanen in July, followed by five Question and Answer meetings. In answer to a question: 'There are so many gurus today both in the East and the West, each one pointing his own way to enlightenment; how is one to know if they are speaking the truth?' K answered in part:

When a guru says he knows, he does not . . . enlightenment is not to be attained. It is not something you can reach step by step as if you were climbing a ladder. . . . One does not like to use the word 'enlightenment'; it is so loaded with the meaning given by all these gurus. . . . Whether they are Eastern or Western gurus, doubt what they are saying, doubt also what the speaker is saying—much more so, because although he is very clear about all these matters it does not mean that he is the only person who knows, which is absurd. The mind must be free from all authority—no followers, disciples and patterns . . . nobody can give guidance, give light to another. Only you yourself can do that; but you have to stand completely alone.[20]

*   *   *   *

In his second talk K made one of those startling statements that caused people to sit up: 'Allegiance to anything is the beginning of corruption.' Other such statements of his have been: 'Ideals are brutal things', 'All thought corrupts', 'There is no such thing as unhappy love', 'If you really loved your children there would be no more wars', 'Time is the enemy of man psychologically', 'There is no intelligence without love', 'God is total disorder'. He maintained that man had invented God, and that one man's God against another man's God had created chaos. In this same Saanen talk he was saying, 'The religious people say there is God and that God has created the world. That God must be a rather miserable God, rather confused, a rather corrupt God to make this world as it is.' As for ideals being 'brutal things', it was one ideology against another that had caused so many wars. Nationalism and patriotism were equally brutal. Over and over again he reiterated that he had no nationality. 'I am not an Indian,' he declared publicly on several occasions. He had to have a passport for the purpose of travel, and at the time of Indian independence, when given the option of retaining his British passport or having an Indian one, he plumped for an Indian one. He could hardly have done otherwise when so many of his Indian friends had suffered persecution under the Raj. The inconvenience, however, with an Indian passport, of having to get a visa for every country he entered, became so tiresome that in the seventies he had seriously considered applying for British nationality but was daunted by the formalities involved. He was then given an Indian diplomatic passport which, though a great honour, was no help with visas. Eventually in 1977 he was granted the so-called 'green card' which accorded him permanent residence in the U.S. and entitled him to apply for American nationality in five years' time. This he never did because it would have required his staying in America for a full year.

*   *   *   *

K and Mary were back at Brockwood on August 20 with Dr Parchure who had been at Gstaad, and ten days later a week's gathering was held there at which K gave four talks and held two Question and Answer meetings. This was a much smaller gathering than the one at Saanen. Most of the people went for the day; all the same, the house was crammed to capacity (the term had not yet started) and there were dozens of campers. The talks took place in a great tent in a field at the bottom of the garden, with an equally large tent adjoining it in which books and tapes were sold and a simple vegetarian meal sold at very low cost.

At one of the Question and Answer meetings K was asked: 'You say, "We are the world", but the majority of the world seems to be heading for mass destruction. Can a minority of integrated people outweigh the majority?' To this K replied:

Are you, are we, that minority? Is there one among us who is totally free of all this? Or are we partially contributing to the hatred of each other psychologically? You may not be able to stop one country attacking another, but psychologically, are you free of your common inheritance, which is your tribal glorified nationalism? Are we free from violence? Violence exists where there is a wall around ourselves. Do please understand all this. And we have built ourselves walls, fifteen feet high and ten feet thick. All of us have these walls around us. From that arises violence and this sense of immense loneliness. So the minority and the majority are you. If a group of us have psychologically transformed ourselves fundamentally we will never ask this question, because we are then something entirely different.

At another meeting he was asked why he continued to go on speaking. He answered:

This has often been asked, 'Why do you go on wasting your energy after fifty years when nobody seems to change, why do you bother about it? Is it a form of self-fulfilment? Do you get energy talking about these things, and so depend on the audience?' We have been through all that several times. First of all, I do not depend on you as a group who come to listen to the speaker. The speaker is not attached to a particular group nor is it necessary for him to have a gathering. Then what is the motive? I think when one sees something true and beautiful, one wants to tell people about it, out of affection, out of compassion, out of love. And if there are those who are not interested, that is all right, but those who are interested can perhaps gather together. Can you ask the flower why it grows, why it has perfume? It is for the same reason the speaker talks.[21]

After the Gathering the Bohms came to stay and the rest of the dialogues took place between K and David Bohm which are included in *The Ending of Time*.

The term started on September 25 and K spoke several times to the entire school before leaving for India. I went to Brockwood for the night of October 3 and talked to him all that afternoon and the next morning. We went deeply again into the question of who and what he was as in the interviews I had had with him the year before and which I fully recorded in *The Years of Fulfilment*.

Seven years earlier, at Ojai, he had spoken with a few members of the American Foundation on the same subject. He had outlined then the Theosophical conception of who he was: the body that the Lord Maitreya, the World Teacher, was to inhabit had been prepared for many, many lives—'not only the body but the face. That was repeated over and over again by both Dr Besant and Leadbeater—the face. To them that was tremendously important— the body and the face . . . the ego of Krishnamurti was put aside . . . but the ego had been preparing, preparing for lives and lives to come to this point.' The coming of the Lord Maitreya, according to the Theosophical concept, was such a rare occurrence in the religious field that the ordinary man could only follow and obey and do his best to live what he was taught. This idea, K said, that an ordinary man had to go through years and years of effort was dangerous and discouraging. 'Discard all that,' he continued, 'forget the past, find out about yourself, be a light to yourself. . . . Forget what the boy was, what he went through. That's irrelevant.'

'You mean forget the Theosophical explanation?' he was asked. He replied:

Theosophical and any other explanation—that's not your concern . . . don't bother about it. Your business is your life. . . . Leave K's personality aside, what he was, how he grew up. . . . I feel we are delving into something which the conscious mind can never understand, which doesn't mean I am making a mystery of it. There is something—much too vast to be put into words. There is a tremendous reservoir, as it were, which if the human mind can touch reveals something—which no intellectual mythology, invention, supposition, dogma, can ever reveal.

I am not making a mystery of it—that would be a stupid childish trick. Creating a mystery out of nothing would be a most blackguardly thing to do because that would be exploiting people. Either one creates a mystery when there isn't one or there is a mystery which you have to approach with extraordinary delicacy and tentativeness. And the conscious mind can't do this. It is there but you cannot come to it. It's not progressive achievement. There is something but the brain can't understand it.[22]

When I went into the subject with him seven years later he seemed eager that the truth about himself should be discovered; he could not discover it himself: 'Water can never find out what water is,' he said. 'There is an element in all this which is not man-made, thought-made, not self-induced. I am not like that. Is this something which we cannot discover, mustn't touch, is not penetrable? I am wondering. I have often felt it is not my business, that we will never find out. When we say it comes into being because the mind is vacant, I don't think it is that either.' Yet he believed that if Mary Zimbalist and I or others 'put their minds to this they can do it. I am absolutely sure of this. Absolutely, absolutely. Also I am sure I can't find it.' But what he would be able to do was to corroborate it if we found it. He also said that 'To find out the truth of the matter you have to have your mind empty.'

He did not want to make a mystery of it yet a mystery remains. For one thing there was the sense of protection he had always had. 'When I get into an aeroplane I know nothing will happen. But I don't do anything that will cause danger.' Then there was the 'process'—that pain in his head and spine which had been so agonising in the first few years after his 1922 experience at Ojai and which still went on in a lesser degree. Thirdly there was the 'vacant mind' which he said he had never lost. 'Only when talking and writing', he told me, 'does "this" come into play. I am amazed. What does it? You can feel it in the room now. It is happening in the

room now because we are touching something very, very serious
and it comes pouring in.'

'Is your mind vacant when you give talks?' I asked.

'Oh, yes, completely. But I'm not interested in that but in why it
stays vacant. Because it stays vacant it has no problems. . . . The
other thing is here now. Don't you feel it? It is like throbbing.'

'The essence of your teaching', I said, 'is that everyone can have
it.' To which he replied, 'Yes, if it is unique it is not worth anything.
But this isn't like that. Is it kept vacant for this thing to say,
"Though I am vacant, you—X—can also have it."?'

'You mean it is vacant in order to be able to say that this can
happen to everyone?'

'That's right. That's right,' he replied.

I then asked him, 'Do you ever feel yourself being used, feel
something coming into you?'

'I wouldn't say that. It comes into the room when we are talking
seriously.'

'How is it related to the pain?' I asked.

'Pain comes when I am quiet, not talking. It comes slowly until
the body says, "That's enough." After reaching a crisis the body
faints; the pain peters out or there is some interruption and it goes.'

'Can we rule out something from outside?'

'I don't. But what is the truth?'[23]

When we went into the matter again on this last occasion in 1980,
he seemed as eager as before to find out the truth about himself and
repeated that if Mary Zimbalist and I could discover it he would be
able to corroborate it. But he could tell us no more.

3

'Unimaginable energy'

K flew by Qantas to Bombay with Mary Zimbalist this year on November 1. Mary's luggage was not unloaded and she discovered that it had gone on to Perth. K was as distressed for her over this as she was herself. Next day they flew on to Madras. The headquarters of the Krishnamurti Foundation in India was at Vasanta Vihar at Adyar, a large house in beautiful grounds. It was quite close to the Theosophical Society but on the Madras side of the Adyar River and further from the sea. Sunanda and Pama Patwardhan lived there, and other friends came to meet K there, including Pupul Jayakar, her younger sister, Nandini Mehta, and their nephew, Asit Chandmal. Pupul and Nandini were the most prominent of the new group of friends K had gathered round him when he returned to India in 1947 after the war and who came into his life just when he needed them most. Pupul, the Vice-President of the Indian Foundation of which K was the nominal President, had a forceful personality. A close friend of Mrs Gandhi, she lived near her in New Delhi and was able to introduce K to many leading Indians in both the political and religious fields as well as to Mrs Gandhi herself. She knew a great deal about many aspects of Indian art and culture and, since Independence, she had been closely associated with the development of handicrafts in India. She was to become the Chairman of the influential Festival of India which involved much travel. Nandini had a gentler nature. For many years now she had been running a Krishnamurti school for poor children in Bombay, Bal Anand. Another prominent member of the Indian Foundation was Achyut Patwardhan, Pama's elder brother. A great freedom fighter, he had suffered much under the British.

Asit Chandmal, whom K had known since he was a child, had been working with computers since 1964, since 1969 with the great

32

Indian Tata group. Earlier in 1980 he had been on their behalf to California and he was soon to start a new company in Singapore for Tata and a Californian company jointly. He had a flat in Bombay which he kept on while living in Singapore. (In 1984 he founded his own computer company.)

Because Radha Burnier was now President of the Theosophical Society K had consented to visit the T.S. Headquarters. Radha came to fetch him late in the afternoon of November 3 and, accompanied by everyone who was then staying at Vasanta Vihar, he drove with her to the gates of the estate where a crowd had gathered to meet him. For the first time for forty-six years he entered the Theosophical grounds and walked through them to Radha's house on the beach, followed by the crowd. He remembered almost nothing of the place, he told Mary afterwards.

The next day K flew to Sri Lanka, where he had been invited to give talks and where he had not been since 1957. He was accompanied by Pupul, Nandini, Mary and the three Patwardhans. Parameswaran, the excellent head cook from the Rishi Valley school who had looked after K when he nearly died in Kashmir in 1960, went with them to make sure that K had the right food. Mary was able to recover her luggage at the Madras airport just in time to catch their flight to Colombo.

They were met by Dr Adikaram, who had arranged K's itinerary, and were driven to the State guest-house where they were to stay. Next day K met the Prime Minister, Mr R. Premadasa, and was interviewed for television by the Minister of State. During the twelve days he was in Sri Lanka he gave a press conference which was fully reported in all the papers, four public talks attended by great crowds, held discussions with thirty Buddhist monks, answered questions at the University and went up to Candy at the invitation of the President, Mr Jayewardene, with whom he talked privately for an hour and a half. It was a triumphant if exhausting visit.

In the middle of November K, with Mary and Dr Parchure, went to Rishi Valley, a five-hour drive from Madras and about ten miles from Madanapalle, K's birthplace. Rishi Valley is the first Krishnamurti school, founded in 1928, situated in a beautiful valley about 2,400 feet above sea-level and dominated by the Rishi Konda mountain. This highly successful, co-educational school has a campus of 300 acres, including a farm. The school also runs a rural centre where children from adjacent villages are educated and given medical care. G. Narayan, a son of K's eldest brother who had become a doctor, was now the Principal and Director of the School. He had previously taught at a Rudolph Steiner school in England. There was something particularly sacred about this valley which K loved so much.

The Patwardhans, Pupul Jayakar and Asit Chandmal joined K at Rishi Valley where he held many discussions with Asit about computers, a subject which had come to fascinate him. Would the human brain atrophy as the computer took over more and more of its functions? At the end of one discussion K spoke of something beyond the brain which he called the mind. The mind could get in touch with the brain but the brain could not get in touch with the mind.

At the beginning of December teachers from the other Krishnamurti schools in India* went to Rishi Valley for a six-day conference which K attended. In the middle of the conference K told Mary that the 'face' had been with him for four days. What was this 'face'? In December 1925 when, at Adyar, the Lord Maitreya was said to have spoken through K for the first time, K's face had changed as his voice had changed. I was lucky enough to have witnessed this thrilling phenomenon. His face had become much sterner, more mature, yet even more beautiful if possible. When my mother described to him afterwards how his face had changed, he said wistfully, 'I wish I could have seen it.' At the Ommen camp in the summer of 1926, this change of face had taken place again on the next occasion when he had suddenly spoken in the first person, and again he had said to the friend who described the change to him, 'I wish I could see it too.' And others since have often spoken to him of the change that takes place in his face at times when he is giving a talk. Is it possible that the 'face' which was often with him now could be the face that he had not been able to see in those early days? He described the 'face' to Pupul Jayakar as 'extraordinary, highly-cultured, refined'.[24]

*   *   *   *

* These were at Rajghat, Varanasi (as Benares was now called), and at Madras, Bangalore and Bombay.

In accordance with K's wishes that the members of the three
Foundations should meet as often as possible, two Trustees from
America, Theodor Lilliefelt and Alan Hooker (who ran a very
successful restaurant at Ojai) went to Rishi Valley that winter, as
did two from the English Foundation, Dorothy Simmons and Mary
Cadogan. Two members of the Brockwood staff were also there,
Scott Forbes, a young American who was responsible for the video,
and Harsh Tankha, an Indian who taught mathematics. A teacher at
Rishi Valley at that time was a Canadian, Ray McCoy. Before going
to Rishi Valley, Ray had taught for a year at K's next most
important school at Rajghat, and in 1981 he was to join the staff at
Brockwood.

There was great excitement when Mrs Gandhi with Rajiv and his
wife and children came to Rishi Valley for the night on December
20. She and her entourage landed by helicopter at Madanapalle.
Preparations for her visit had been going on for some days. Pupul,
as her best friend, acted with K as joint host. On arrival, Mrs
Gandhi planted a tree and then spoke to the assembled school. She
toured the grounds and afterwards went for a walk alone with K
while armed guards were hidden from their sight in the bushes. In
the evening there was student dancing and Mordangan playing
(drums) under the great banyan tree, followed by a moonlight
supper.

Between December 27 and January 11, K, back in Madras, gave
six public talks in the grounds of Vasanta Vihar, followed by a
three-day discussion with some Indian scholars. (His talks in India
were always held in the evenings out-of-doors.) His Indian talks did
not differ from his talks anywhere else. In a series of talks in India
he would cover, as he usually did, the whole spectrum of living; nor
in India did he make any concessions to the fact that some of his
audience could not understand English. The one difference was that
in India his voice had to compete with the continual raucous noise
of the crows, a nostalgic sound for anyone who loves India.

K also talked further with Asit while in Madras about computers.
Before leaving for Bombay he made two more visits to the
Theosophical Society estate at Radha Burnier's request. The T.S.
Convention was going on there and she wanted him to walk from
her house to the gates of the compound so that the T.S. members
could greet him. On the second occasion he went inside the

Headquarters building where Mrs Besant had lived, and visited the room Mrs Besant had built for him and Nitya on top of an adjoining house, connected to the Headquarters at first-floor level. (My mother and I had stayed in that room for a month in 1923 at K's request while he was at Ojai, and I remember it as the most beautiful room I have ever been in, with a view of the wide Adyar river where it joins the sea.) This room brought back no memories for K, though he did remember the *chowki* in Mrs Besant's room where he had so often sat and watched her at her writing desk.

On January 21, 1981, K and Mary flew to Bombay where they stayed with Asit Chandmal in his comfortable flat in Sterling Apartments, Peddar Road. The next day Asit asked some computer experts to lunch whom K was fascinated to talk to. Another day K was interviewed by Pupul Jayakar on television. Between January 24 and February 8 he gave six public talks to audiences of about 5,000 people. Indian audiences were far more demonstrative and reverential than Western ones and after a Bombay talk K would be mobbed by crowds, all frenziedly trying to touch him or his garments. It would take him a long time to walk to the car, parked close by, and when he was at last inside it the chauffeur could only crawl forward in order not to crush the people clinging to the sides and the bonnet, still trying to touch him.

After the third talk K said that he felt no communication with his audience and had almost stopped speaking, but after the last one, during which the audience sat so still that they seemed hardly to breathe, he asked Mary whether there had been something special about it. 'It has done something to me,' he said. Perhaps the most remarkable thing about this last talk was the vehemence with which he spoke. After reviewing what he had said in the five previous talks, he began to speak of meditation and thought:

Meditation is the understanding of knowledge, not sitting repeating some phrase, following a system that someone else has laid down or the particular form of meditation your guru has put out. That is all based on thought which is the outcome of knowledge and knowledge is never complete so thought is never complete. The speaker is not a guru, he has no followers. The disciples destroy the guru and the guru destroys the disciples. . . . One of the strange things in this country is personal worship. To prostrate yourself to another, to worship another human being is the most undignified, the most inhuman thing you can do. . . . There is nothing

36

Mary Zimbalist on the verandah of Pine Cottage

View from K's bedroom at Rajghat

K at Rishi Valley School, December 1980

K under the cedar tree at Brockwood, October 1984

sacred that thought does not produce—the temples, the churches. Thought itself is not sacred but the things that thought has produced we worship, we follow. And thought has brought about disorder in our private life and disorder outwardly. This disorder cannot be made into order by any government, by any religion, by any guru because what they do and say is all based on thought and thought is a material process. . . . Thought has caused disorder and discord and cannot possibly bring about order. . . . Meditation is the ending of knowledge. Our consciousness is the storehouse of knowledge. . . . Meditation is the way we live; meditation is part of our daily life, not something separate but an actual activity of our daily life, and our daily life is based on knowledge, on memory, so our life is based on the past. We are always operating from the past which is the known. As long as we act in the field of knowledge our brains become mechanical. We know we are afraid, we know we are lonely, we know we have great sorrow, we know we are anxious, uncertain, unhappy, trying to fulfil, trying to become, trying to get something all the time. . . . Now we are asking whether knowledge—we are talking of course about psychological not practical knowledge—can ever end.?

Towards the end of the talk he said with tremendous emphasis,

Don't accept a thing the speaker is saying. Follow his reasoning and all the subtleties involved in it, but doubt it, be a light to yourself. Religion is the sceptical enquiry into the whole of our existence which is our consciousness. If there is fear your meditation is utterly meaningless. A free mind is essential for enquiry and when there is fear there is no freedom.[25]

At the end of the talk, one can hear on the cassette the deafening hubbub of voices which broke out until the machine was turned off.

Even before K had gone to Bombay, Dr Parchure had told Mary that he was really too tired to do his exercises but that he refused to cut them down. He was immensely stimulated by his visits to India although exhausted by them, for when he was not giving talks he was taking part in endless discussions.

After nearly four months in India K and Mary flew to England on February 15, where K had only five days' rest at Brockwood before they went on to Los Angeles. When Joe and I went to Brockwood to see him he immediately told us about Mrs Gandhi's visit to Rishi Valley and the time in Sri Lanka where he had much enjoyed being treated as a V.I.P. He seemed really impressed that the President of Sri Lanka should have wanted to see him. There was such a human side to him, coupled with true humility. He had a great respect for successful people and for academic honours regardless of the fact that worldly success and university degrees were the result of competition and personal striving which he deplored. On the other hand he was repelled by anyone who boasted of his fame or accomplishments or showed any sign of self-importance. These anomalies in him I make no attempt to resolve. If there had not been such contradictions in his make-up he would have been far less lovable and certainly less interesting.

*   *   *   *

Throughout March and April at Ojai K helped Alasdair Coyne to plant a new garden at Pine Cottage. (Alasdair had looked after the huge walled kitchen garden at Brockwood before going to live at Ojai and starting a practice there as a landscape gardener.) K was perhaps never happier than when working in a garden. He was particularly happy planting trees. He had helped to plant them at Rishi Valley, Rajghat, Vasanta Vihar and round the Oak Grove School.

K was delighted when two black granite *nandis* (sacred bulls) arrived which had been given to him in India the year before. They had been shipped from Madras and it took six men to unload them and place them on either side of the approach to the new house whose front door had just been painted Pompeian red. K crowned them with pink flowers. He told Mary how much gardening agreed with him and that he must take it up at Brockwood. (Unfortunately he never did, principally because he suffered badly from hay fever there.)

Soon after his arrival at Ojai K telephoned to me in London to ask me to become Chairman of the Publications Committee in place of George Wingfield Digby who, with his wife, had retired. It was a great blow to lose the Digbys who had both been excellent editors. It reduced our little editorial team to Ian Hammond, Sybil Dobinson (who edited the Bulletin) and me. Jane Hammond was fully occupied with transcribing tapes and Mary Cadogan had not yet taken up editing. We looked for new editors, preferably young. Editing K's talks is not just a matter of putting them into good English, nor even of understanding, at least intellectually, what he is saying. The chief difficulty is to retain the authentic cadence of his voice while putting order into what are often disjointed sentences.

In 1983 we were able to recruit Felix and Elena Greene who worked from Mexico. Felix died in 1985 and Elena, who now lives in London, has become a valuable member of the Publications Committee as are also Ray McCoy, the archivist at Brockwood, and Scott Forbes's wife, Kathy.

The voice is such a vital part of a person and it is of course impossible to transfer anyone's voice to paper. One may succeed in capturing K's way of speaking but what cannot be transmitted is the emphasis he puts on certain words and phrases, the fire, the enthusiasm, the earnestness, the urgency, the *passion* that comes from his whole being.

*   *   *   *

Several scientists and psychologists went to Ojai in April and K held discussions with them for three days; after that he talked to teachers and parents of pupils of the Oak Grove School for four days running. After so many discussions it was a relief to him to drive up into the mountains with Mary. He wished he could have a cabin up there 'away from everything'. He felt like 'disappearing'. He so often longed for this—to become anonymous, not to see anyone who knew him. Yet coming in from the garden a few days later he declared how young he felt. (This was a fortnight before his eighty-sixth birthday.) On the same day he said to Mary, 'You must outlive me.' 'Why?' she asked. 'To look after this person.' 'Others would line up to do that,' she said. 'I don't want them,' he replied.

During the talks and Question and Answer meetings in the Oak Grove in May, K woke one morning with a feeling of 'tremendous power—not to do anything, just power'; as he told Mary, he would quite often wake with some extraordinary feeling of new and vast energy. There was the instance of this described on page 15. Four years before that he had allowed Mary to write down another experience:

Before beginning *asanas*, he [K] generally sits very quietly, thinking about nothing. But this morning a strange thing took place, most unexpected and in no way invited—and besides you can't invite these things. Suddenly it appeared as though in the very centre of the brain, the head, right inside, there was a vast space in which was unimaginable energy. It is there, but nothing whatever is registered, for that which is registered is a waste of energy. If one can so call it, it was pure energy in a limitless state, a

39

space that had nothing but this sense of immensity. One doesn't know how long it lasted but all during the morning it was there, and as this is being written it is as though it was taking root and becoming firm. These words are not really the thing itself.[26]

And in 1972 he had tried to express what that energy might have felt like physically: 'I woke at three [a.m.] with a sense of extraordinary fire, light burning in the mind. There was no observer. The testing was from the outside but the observer didn't exist. There was only that and nothing else. The power penetrated the whole being. I sat up and it lasted three hours.'[27]

4

The Meaning of Death

K and Mary returned to Brockwood on May 21 where they found Dr Parchure who had just come from India. I went there for the day on the 23rd and sat with K and Mary at the kitchen table in the West Wing talking at great length. In spite of the large and beautiful drawing-room below, we almost always found ourselves talking in the first-floor kitchen. As I have said, K would usually plunge straight into telling me all that had been happening to him since we last met, but on this occasion it was a little different because my eldest sister, Barbara, whom K had known in the early days, had committed suicide in April by taking an overdose of barbiturates and K wanted to hear all about it. Barbie was eighty-two and had lost her first husband, her three sons and the two stepsons she had brought up since they were little. She had no other children and no grandchildren. When her second husband died she felt that she had had enough. Having made her decision, she rang me up the evening before she was found dead to tell me that she was happier than she had been for years. K was particularly interested in the instructions she had left to have no funeral; she was to be cremated with no one present except the undertaker who was to scatter her ashes. (At a meeting of the Joint Foundations at Brockwood in 1972 K had said that he wanted to be cremated and have his ashes scattered wherever he happened to die. This had shocked the Indian Trustees who wanted his ashes scattered in the Ganges.)

I now went on to tell K about the Voluntary Euthanasia Society Joe and I belonged to which had issued a booklet to members, listing lethal drugs and explaining how their use could be facilitated by the help of a plastic bag. What I told him about this evidently remained in his mind, for the following January, in India, he was telling Pupul Jayakar and Nandini Mehta all about it, even remembering the details of how the plastic bag should be used after taking the overdose.[28]

The idea of suicide did not shock K but to him death was something to be lived every day. Death was not the ending of life. In a talk he was to give in Amsterdam in September, he said:

Death means the ending of the known. It means the ending of the physical organism, the ending of all the memory which I am, for I am nothing but memory. And I am frightened to let all that go, which means death. Death means the ending of attachments, that is, dying with living, not separated by fifty years or so, waiting for some disease to finish you off. It is living with all your vitality, energy, intellectual capacity and with great feeling, and at the same time for certain conclusions, certain idiosyncrasies, experiences, attachments, hurts to end, to die. That is, while living, also live with death. Then death is not something far away, death is not something that is at the end of one's life, brought about by some accident, disease or old age, but rather an ending to all the things of memory—that is death, a death not separate from living.[29]

And in 1968 he had written, 'The one who dies each day is beyond death. To die is to love. The beauty is not in past remembrances or in the image of tomorrow. Love has no past and no future; what has, is memory, which is not love. Love with its passion is just beyond the range of society, which is you. Die, and it is there.'

* * * *

On going again to Brockwood in June, I found Pupul Jayakar staying there with her daughter Radhika and Radhika's Canadian husband, Hans Herzberger, a professor of Philosophy who was then at All Souls, Oxford, as a visiting Fellow. Radhika had lived in the United States and then Toronto since 1957, first as a student, but had never lost the feeling that her roots were in India. In 1978 she had been to Rishi Valley for a year with her two daughters who were at school there. The following year her husband went back with her to India and the idea of her living and teaching at Rishi Valley was discussed. During this visit to Brockwood it was decided that after taking her doctorate in Sanscrit and Buddhist studies in 1982 she should go permanently to Rishi Valley. Her husband arranged to teach for one term at his university and spend the second term at Rishi Valley doing research work in his own field.

On June 20 an interview with K by Bernard Levin was broadcast on television at 9 p.m., the last of a series of ten Levin interviews. We had had high hopes of this but it was not a success. Levin had evidently not done enough homework or had not spent enough time talking to K before the actual recording when he and the television crew had gone to Brockwood in May. K started with the words, 'All thought is corruption.' He was given no chance to develop his theme and the critics did not get beyond ridiculing this bald statement. K merely glanced at the screen and then went off to clean his teeth as it was after supper. He never liked to look at himself on television or video, just as he never read his own books. He had often explained this statement about thought in his talks and writings. For instance:

Ideals corrupt the mind; they are born of ideas, judgements and hopes. . . . We are using the word mind to imply the senses, the capacity to think, and the brain that stores all memories as experience, as knowledge. . . . We said ideals corrupt. Knowledge also corrupts the mind. Knowledge is the movement of the past, and when the past overshadows the actual, corruption takes place. . . . We are using the word corruption to mean that which is broken up, that which is not taken as a whole.[30]

K came to London quite frequently that summer. On one occasion it was to see David Bohm who was to undergo triple heart surgery on June 25. Bohm was in a critical condition for several days afterwards. K had sat with him at Birkbeck College for an hour a couple of days before the operation. This had been an immense comfort to him for he had a great fear of dying. K was to talk more and more about death and the fear of dying in his last years.

Before going to Gstaad this summer, K and Mary stayed in Paris for a week in a flat above the Tour d'Argent restaurant, lent to them by Mary's brother. Practically every day they saw Jean-Michel Maroger, who had become a Trustee of the English Foundation in 1980, and his wife Marie-Bertrande. Their daughters had been at the Brockwood School. Jean-Michel was a marine consultant with a beautiful house at Pontlevoy near Blois as well as an apartment in Paris. He had had an English nanny and he could speak perfect English; Marie-Bertrande spoke almost as well and they were invaluable in translating K's books into French. Jean-Michel also translated K's talks at Saanen. It was his mother who had

43

introduced him to K's work, and in 1976 she had rented a chalet near Saanen so that the family could attend K's talks. After K's death Jean-Michel was to write to me:

I must say that what struck me most at first was the man, more than what he said, his charisma, his intensity, the emotion that one could feel in the audience, the whole atmosphere. I was probably then most sensitive to the non-verbal aspect of the communication; the rest followed later. I recall that at the end of the second or third talk I rushed out of the tent, walked up to him, took his hand and thanked him with tears in the eyes.

I cannot resist the temptation of recalling some events which nourished my fascination with Krishnaji. In October 1979 he came with Mary to spend ten days at La Mahaudière. I had called for them at Ch. de Gaulle airport and I was struck by the intense interest with which he was watching everything there, the escalators, the modern luggage-conveyor system, etc., etc. Nothing escaped his attention; it was like a wide-awake young boy discovering everything around him.

On our way home, I was driving, Mary was sitting next to me and Krishnaji was alone on the rear seat. We were going through the Beauce plain and on the right, the sun was setting in a glory of colours. Suddenly, we heard a Sanscrit chant coming from the back of the car. We arrived rather late, but he insisted on having dinner with us in the dining room and even tasted our local wine. For me, for all of us, this stay was a blessing and perhaps you are aware that the first twelve Letters to the Schools were dictated here.

For the first time for many months while K was in Paris he had the pleasure of going to the cinema—a thriller, *Shogun*. He had so few amusements in his dedicated life. It was a real delight to go with him to a good film, a thriller or a Western, and take part in his intense enjoyment.

On their last day in Paris, K suddenly asked Mary to write a book about him. The next day he talked more about the kind of book it should be—what it was like to be with him. One can only hope that one day Mary will feel that she can write such a book, for nobody has been so close to him. Later that summer he was to tell her again that she must outlive him. 'You are responsible to *that*,' he said.

*   *   *   *

Vanda Scaravelli had opened Chalet Tannegg as usual but she

returned to Florence in the middle of the Saanen Gathering which took place between July 12 and 31. Before the seven talks started, K had dictated to Mary more of his *Letters to the Schools*, Nos. 38 and 39. The year before at Saanen he had dictated only one, No. 37. He dictated these letters in batches but they were sent our singly to all his schools at regular intervals and bore the date of their despatch. The first thirty-seven Letters, dated September 1, 1978 to March 1, 1980, had been published in June 1981. The last eighteen Letters, sent out monthly and dated November 15, 1981 to November 15, 1983, were published in 1985. K began the second of these later Letters, dictated at Tannegg:

A school is a place of learning and so it is sacred. The churches, temples and mosques are not sacred for they have stopped learning. They believe; they have faith and that denies entirely the great art of learning, whereas a school like those to which this letter is sent, must be entirely devoted to learning, not only about the world around us, but essentially about what we human beings are, why we believe the way we do, and the complexity of thought. . . . Learning and the accumulation of knowledge are two very different things. Knowledge must always be incomplete, whereas learning is order. Disorder is essentially conflict, self-contradiction and division between becoming and being. Order is a state in which disorder has never existed. Disorder is the bondage of time.[31]

In the earlier volume he had written in a Letter dated March 15, 1979:

When you wander through the woods with heavy shadows and dappled light and suddenly come upon an open space, a green meadow surrounded by stately trees or a sparkling stream, you wonder why man has lost his relationship to nature and the beauty of the earth, the fallen leaf and the broken branch. If you have lost touch with nature, then you will inevitably lose relationship with another. Nature is not just the flowers, the lovely green lawn or the flowing waters in your little garden, but the whole earth with all the things on it. We consider that nature exists for our use, for our convenience, and so lose communion with the earth. This sensitivity to the fallen leaf and to the tall tree on a hill is far more important than all the passing of examinations and having a bright career. Those are not the whole of life. Life is like a vast river with a great volume of water without a beginning or an ending. We take out of that fast-running current a bucket of water and that confined water becomes our life. This is our conditioning and our everlasting sorrow.

*   *   *   *

The seven Saanen talks were a series covering the whole of K's teaching in detail and moving from one aspect of it to another in logical sequence, therefore the book in which they were published should be read as a whole.[32] At one of the Question and Answer meetings K was asked: 'Intellectually we understand that the observer is the observed, but what is necessary to perceive this so that it goes beyond the intellectual level?' K replied:

First of all do we even intellectually accept it? . . . or is it just a lot of words floating around? When you say, 'intellectually I agree with you' what does it mean? It means absolutely nothing. It is just a form of social acceptance . . . but the fact is that the observer is the observed. That is the truth. That is: I am lonely [for example]; my self-centred activity, my ambition, my image about myself, all that has brought about this sense of isolation which I call loneliness. That loneliness is not separate from me. If it is separate from me I can act on it, run away, suppress it, but if it is me— please understand this—if this state is me what is one to do? You understand my question? I may be married, have children, but I am basically terribly lonely. If that loneliness is something separate from me, then I am in conflict with that loneliness. I fight it, I try to fill it by knowledge, by excitement, by this or that, but if it is me I can't do anything about it. Right? . . . Because I cannot do anything about it the conflict ends, but the thing remains, the thing is there. So can my thought remain with it completely, not run away from it but remain with that loneliness with all its complexity of anxiety, fear, remain with it totally without any movement, look at it. If you look at it as an observer looking in, then again the problem arises. But the fact is that loneliness is you, so you have to look at it without the observer, as a whole. When you do that completely, loneliness disappears totally, never to come back.[33]

During the talks, K suffered a great deal from stomach aches. At the end of the Gathering Dr Parchure went with him to the Saanen hospital but tests showed nothing to account for the pains.

*   *   *   *

In late August and early September, after the Brockwood Gathering, K held a seminar at Brockwood on education attended by

46

Maurice Wilkins of King's College, University of London, who had won a Nobel Prize for Medicine in 1962, Rupert Sheldrake the biologist, author of *A New Science of Life:the Hypothesis of Formative Causation*, and Stuart Holroyd, author of *The Quest of the Quiet Mind*, an excellent short exposition of K's teaching. K held firmly during the seminar to the contention that the purpose of education was to bring about the total flowering of a new human being. He was not interested in discussing more practical matters such as the curriculum of a school. From Dr Wilkins he learnt something about genetic engineering.

Dr Parchure returned to India on September 16, the day before K flew to Amsterdam, where he had not been for ten years, to give two talks at the huge RAI Hall there. Accompanying him were Mary Zimbalist, Mary Cadogan, Dorothy Simmons and I. There was some amusement at so many Marys on the part of the travel agent with whom Mary Cadogan booked all our tickets, especially as Dorothy's full name was Dorothy Mary. (K called Mary Zimbalist Maria, pronounced Mareea, to distinguish her from me.) We were met at Schipol by Dr Hans Vincent and K's old friend Anneke Korndorffer. We stayed in a small, comfortable hotel in the midst of pine woods, the Kastanjehof at Laage Voorsche near Hilversum, where the specially prepared vegetarian food was delicious, though over-abundant. On the way to the hall next day in a large hired car, driven by Mary Zimbalist, K suddenly said, 'What am I going to talk about?' 'Haven't you any idea?' I asked. 'None.'

We found the hall packed, the audience overflowing into another hall with closed-circuit television. The thought of a man who had no idea what he was going to say facing this great crowd filled me with panic, and when the small figure appeared, to sit alone on the huge platform on a hard chair, my sense of protection towards him was so great that I could hardly keep back tears. As always he remained quite silent for a few moments, looking from side to side at his audience as if assessing them while they remained tensely expectant. Then he began: 'Most unfortunately there are only two talks and so it is necessary to condense what we have to say about the whole of existence. . . . We are not bringing something exotic from the East like the nonsense that goes on in the name of the gurus and those people who write strange things after visiting India—we do not belong to that crowd at all.' More and more he was emphasising at this time that the difference between human beings was only superficial. He explained this later in the talk:

The content of our consciousness is the common ground of all humanity. . . . A human being living in any part of the world suffers, not only physically but also inwardly. He is uncertain, fearful, confused, anxious, without any sense of deep security. So our consciousness is common to all mankind . . . and therefore we are not individuals. Please do consider this. We have been trained, educated, religiously as well as scholastically, to think that we are individuals, separate souls, striving for ourselves, but this is an illusion. . . . We are not separate entities with separate psychological content, struggling for results; we are, each one of us, actually the rest of humankind.

Although most Dutch people could speak English well, many of that large audience must have been unable to understand the language, let alone the complexities, of what K was saying, yet there was an even larger attendance for the second talk. He began this talk next day:

We are like two friends sitting in the park on a lovely day talking about life, talking about our problems, investigating the very nature of our existence. . . . So let us go into the question of why we human beings live as we do . . . always the brain, the mind, constantly occupied. There is never a quietness, never peace but always this occupation with something or other. That is our daily, monotonous, lonely rather insufficient life. And we try to escape from it through religion, through various forms of entertainment. At the end of the day we are still where we have been for thousands and thousands of years.

Later in the talk he was saying:

First of all we should observe that our brains never act fully, completely; we use only a very small part of our brain. That part is the activity of thought. Being in itself a part, thought is incomplete. The brain functions within a very narrow area, depending on our senses, which again are limited, partial; the whole of the senses are never free, awakened. I do not know if you have experimented with watching something with all your senses, watching the sea, the birds and the moonlight on a green lawn, to see if you have watched partially or with all your senses fully awakened. The two states are entirely different. When you watch something partially you are establishing more the separative, egotistically centred attitude to living. But when you watch that moonlight on the water making a silvery path with all your senses, that is with your mind, with your heart, with your nerves, giving all your attention to that observation, then you will see for yourself that there is no centre from which you are observing. . . . Man has always sought something beyond the physical existence. He has always searched, asked, suffered, tortured himself, to find out if there is something that is not of time, which is not of thought, which is not belief or faith. To find that out one must be absolutely free, for if you are anchored to a particular form of belief, that very belief will prevent the investigation into what is eternal—if there is such a thing as eternity which is beyond all time, beyond all measure. . . . A religious mind is a very factual mind; it deals with facts, with what is actually happening with the world outside and the world inside. The world outside is the expression of the world inside; there is no division between the outer and the inner. A religious life is a life of order, diligence, dealing with that which is actually within oneself, without any illusion.[34]

K was very happy to be in Holland where he had spent so much time when he was young. On September 21 we all went to Deventer to see the Krishnamurti Archive Centre at the Atheneum Bibliotek. It was fascinating for me to see albums full of photographs of the Eerde and Ommen days of the twenties. On the way back to the hotel, after lunching at Deventer, we went to see Castle Eerde, now a school, where small gatherings had been held from 1926 until 1929 when K dissolved the Order of the Star. He had then returned the Castle and its 5,000 acres of land (except for the land on which the Ommen camps were held up to the war) to Baron van Pallandt who had made it over to a Trust to be used for K's work. As we drove through the beautiful beech woods leading to the Castle, K wondered, half seriously, why he had ever given it back, but when he got to the Castle he refused to get out of the car for fear of being seen and recognised.

On his return to Brockwood it was found that K had a high temperature. The school doctor attended him in Dr Parchure's absence. For over a fortnight he was ill with a very bad attack of influenza through which Mary nursed him. It was not until October 14 that he dressed and went down to lunch with the school. When he came to London two days later he told me what he had told Mary on the 11th: at four a.m. he could have 'slipped away. The door opened and then shut.' He had always felt that his hold on life was very weak; that if he let go he could easily 'slip away'; it was harder for him to stay alive than to die.

During his illness he talked to Mary at some length about his odd memory. He had two distinct memories, he told her—one of standing alone by the river at Adyar without a thought in his head (as described in his journal, see p. 3) and the other of Mrs Besant taking him by the hand, sitting him down beside her on her *chowki* and asking him whether he would accept her and the others present as his disciples. He had said he would accept only her. (This was in 1925)

K was well enough in a day or two to dictate another Letter to the Schools (dated January 15, 1982). In this Letter he asked, 'What does it mean to look at life as a whole? It means to observe human beings, ourselves, without any division of nationality, to see life as one single movement without a beginning and without an end, without time, without death. This is a difficult thing to understand because we think of the part not the totality. We divide, hoping to understand the whole from the part.'

'What is it to be transformed?'

Before K flew to Delhi on October 25 I had talked to him about a friend of mine, Anita Desai, who lived in New Delhi with her husband and four children. She was a distinguished writer whom I had first met at a party in London to launch one of her books (another, *In Custody*, was to be short-listed for the Booker Prize in 1984). I had spoken to her about K and knew that she wanted to meet him, and I felt sure that he would like her, for not only was she young, talented and beautiful, but very gentle and graceful. Her mother had been German and her father Indian and she had been brought up in India.

Asit Chandmal, who had come to Brockwood from San Francisco, flew with K to Delhi, and shortly afterwards Mary Zimbalist returned to Ojai. Dr Parchure was able to report to her from India that K's energy was good, though the tremor in his hands, which he had had for some time, had increased. This shakiness of the hands was to get worse as time went on. K stayed in New Delhi with Pupul Jayakar at her house in Safdarjang Road, in the same street as Mrs Gandhi. After K's death Anita sent me some notes about her meetings with him which are given below:

I had a telephone call from Pupul Jayakar's secretary, asking me to come to a small private meeting in her garden one October morning in 1981. There were actually a few hundred people seated there on the grass under a coloured 'shamiana' but of course that made a smaller crowd than the public meetings that Krishnaji addressed. He spoke, then invited questions from the audience. When the meeting was over, someone asked on the loud speaker whether I was present and if I would come and meet Krishnaji. I did that and he greeted me as 'Mary's friend—Mary spoke of you.' He said he had heard I walked in the Lodi gardens in the evenings and asked if I would meet him there. I used to take my dog Tensing to the park at the same hour of the evening that he was there. I saw him appear at the head of a small group of people, striding along at great speed that the others could not keep up with. We met at one end of the park and then walked together and it became a part of our routine to meet in the evenings and walk together during his stay in Delhi. The only evenings when he did not walk there were the ones when he gave public addresses. He was never alone. Usually members of Pupul's family accompanied him (although she never did herself)—her sister Nandini Mehta always, sometimes her daughter Radhika Herzberger and Radhika's daughters, always Mr Patwardhan of the Krishnamurti Foundation in Madras, occasionally Pupul's nephew [Asit Chandmal], once or twice Radha Burnier. What struck me was that they neither walked beside K, nor talked to him (with the exception of Radhika Herzberger and Mr Patwardhan), and all tended to follow him at some distance. I wondered if he really liked striding ahead alone and feeling them trailing behind him. Since that seemed to be their custom, it embarrassed me somewhat to walk beside K and talk to him. I imagined it would be difficult but he talked volubly and with great charm and a lack of self-consciousness, something of his childhood (for instance, of how close he had been to his brother and how his death had affected him), of different episodes of his life, of people he had known (e.g. a visit to Bernard Berenson at I Tatti*), and a great deal of time about his schools, what his aspirations were for them, of the children who came to them, what he hoped for them. He seemed concerned above all about young people today, the environment of violence and fear, and what he could do to change that. (He liked talking to my daughters if they came along; he was interested in my older daughter's stories about her college, and the bad behaviour of young men on the bus; he told her with great passion, 'You should hit them; if I were there, I would have hit them.')

He asked me to go to Rishi Valley, the school of which he seemed particularly proud, and wanted me to stay for a while and talk to the students. My last meeting with him haunts me because it had no sequel and therefore cut off our dialogue, promising an answer that never came. I think we must have been arguing more and more passionately as we walked along in the autumn dusk. I couldn't understand his very ambivalent attitude to

* The entry in Berenson's diary for May 7, 1956, when he was ninety, reads: 'Krishnamurti to tea: affable, responsive, conceding all my objections, and indeed our discussion was scarcely controversial. He insisted nevertheless on a Beyond, and that this was a state of immobile, uneventful existence, no thought, no questioning, no—what? He rejected my contention that such a state was something beyond my Western cast of mind. I went so far as to ask him whether he was not after something merely verbal. He denied it firmly, but without heat.' (*Sunset and Twilight*, edited by Nicky Mariano, Hamish Hamilton, 1964.) K was staying at Il Leccio with Vanda Scaravelli who had taken him to I Tatti. She had often taken him there before.

art and literature and learning—he often praised people of scholarship and achievement, and although he claimed to read nothing but the dictionary and detective stories, he did tell me of a time when he was quite alone at Ojai and played Beethoven's last symphony over and over again on his record player, just lived with Beethoven's music and was perfectly content. Yet he often said it was not necessary to read or write, one ought to be able to live in complete solitude, happy with the trees and plants and birds, and not requiring anything else. I must have been trying to tell him what books meant to me, how I felt they were an indispensable part of my life, both the reading and writing of them. It was quite dark; he stopped at the foot of the Lodi tomb and said, 'Let me ask you a question—why do you write?' I began to mumble and stutter and ran several answers into one, muddling them. I said my life would be incomplete if I did not write, that ever since I was a child no experience seemed complete to me till I had written it down, that I found I could put my thoughts in order as I wrote them down, that it was a way of bringing order and harmony to chaos and meaninglessness, and that I felt this was what I was made to do and that by it I could justify my existence. Naturally he got very impatient with my answer. 'No, no, no, that is not right,' he said with great passion. 'An artist should be like Beethoven—he felt the music inside him and it poured out of him and he could not stop it or control it, it just rose up and poured out.' Pupul's nephew was with us that evening, following us around with a camera, not taking part in the conversation but listening and nodding. He indicated that they had to leave, it was dark, and they were leaving Delhi next day. Krishnaji put his hand on my shoulder and said, 'But you will come to Rishi Valley, and when you come, I will tell you something.' I felt intensely curious to know what he wanted to tell me since it seemed it would bear on my writing and my life, and I thought he would also explain the ambiguities of his own response to art. But I did not go to Rishi Valley and he did not tell me any more on the subject.

I want to tell you of a few pictures I have in my mind of him: once my dog stalked and started to chase a squirrel; K immediately lifted his arms and started to flap them, shouted and ran after the dog while I ran after them crying, 'No, no, no, no, he never catches them, don't worry, he won't catch it.' He liked throwing a ball or stick for Tensing to fetch. Then I remember a group of people waiting for him to come up and K, on seeing them, looking around desperately, 'I wish I could hide. I hate—I hate— having to meet people.' I thought that strange, after so many years of public life. But the dislike and fear were plain to see on his face as he tried to suppress it and smile. A baby was lifted up to be blessed and he patted its cheek with evident embarrassment.

Twice Pupul invited me to lunch; she often gave small luncheon parties at which he could meet a cross-section of society in Delhi. Once the other guest was a suave civil servant who kept up the kind of conversation one might hear at a diplomatic cocktail party. K, not to be outdone, traded one joke for another with him. [K's jokes, and he loved telling jokes, were mostly irreverent.] There were usually four to six people at these lunches and after them K would go to his room to rest.

Then there were the 'private meetings' in her drawing-room for some 50–100 at a time. Two or three of the audience, and Pupul herself, would sit beside K and put questions to him. Once there was a Buddhist priest whom K greeted with great respect and affection; the two seemed very happy in each other's company. The other guests frequently made him irritable and impatient. The meetings would last for an hour. They were always held in the morning, at that pleasant time of year when it is beginning to get cool, the sun filtering through the bamboo screens beginning to feel mild and gentle, and one could hear the calls of the birds in the garden. In my mind I always associate K with gardens and bird calls.

Then I'd like to tell you about a documentary I saw on television some time ago, in India. There was a scene of him crossing a bridge—perhaps in Benares—leaving others behind, and crossing it alone. And of the question put to him: 'You have spent all your life travelling and meeting people and talking to them. Please tell me, why do you do it?' He laughed, half-swung around as if looking for an answer, then said something unexpected: 'Out of affection, I suppose.' The words sounded both shy and impulsive.

The reference to the dictionary in Anita's notes is interesting. In early years K had used words in common parlance which his audiences readily understood. Later he became fascinated by the derivations he found in etymological dictionaries and often referred to definitions and usages which had become obsolete. This was a very rare instance of K relying on something he had read. For some, no doubt, these references to 'the dictionary' clarified his meaning; others, myself I must admit included, felt that the introduction of outside thought was a loss rather than a gain. As for the detective stories, reading them was perhaps the only true recreation K indulged in. They were a distraction and left no impression whatever. Every now and then he finished one without realising that he had read it before.

Anita did not see K after 1984 because she was lecturing in America the last time he went to Delhi in 1985. He wrote to me after first meeting her to say how much he liked her and how much he wished she would go to Rishi Valley.

K's ambivalent attitude to art and literature was always a puzzle. He loved certain classical music, Mozart almost as much as Beethoven, and Indian music, especially chanting (he would chant many of the ancient Sanscrit mantras himself). He loved the poetry of Shelley and Keats and certain passages from the Old Testament which my mother had read aloud to him (at one time he knew the 'Song of Solomon' almost by heart), but it is doubtful whether he ever read modern poetry. He had been deeply moved by some buildings and sculpture—the Parthenon, Chartres Cathedral, the statue of Themis in Athens, a stone head of Buddha in the Boston Museum, the Winged Victory at the Louvre, the huge Maheshmurti statue of Shiva in the Elephanta Caves near Bombay. (He kept a photograph of this in an envelope, for he said one must only look at it afresh and not get used to it.) But I never heard him praise a picture and I wonder whether any work of art moved him as much as a sunset.

*   *   *   *

In India that winter K was kept very busy as usual. As well as public talks in Delhi, at Rajghat (his second-oldest school at Varanasi), at Madras and Bombay, and talking to students and teachers at Rishi Valley where he spent a fortnight in December, he held long discussions with various swamis and pandits and the group of friends who usually surrounded him. (Many of these discussions are given in Pupul Jayakar's *Krishnamurti*.) At Ojai, Brockwood and Gstaad he would have breakfast quietly in bed and not get up until midday unless he had an appointment. It was these quiet mornings that enabled him to dictate his *Letters to the Schools* and write his Journal. (It is only in his writings that we have his lovely descriptions of nature.) In India, however, he got up for breakfast and the talk would start then.

Discussions with several people taking part and asking questions were the favoured way in India of delving into philosophy or religious teaching. The Indian way is no doubt the best way of reaching intellectual understanding, but it seems to preclude those leaps of intuition by which some people grasped more readily what K was talking about. Those who followed the way of discussion could probably explain his teaching better to others; the intuitive grasp serves only for oneself. However, as K himself had said over and over again that he wanted no interpreters, the intuitive way may be as good as the other. K himself enjoyed these discussions and was stimulated by them. He liked to go slowly, step by step, into his teaching, though he had told me that it came to *him* in the form of 'revelation'. I had said to him while I was writing his biography, 'Knowing you as K, the man, it is hard for me to think of you making the teachings,' to which he had replied, 'If I deliberately sat down to write it, I doubt if I could produce it. . . . There is a sense of vacancy and then something comes. . . . If it were only K—he is uneducated, gentle—so where does it come from? This person [K] hasn't thought out the teachings. . . . It is like—what is the Biblical term?—revelation. It happens all the time when I am talking [giving talks].'[35]

It was also the Indian way to doubt everything that was said and question it. This K thoroughly approved of since faith, accepting unquestioningly the words of another, was to him an impenetrable barrier to truth.

At a Question and Answer meeting in Madras, K was asked, 'What is it to be transformed?' To this he replied:

When you are observing, seeing the dirt on the road, seeing how the politicians behave, seeing your own attitude towards your wife, your children and so on, transformation is there. To bring about some kind of order in daily life, that is transformation; not something extraordinary, out of this world. When one is not thinking clearly, objectively, rationally, be aware of it and change it, break it. That is transformation. If you are jealous watch it, don't give it time to flower, change it immediately. That is transformation. When you are greedy, violent, ambitious, trying to become some kind of holy man, see how it is creating a world of tremendous uselessness. Competition is destroying the world. The world is becoming more and more competitive, more and more aggressive and if you change it immediately, that is transformation. And if you go very much deeper into the problem it is clear that thought denies love. Therefore one has to find out whether there is an end to thought, an end to time, not to philosophise over it and discuss it but find out. Truly that is transformation and if you go into it very deeply, transformation means never a thought of becoming, comparing.[36]

When K stopped at Brockwood for a few nights in February 1982 on his way to Ojai he was feeling very strong and looked wonderfully well although his weight was down to 109 lb.

*   *   *   *

K had known before he went to India that he was to have a hernia operation as soon as he returned to America. Mary Zimbalist had written to me from Ojai on January 12, 1982:

I have been arranging K's stay in hospital for this hernia repair and it turns out to be more than the equivalent of a visit to Mr Thompson [his dentist in London], which I suspect is rather what K imagined when he told me to arrange things. He will see our regular doctor three days after his arrival here on the 14th February and then is booked to go into hospital the following Saturday for the usual gamut of tests, etc. before surgery on the Monday. I have taken a 'suite', which means two rooms, one of which I will inhabit to try to make hospital life as uncomplicated as possible for him. The surgeon sounds nice on the telephone but we won't actually see him until K is already admitted to hospital. That is the way things are run these days. He is, however, chosen by our regular doctor as the very best and also as a sensitive, nice man as well. My concern now is the amount of time to recover from a hernia operation because the New York Talks loom at the end of March. There have been varying opinions on length of convalescence but the surgeon himself says 3–4 weeks should be enough. There is too little leeway in all this but I don't know what to do except to leave the plans in place. The priority of course is to get the hernia repaired as it is too dangerous for him to travel around the world with a possibility that a loop of intestines could slide down and be caught in the hernia. That would be serious and require immediate surgery of a more serious kind.

This was not the first operation that Mary had had to arrange for K. He had undergone a prostate operation in 1977. At Ojai and Brockwood, Mary not only acted as K's secretary and chauffeur but prepared his breakfast and supper, shopped for him, washed and ironed his clothes and looked after him when he was ill. He insisted on helping her by taking his breakfast and supper trays from his bedroom to the kitchen, stacking and unstacking the dish-washer, swabbing the formica surfaces and polishing the electric kettle every evening. He was always intensely interested in what she bought when she went shopping, and even liked to help unpack her basket of groceries.

On February 20, a few days after arriving at Ojai, K went into the UCLA Medical Center where Mary stayed on a couch in his room for the four nights he was there. The operation took place under a spinal anaesthetic as had his former operation. It was a great ordeal for him and as the anaesthetic wore off the pain became intense. He spoke of the 'open door'. Mary asked him to close it. Later on in the day he told her, 'It was very close. I didn't know whether I had the strength to close the door.' By the evening, however, he was sitting up reading a detective story.

He was allowed to go back to Ojai on the 24th but suffered some pain on and off for a fortnight and did not go for his first walk until March 7. On that day he spoke to Mary again about 'the impulse to slip off'. But, 'Not now,' he added. 'I still have too much to do.'

A few days before he flew to New York on March 20, it was discovered when he went to the Ojai Hospital for a check-up that his blood-sugar count was too high. He was put on a diabetic diet. He and Mary stayed in New York at the Hotel Parker-Meridien near Carnegie Hall where he was to give two talks. They heard that the hall had been sold out for the first talk, and, the following day, that tickets were being 'scalped' outside at $85 for the second talk. K had several times before spoken in New York, the last time in 1974, but this was the first time that the cost of renting a hall had made it necessary to charge $10 for a ticket.

On March 26 K was interviewed at the hotel by Paul L. Montgomery for the *New York Times*. The article appeared, with a photograph of the speaker on the platform, on the morning of the second talk on March 28, a Sunday. It stated that every one of the 2,780 seats in Carnegie Hall had been filled for the first talk and that hundreds had stood outside the hall unable to get in. It then gave a résumé of K's early life, mentioned his Foundations and his present mode of travelling from place to place lecturing, then quoted what Henry Miller had once said about him: 'Here is a man of our time who may be said to be a master of reality. He stands alone. He has renounced more than any man I can think of, except the Christ.'

K told Montgomery, 'You see, I never accepted authority, and I never exercised authority over others. I'll tell you a funny story. During Mussolini's time, one of his chief workers asked me to speak in Stresa, by Lago Maggiore. When I got to the hall, there were in front of me cardinals, bishops, generals. They probably thought I was a guest of Mussolini. I talked about authority, how pernicious it was, how destructive it was. The next day, when I spoke again, there was one old woman in the audience.' On being asked by Montgomery 'if he thought his lifetime of work had made any difference in the way people lived', K replied, 'A little, sir. But not much.'

In the first talk K began by saying he was not giving a lecture but, 'Together, as two friends walking in a quiet lane, on a summer's day, we are conversing and seeing clearly why human beings throughout the world are behaving in the way they do. . . . We are going to take our human existence as it is and find out for ourselves if there's any possibility of radical change in the whole human condition.' He then went into the subjects of knowledge, conditioning, freedom, human consciousness, thought, relationship, security, fear, desire, time, images, analysis. One reason for psychological fear, he said,

is comparison, to compare yourself with another. Or comparing yourself with what you have been and what you will be. . . . Have you ever tried never to compare yourself with another, either physically or psychologically? When you don't compare you're not becoming. You understand this? Our whole cultural education is to become something, to be something. . . . Religiously, socially, we're always wanting to become something. To live without any comparison whatsoever is an extraordinary thing that takes place when you have no measure.

About relationship he said that we all had images about ourselves and others and that there could be no real relationship between images. For instance, as long as you had an image about your wife and she had an image about you there was bound to be conflict. He went on:

As long as you have an image about yourself, you're going to get hurt. It's one of our miseries in life, from childhood through school, college, university (if you're lucky)—right through life, you're getting hurt. . . . And what is it that is hurt? It is the image that you have built about yourself. . . . Is it possible to be totally free of all image? Then there is no hurt, no flattery. But most people find security in the image they have built for themselves, which is the image that thought has created.

He then spoke of analysis, so pertinent to American life: 'If there is any trouble, we trot off to the analyst—he's the modern priest— we think he's going to solve all our stupid little problems. Analysis implies that there is an analyser and the analysed. Who is the analyser? Is he separate from the analysed? Or is he the analysed?' K was saying about the analyst and the analysed what he had been saying for years about the observer and the observed, the thinker and his thought. They were inseparable. There was no difference between them. This was true, he maintained, of all inward fragmentation. 'When you're angry,' he said, 'anger is you. You are not different from anger. When you are greedy, envious, you are that.'

A short way through this long talk, he pleaded, 'Please, please, if I may request you in the most friendly way, do not clap before or after the talk—it isn't worth it. If you clap, you are clapping for your understanding. It's not that you are clapping for the speaker. The speaker is not interested in any way in being a leader, in being a guru—all that stupid nonsense. We are together understanding something in life, life which has become so extraordinarily complex.'[37]

In the second talk, which was shorter, he spoke of the wholeness of life and asked why it was that we had made pleasure 'something totally separate from the rest of life'. From there he went on to discussing time and pointed out that psychological time did not exist at all.

Time as skill, knowledge, that is necessary, but psychological time has no truth in it; it is not a fact. Psychological time is an illusion, it has no reality. What has reality is the transformation of 'what is'; for example, I am violent; the desire to be non-violent is time. During that time I am still violent, whereas the observation of violence in myself requires no time. The attention to 'what is', which is violence, dissolves completely, instantaneously, that which is. You work it out if you are interested in it.

He continued with the subject of love, saying again that one could come upon love only by negating what love was not. 'One has to negate totally all self-centred activity. Then only that which is love blossoms into compassion. Compassion cannot exist if you are attached to any particular theory, to any particular belief, to any particular religious organisation. . . . Out of that love, whatever you do is right, correct, true, for love is holistic, it is not divisive.'

He then turned to death and meditation, saying about them what he had said before, though in different words.

At the end of the talk he asked if he might get up and go, and was evidently a little dismayed when questions were put to him. He begged for no more than two. The last one was, 'Sir, could you describe to me God. Does God exist?' To this K replied:

We have invented God. Thought has invented God, that is, we, out of our misery, despair, loneliness, anxiety, have invented that thing called God. God has not made us in his image—I wish he had. Personally I have no belief in anything. The speaker only faces what is, what are facts, the realisation of the nature of every fact, every thought, all the reactions—he is totally aware of all that. If you are free from fear, from sorrow, there is no need for a god.[38]

In spite of his request for no clapping there was applause as he stood up.

6

The Art of Meditation

On K's return to Ojai a check-up at the UCLA Medical Center found that his blood-sugar count was till too high but that otherwise he was perfectly fit. A visit to the oculist, however, discovered the beginnings of cataract in both eyes and a threatening of glaucoma in his left eye for which he was given drops to put in daily.

David Bohm, fully recovered, and his wife now came to Ojai and on April 16 the first of four, hour-long discussions took place on 'The Nature of the Mind' between K, Bohm, Dr John Ridley, a psychiatrist in private practice in Ojai, and Rupert Sheldrake who was at this time a consultant to the International Crops Institute in Hyderabad. The first discussion was on 'The Roots of Psychological Disorder', the second on 'Psychological Suffering', the third on 'The Need for Security', and the fourth on 'What Is a Healthy Mind?'. These discussions, video-recorded in colour, had been sponsored by the Robert E. Simon Foundation, a private body giving substantial grants towards the furthering of mental health. There were immediate requests for these tapes from various university and training centres throughout the country who could either buy or borrow them to show. They were also shown on several Cable TV stations, including New York.[39]

K's birthday, his eighty-seventh, fell as usual in the middle of the Oak Grove Talks between May 1 and 16. (Mary kept his birthday on the 12th, the day on which he was born by Western time.) It was his only free day and they drove to Beverly Hills along the beach road where they had a picnic lunch and did some errands. He looked well and was particularly full of energy. He told Mary, 'Every night now meditation wakes me.' It was during his meditation that the 'other' was most present to him. What he meant by meditation, though, was very different from most people's understanding of the word. He spoke about it in at least one of every series of talks he gave. Each time he described it differently. The meditation that had woken him may have been as he described it in one of his books:

Meditation at that hour was freedom and it was like entering into an unknown world of beauty and quietness; it was a world without image, symbol or word, without waves of memory. Love was in the death of every minute and each death was the returning of love. It was not attachment, it had no roots; it flowered without cause and it was a flame that burned away the borders, the carefully built fences of consciousness. Meditation was joy and with it came benediction.[40]

In a talk given at Saanen he observed, 'Meditation is the emptying of the mind of the activity of the self, and this cannot be done by any practice, by any method, or by saying, "Tell me what to do."'[41]

On another occasion he wrote: 'Man, in order to escape his conflicts, has invented many forms of meditation. These have been based on desire, will and the urge for achievement. This conscious, deliberate striving is always within the limits of a conditioned mind and in this there is no freedom. All effort to meditate is the denial of meditation. Meditation is the ending of thought. It is only then that there is a different dimension beyond time.'[42]

And again:

Meditation is one of the greatest arts in life—perhaps the greatest, and one cannot possibly learn it from anybody. That is the beauty of it. It has no technique and therefore no authority. When you learn about yourself, watch yourself, watch the way you walk, how you eat, what you say, the gossip, the hate, the jealousy—if you are aware of that in yourself, without any choice, that is part of meditation. So meditation can take place when you are sitting in a bus or walking in the woods full of light and shadow, or listening to the singing of birds or looking at the face of your wife or child.[43]

And in 1984, in a talk to scientists at Los Alamos (see p. 81), he was to say:

Meditation is not conscious meditation. What we have been taught is conscious, deliberate meditation, sitting cross-legged or lying down or repeating certain phrases, which is a deliberate, conscious effort to meditate. The speaker says such meditation is nonsense. It is part of desire.

Desiring to have a peaceful mind is the same as desiring a good house or a good dress. Conscious meditation destroys, prevents the other form of meditation.

*   *   *   *

In June K was to give two talks at the Barbican Concert Hall in London. It was the first time he had spoken in London in any hall larger than the Friends' Meeting House and the Wimbledon Town Hall. On June 3, Joe and I met him and Mary Zimbalist at Waterloo (they had come from Brockwood) and drove them to the Savoy Hotel where they were to stay for three nights. The next morning we drove them to the Barbican. We had surveyed the Hall beforehand, discovering that there was no separate entrance for the artists. The only way K could get from the street to the Hall without going through the crowd in the foyer was by the service lift.

The Hall was packed, the overflow watching in the cinema on a lower level. I did not hear the talk because, with the help of one of my grand-daughters, I was manning the bookstall where K's books were on sale outside the auditorium. In spite of the exorbitant price asked for the hire of the Hall (there was no charge for tickets) the loudspeaker failed to work. Terence Stamp, who had been an admirer of K's for many years, came storming out saying that it was a disgrace. The books sold very well, however, and so did the cassettes of K's talks which were being sold by Ray McCoy.

In the course of the second talk K said:

Perhaps some of you have heard the speaker for the last fifty years or more and are still caught in the old tradition, the old habits of attachment and attempting to become detached, struggling to be detached. Detachment leads to cynicism, cruelty, whereas if one understands the nature of attachment and goes into it deeply and sees the consequences of it, then that which is false drops away. One hasn't time to go deeper into this, because there is something more to talk over together if you are not too tired.

We ought to talk over together the very complex problem of what is death—why human beings throughout the world, of whatever colour, whatever nationality, whatever race, whatever religion, are scared of death. Those who are really quite serious in their intent to find out the whole meaning of death must enquire, not only into the fear, but also into what is the ending—which means the ending of everything, ending of your possessions, ending of all your remembrances, of all your attachments, ending of all the pleasurable or unhappy habits. We ought to enquire not into what death is but rather into what is the ending of the known because one's mind, one's brain, is always functioning within the known, and when it is challenged, which is the ending of the known, which is death, it is scared, it is frightened, it shrivels up.

So is it possible to end it while living—not commit suicide, I'm not talking about that—but to end attachment, for example, attachment to one's work, to one's neighbour, to one's family, to one's ideas, beliefs and doctrines, to end one's god, if one has a god, to deny totally all the known, for that is the essence of death? The ending of the known is death. So can we live with death all the time? I wonder if you understand what I am talking about? While living, with plenty of vitality, energy, drive, live at the same time with this constant ending of accumulation, constant ending of every record. That requires a great deal of attention, awareness, energy. When once you perceive that, then it becomes like a river full of water that is flowing.[44]

Although the loudspeaker was working for this second talk, K disliked the atmosphere of the Hall so much that it was not one of his best. We felt disgusted with the whole Barbican complex.

*   *   *   *

Vanda Scaravelli and Fosca had opened up Chalet Tannegg by the time K and Mary arrived on July 4, but as this year the downstairs flat had not been rented, Vanda insisted that Dr Parchure should stay at Tannegg while she herself stayed in a room in another chalet. K gave six talks at Saanen this year, followed by the usual Question and Answer meetings. Dr Dagmar Liechti, former Head of the Bircher-Benner Clinic at Zurich where K had been in 1960, was at the Saanen Gathering and went to Tannegg to discuss K's health with Dr Parchure, his blood-sugar count being still too high. They suggested to him that he should cancel the seminar of scientists arranged to take place at Brockwood in September after the Gathering there. K agreed to this; he felt that he ought to space out his activities better. In spite of feeling tired after the Saanen talks he dictated to Mary another batch of *Letters to the Schools*, one a day between August 1 and 12. He was also talking at this time about the possibility of building adult centres where people might come for the sole purpose of studying his teaching; there might be one in

India, one at Ojai and one at Brockwood. He envisaged beautiful buildings, quite separate from the schools.

Instead of the seminar after the Brockwood Gathering, K, with Mary and Dorothy Simmons, went for a holiday to France. They were met in Paris on September 10 by Jean-Michel Maroger who drove them to Cellettes, near Blois, where he had taken rooms for them at the Château Lutaine, close to the Marogers' own place, La Mahaudière. (The Marogers could not have them to stay again because their eldest daughter was about to get married.) K and Mary stayed at the Château for over a fortnight (Dorothy had to return earlier because of the beginning of the school term), visiting Chaumont, Amboise and Chenonceau as well as seeing a good deal of the Marogers. It was a most successful holiday—no talks for K, no serious discussions, no dictations, no schools, no one who knew him except the Marogers—a rare occurrence in his life.

Before K went to India that year at the end of October, I begged him to go on with his Journal. I felt that he was talking too much and not writing at all nowadays. It was so much easier to talk than to write. Writing needed discipline; his talks were discursive, and the easiest form of talking was answering questions. Besides, his talks and discussions had to be edited for publication and that inevitably put a filter between him and his reader, whereas not a word had had to be altered in his *Notebook* or his *Journal* which he had written by hand. And added to that was the greatest boon of all to my mind—his descriptions of nature which made his writing infinitely precious. When he said that writing was difficult now with his shaky hand, I suggested that he should dictate, while alone, into a tape-recorder, holding a pencil in his hand so that his words would flow as if he were writing. He liked the idea but said, as I feared, that he would have no time while he was in India. However, he said he would try it when he got back to Ojai.

This year K flew most of the way alone to India. Rita Zampese, Manager of public relations for the United Kingdom for Lufthansa in London, with whom Mary Zimbalist had made friends, went with him as far as Frankfurt and saw him on to the Lufthansa flight to Delhi where he arrived on October 24 to stay with Pupul Jayakar. His programme in India that winter was fuller than ever, for as well as giving talks in Delhi, Rajghat, Madras and Bombay, taking part in discussions with pandits and others and talking to the staff and pupils at Rajghat and Rishi Valley, he went to Calcutta in November to give four talks. He had never spoken there before.

Sunanda and Pama Patwardhan went ahead with Parameswaran, the cook from Rishi Valley, to get ready the house that had been put at K's disposal in Calcutta. K followed from Rajghat with Achyut Patwardhan and Dr Parchure on November 18. He wrote to Mary Zimbalist next day that 'tremendous publicity' was 'going on', and on the 20th, the day of the first talk, he wrote: 'The papers are full of so-called teaching.' After the second talk on the 21st, he continued this diary letter: 'Huge crowds. On dit, the audience is larger than Bombay, between five and six thousand, absolutely quiet and silent, which they say Calcutta has never seen before. The papers are making a résumé of the talks. One wonders why. Newspapers don't usually do this kind of thing. Two prominent industrialists came to lunch today and we talked seriously. It's all rather odd.'

Pupil Jayakar went to Calcutta for two nights on the 25th, and Radha Burnier also arrived on the 25th and stayed until K and the others flew to Madras on the 30th en route for Rishi Valley. K told Mary that Calcutta was 'a filthy, noisy city, over-crowded; it's quite appalling. They have a communist government here, but fortunately quite ineffective, in name Marxist, opposed to Mrs Gandhi. It's such a chaotic mess. Chacun pour soi. Electricity goes off for hours on end and general darkness prevails mentally too.'

There were two more talks on the 27th and 28th. The Calcutta press gave both K's life and his talks full coverage. He spoke on all his usual themes, stressing the urgent need for self-transformation at a time of crisis for the world threatened by total extinction. Men as well as nations were becoming more isolated and there was no security in isolation. 'When you see the truth of something,' he said, 'you are absolutely alone.' Standing alone, according to him, was very different from being isolated. He spoke of the nature of intelligence: 'Knowledge, cleverness, is not intelligence. Where there is compassion, love, it has its own intelligence. Intelligence is the activity of the wholeness of life, not the fragmentation'. This meaning of the word 'intelligence' is important for an understanding of the teaching. 'Most of us have lust only,' he went on, 'and not passion. Only with the ending of sorrow is there passion.'[45] And sorrow could never end so long as there was attachment.

The Art of Meditation

Unlike the crowds in Bombay, the Calcutta audience dispersed quietly after a talk, impressed apparently but rather bewildered. As the reporter for the *Economic Times* wrote: 'In the final analysis it must be said that no one can comprehend, in its entirety, the philosophy of J. Krishnamurti (or is it non-philosophy?) by merely attending a series of four talks.'

At Rishi Valley, where K went in December, Radhika Herzberger was now installed as Director of Studies, working closely with Narayan who was still the Principal. K was very pleased by the way things were going at the school. After speaking in Madras and Bombay, he returned to Ojai in February, 1983, in excellent spirits although tests in Madras had shown that his blood-sugar count was as high as it had been just after his operation.

*   *   *   *

K had not forgotten his undertaking to try dictating alone as if he were writing, and on February 25 at Ojai, while in bed after breakfast, alone in his room, he dictated the first piece into a Sony-Walkman cassette-recorder. This piece began:

There is a tree by the river and we have been watching it day after day for several weeks* when the sun is about to rise. As the sun rises slowly over the horizon, over the trees, this particular tree becomes all of a sudden golden. All the leaves are bright with life and as you watch it as the hours pass by, that tree whose name does not matter—what matters is that beautiful tree—an extraordinary quality seems to spread all over the land, over the river, and as the sun rises a little higher the leaves begin to flutter, to dance. And each hour seems to give to that tree a different quality. Before the sun rises it has a sombre feeling, quiet, far away, full of dignity. And as the day begins, the leaves with the light on them dance and give it that peculiar feeling that one has of great beauty. By midday its shadow has deepened and you can sit there protected from the sun, never feeling lonely, with the tree as your companion. As you sit there, there is a relationship of deep abiding security and a freedom that only trees can know.

Towards the evening when the western skies are lit up by the setting sun, the tree gradually becomes sombre, dark, closing in on itself. The sky has become red, yellow, green, but the tree remains quiet, hidden, and is resting for the night. If you establish a relationship with it, then you have relationship with mankind.[46]

* He was evidently describing a tree in some other part of the world, probably at Rajghat since he mentions a river.

K went on with these dictations, though not every day, until April 6 when he, Mary and the Lilliefelts flew to New York for two more talks. Most of the pieces he dictated begin with a description of nature, showing how every day was indeed for him a new day, a day such as had never been before. For me, these descriptions quieten one's entire being, making it intuitively receptive to the teaching that follows.

In March, Dr Jonas Salk, the discoverer of the polio vaccine, was at Ojai to hold a video-taped discussion with K. The discussion was started by Dr Salk: 'I would like you to tell me what is your deepest interest, your deepest concern.' After a little hesitation, K answered, 'I think any serious man must be concerned about the future, what's going to happen to mankind.'

A long exchange followed about the need for a transformation of the human psyche as the only hope for humanity, Dr Salk arguing that change was a process of evolution but that evolution could be accelerated, K maintaining that that involved time; change must be immediate or it would be too late to save humanity from destruction. K asked if time could end, psychological time, that was. There was no *means* by which one could bring about self-transformation but when once 'you actually see the truth that you are the rest of mankind—feel it in your guts, in your blood, then your whole activity, your whole attitude, your whole way of living changes.'

They both agreed that you could not change anyone by telling him what do do; compassion, though, might bring about change in another; and 'compassion,' K averred, 'could not be put together by thought. How can compassion exist when I have hate in my heart, when I want to kill somebody, when I am crying? . . . It's like the sun. Sunshine isn't yours or mine. We share it. So if you want to help change another, be like the sun. Give him compassion, love, intelligence, nothing else. Don't say, do this, do that; then he falls into the trap that all religions have set.'

Dr Salk grasped the point: 'I hear you say something very positive, very important, very significant. I hear you say that people, individuals, a group of people exist who possess the qualities for emanating something that could help the rest of mankind.'

'You see,' K said, 'that's the whole conception—that there are

69

such people who help. Not guide, not tell you what to do, because that's too silly. But, just like the sun, give light. And if you want to sit in the sun, you sit in it. If you don't, you sit in the shadow.'

'It's that kind of enlightenment,' Dr Salk said.

'It is enlightenment,' K replied.[47]

*   *   *   *

This year in New York K stayed in a suite in the Dorset Hotel on West 54th Street and gave his talks on April 9 and 10 at the Felt Forum in Madison Square Garden which held over 4,000 people. On the 12th he gave an interview at the hotel for an hour and a half to two reporters for *East West Journal* (it appeared in the July number). In an introduction to the interview, one journalist wrote, 'Having been warned that "he is an extremely difficult man to interview and does not tolerate small talk" we wondered how we would manage. Yet we met a polite and shy man who seemed to have infinite patience, yet at the same time exhibited a fierceness and sense of mission. . . . His clarity and insightful comments put us on the spot many times, leaving us with the feeling that here was a truly free man who, without trying, had achieved what I feel is a type of spiritual anarchy—a deeply moral and sacred outlook completely independent of orthodox ideologies or religions.'

K *was* quite fierce at first:

EWJ: Now that we have massive worldwide communications, unique in history, do you think that a transformation of consciousness will emerge? I mean, specifically, using the media as a tool to raise consciousness. For instance, this film 'Gandhi' that has just won the Academy award is basically about peace and about Gandhi's main message of non-violence.

K: That's rubbish. Unless you go to the root of the matter you're merely scratching the surface.

EWJ: But perhaps people could be inspired by scratching the surface to then try to go to the root.

K: Inspiration only lasts for a very short while. Very few people ever affect the psyche. Very few. Gandhi is totally forgotten in India.

EWJ: There was an article that said that the Indians were very impressed by the movie, but were somewhat bemused by the non-violent aspect of it.

K: That's right. He was a very violent man. They're trying to make a saint out of him as the only man who was helping India to be free, which isn't true. There were hundreds. Annie Besant was one. She worked for forty years helping the country to be free. She is never mentioned. It's all so lop-sided.

K went on to talk about human consciousness and asked whether one person who was 'illuminated', free from all conditioning, such as Buddha or Jesus, could affect the consciousness of the rest of mankind? He answered his own question; it had never been done:

Unless we radically change, the future is what we are now. It's a serious fact. And nobody wants to change radically. If you want peace, you live peacefully. But nobody wants to live peacefully.

EWJ: It appears that we are at a unique time in history.

K: Yes, but the crisis is not in the world out there. Rather, it is inside us, in our consciousness. Which means that man has to change.

EWJ: Has your teaching and your writing made a change?

K: With some, perhaps. I'm not looking to see if somebody's changed or not. It's like this: you give food to me and if I'm hungry I'll take it. And if not, I look at it, smell it, say 'It's very nice', and then wander off. Very few people are hungry for this kind of stuff.

EWJ: Do you feel that your teaching has made a deep impression?

K: Some have given up their jobs, have said, 'We'll come to your schools.' They are doing it because they are schools—not monasteries, not ashrams, but schools.

EWJ: So you feel that education is a place to really effect a change?

K: If teachers were concerned, if education all over the world was concerned, to bring about a new generation they could do it. But they are not concerned. They want to stuff the children with mathematics, biology, chemistry to make them become good engineers. Society wants good engineers—there's money in it. Educators have an enormous responsibility because they hold the future. More than the parents. Educators must be concerned with the holistic view of life.

At the end of the interview K was asked, 'When you meet someone who is sick physically what is your approach? Do you heal?' K replied, 'Yes, but please, I want to make this quite clear. Healing is not my profession, my work.' K definitely had a power of healing but he rarely used it since he did not want people to come to him as a physical healer.

*   *   *   *

Pupil Jayakar was in New York at this time in connection with the Festival of India, and while having dinner one evening with K and

Mary in the suite at the hotel they began to talk about how K had become what he was, though without reaching any conclusion. A strange 'something' was felt in the room which always came when this subject was seriously broached. It had come at those times when I had talked to him at Brockwood about who and what he was. But on this occasion in New York he said what he had not said before, that the 'something' always came from the left.

When K returned to Ojai he began his dictations again while alone in the mornings. At this time he told Mary once more that she must write a book about him, writing a bit each day. He also discussed with her and Erna Lilliefelt his idea of starting a study centre at Ojai and wondered whether he should spend more time there, holding seminars. But ten days after returning from New York he was off with Mary to San Francisco where he had last spoken in 1975 and where he now gave two talks in the Masonic Hall. They stayed at the Huntington Hotel. As well as short interviews in *The Examiner* and *The Chronicle*, K gave an hour's interview on 'New Dimensions' radio on April 28 which was syndicated to fifty other radio stations round the country. The self-effacing interviewer allowed him to develop his themes with hardly any interruption, merely probing occasionally with an intelligent question, so that is was more like a talk, and one of his best. Whenever K was in San Francisco he saw Alain Naudé who had been his secretary and travelling companion in the sixties and with whom he remained good friends.

K was still in San Francisco when Dorothy Simmons telephoned to say that there had been a bad fire in the West Wing at Brockwood. It had started in the attic above K's bedroom which faced south. The attic, which comprised a small dormitory and a self-contained flat, was entirely burnt out, and K's bedroom was badly damaged, though some of the furniture and all his clothes had been saved. The drawing-room, under his bedroom, had suffered more from the water than the fire. The cause of the outbreak was presumably from a blow-lamp used by a workman repairing one of the attic windows; it seemed that an old bird's nest under the eaves had been set alight and left smouldering. If the school had not been in full operation that afternoon the whole house might have gone, for when the fire engines arrived from Alresford their hoses could not reach the swimming pool, the main supply of water. (The water for Brockwood is pumped up from a well into a tower.) While more fire engines were on their way from Winchester, teachers and pupils at the school kept the flames under control by a bucket-chain. K said that he had had a premonition of the fire. The insurance did not cover all the damage. Does it ever?

*   *   *   *

In April the English Publications Committee received the first typescript from India produced within the three-year cycle agreement with the India Committee (p. 25). We had been eagerly awaiting it, for we were most anxious to have an international book from India. It was a very bulky volume of discussions between K and others, entitled *Intelligence and the Mechanical Brain*. After reading it, I asked Mary Cadogan to send it to every member of our committee, including Alan Kishbaugh in California, without comment. The reports were unanimous: it needed a great deal of cutting and much more careful editing before we could submit it to Gollancz; therefore we most reluctantly returned it with this recommendation. The following year, the Indian Foundation brought out for the Indian market a short and impeccably edited book containing K's talks in India between October 1982 and January 1983. If only this manuscript had been sent to us for the international book all the later publication difficulties with India might have been avoided.*

This month, my last sister, Elisabeth, the one nearest to me, died. K had known her well because she had been with us at Ehrwald and Pergine and twice in India. She had been ill since her flat caught fire two years before as the result of a faulty electric blanket and she had been rescued, unconscious from smoke, just in time. With my three sisters and my brother all dead, I was left with the irrational and sentimental feeling that K was the only remaining member of my family, so closely entwined had he been with my childhood and youth. He had always been there, dearer to me than my father or any of my siblings, the most abiding influence of my life. Yet when I turn to his *Notebook* it seems incredible that I could have felt so close to a being who had lived most of the time in another dimension—in a consciousness of sustained ecstasy. He had

---

* We afterwards discovered that an Indian working for the Oxford University Press had helped with the editing of this book.

written, 'There is no reason for this ecstasy—to have a cause for joy is no longer joy; it was simply there and thought could not capture it and make it into a remembrance. . . . It came wave upon wave, a living thing which nothing could contain and with this joy there was benediction. It was so utterly beyond all thought and demand.'

7

The New Centre

Dorothy Simmons and Mary Cadogan went to Ojai for the Oak Grove talks in May this year in fulfilment of K's wish that the trustees of the different foundations should meet as frequently as possible. One afternoon during the Gathering K sat through the whole showing of an hour-long colour film on his life and teaching which had taken five years to be made by Evelyne Blau, one of the American trustees. This film, called *The Challenge of Change*, produced by Michael Mendizza, is startling in that the supposed voice of K, reading from the essay he had written in 1913, is that of the America actor Richard Chamberlain. To have heard K impersonated by an Englishman would have sounded strange enough. But the film has been very well researched and there are some beautiful shots of K, especially in Switzerland and India. The film has not yet been shown on any wide commercial network but it has had some very successful public showings in various towns in America.

By the time K and Mary went back to Brockwood on May 28, the smell of burning had almost disappeared. K slept in the small room in the West Wing, facing north, looking on to the main entrance to the house. Mary's room was undamaged. Dr Parchure had arrived from India before them to stay with K for the rest of the summer.

K dictated one more piece alone in his room at Brockwood on May 30, the only one of this series that was done away from Ojai and the last of 1983. In this piece he described Brockwood:

It has been raining here for over a month every day. When you come from a climate like California where the rain stopped over a month ago, where the green fields were drying up and turning brown and the sun was very hot (it was over 90° and would get hotter still though they say it is going to be a mild summer)—when you come from that climate it is rather

75

startling and surprising to see the green earth, the marvellous green trees and the copper beeches, which are a spreading, light brown becoming gradually darker and darker. To see them now among the green trees is a delight. They are going to be very dark as the summer comes on. And this earth is very beautiful. Earth, whether it is desert or filled with orchards and green bright fields, is always beautiful.

To go for a walk in the fields with the cattle and the young lambs, and in the woods with the song of birds, without a single thought in your mind, only watching the earth, the trees, the sheep and hearing the cuckoo calling and the wood-pigeons; to walk without any emotion, any sentiment, to watch the trees and all the earth: when you so watch, you learn your own thinking, are aware of your own reactions and do not allow a single thought to escape you without understanding why it came, what was the cause of it. If you are watchful, never letting a thought go by, then the brain becomes very quiet. Then you watch in great silence. And that silence has immense depth, a lasting incorruptible beauty.

K stopped dictating because on June 6 Dorothy Simmons suffered a heart attack and was taken to hospital. Thereafter he was fully occupied with the question of who was to run the school while she was ill. There was no deputy Principal so K appointed a committee of four—Scott Forbes, Stephen Smith, who taught English, Harsh Tankha, the mathematics teacher, and Ingrid Porter, the Secretary of the School. Montague Simmons was too old to take charge.

Brockwood now had video colour equipment which was used for the first time to record two dialogues between K and David Bohm on June 11 and 25 for Bohm to show at a conference at Davos on 'The Future of Humanity' to which K had been invited but which he felt unable to attend.[48] Svetlana Peters (Stalin's daugher) was staying at Brockwood for the weekend and listened to the second dialogue. (Many paying-guests would come to stay at Brockwood for a night or two in cell-like rooms, each with its own shower and W.C., in what are called The Cloisters, separate from the main house.)

I had recently become friends with Svetlana who had written to me out of the blue about the first volume of my biography of K. She was living at Cambridge then and had arranged with Dorothy Simmons to go to Brockwood before Dorothy had her heart attack. Svetlana was very lonely after twelve years in America. Her daughter, Olga, by her American husband from whom she was divorced, was at a Quaker boarding school and she was grievously missing the son and daughter she had left in Russia and her grandchildren whom she had never seen. She had written two best-sellers, one about her childhood and youth which she had managed to smuggle out of Russia, and the other about her defection and escape via India. She was now writing a third book, her impressions of life in America. By now, she told me, she had no language to write in—her English was very faulty and she felt she could no longer write in Russian, so she was trying to find someone to turn this new book into good English. She was distressed because the publishers she had approached seemed only to want more about her father and she was longing to get out of his shadow. She was very talented and well-educated and had great charm, warmth and simplicity, and I found her Russian accent irresistible.

I had told K about her and he was looking forward to meeting her. She arrived just as he was setting out on his afternoon walk and he immediately asked her to walk with him. K never saw her again after that weekend.

Her return to Russia was a complete surprise to me, but understandable, knowing how much she longed for her children. I wrote to her through the Soviet embassy in London wishing her happiness, and in due course a card came back posted in Moscow, acknowledging my letter and hoping that 'our friend' was well. In June 1986 I was to receive a long and beautiful letter from her from Wisconsin, saying that she had only just heard that 'our Krishnaji is no more' and going on to tell me what a terrible time she and Olga had had in Russia. It was only the thought of K and reading his books that had kept her going. She had made translations into Russian of some chapters from his *Commentaries on Living*, the *Notebook* and the *Journal*. Soon, one hopes, there will be a book on her experiences after her return to Russia and what she called 'the MIRACLE' of being eventually allowed to leave. '*The MIRACLE*', she wrote, '*happened because K helped me to concentrate, to push, to collect all energy and not to give up.*'

       *   *   *   *

Every day until he left Brockwood for Gstaad, K talked to the assembled school and staff, giving all his energy to trying to bring about harmony in the school which was torn between rival groups following Dorothy's illness. He was not well during much of the time at Gstaad that summer, suffering chiefly from a feverish cough. His indisposition did not, however, affect the quality of the Saanen talks. He told Mary that he was going to live to be a hundred 'to see what it was like'.

On August 1, after the Gathering, K was to meet yet one more person who came into his life at just the right time. This was Friedrich Grohe. Mr Grohe was then fifty-four, a widower, born in Germany, who, four years ealier, had retired from the family business, known internationally for its manufacture of bathroom and kitchen taps. Reading one of K's books in 1980, *The Impossible Question*, determined the course of his life from then on, to use his own words. He was later to become a Trustee of the English and Indian Foundations, to support the schools at Brockwood and Ojai and the proposed study centres in Brockwood and India. At the time of his first meeting with K he was staying in a flat at Rougemont near Saanen (his main home was near the Lake of Geneva) and had come to see K because he wanted to start a Krishnamurti school in Switzerland. K advised him against the school idea; instead, Mr Grohe responded to K's suggestion of building a study centre at Brockwood.

On the way back to England Mary persuaded K to use a wheelchair at the airport for the first time. It was a great success for they swept past long queues at Heathrow on arrival. They found Dorothy back at Brockwood, looking much better, but K felt that she should no longer be burdened with all the business of the school.

A larger tent was needed that year for the crowds who attended the Brockwood Gathering. It had always amused K to look out of his window at the campers who would be staying for the whole week, setting up their tents, and at the people arriving on the days when the talks took place. This year, having to sleep in a room looking north on to the drive, he missed the view across the lawn to the campers, the two great marquees and the crowds assembling. He would speak at 11.30 for an hour; then, as the crowd waited for lunch to be served in the adjoining marquee, he would go back to the house for fruit and salad in the West Wing kitchen and return afterwards to the marquee to toy with a cooked dish on a paper plate with a plastic fork while he walked about talking for half an hour to the people who came up to him. He was very shy and shaky on these occasions.

Friedrich Grohe went to Brockwood for the night of October 1 and donated £50,000 to the school (this was quite apart from the money he was to put up for the study centre). K called him his A.G. (*Ange Gardien*). Brockwood, like the other Krishnamurti schools, was a fee-paying school with a certain number of free places financed by a special scholarship fund. It was not self-supporting; the building itself needed a great deal of maintenance and money was always short.

Until K flew to Delhi with Dr Parchure on October 27 most of his time was taken up with the many difficulties of reorganising the school. Mary was going to stay on at Brockwood for three weeks after his departure to see to the redecorating and refurnishing of his bedroom, and he rather left to her the responsibility of bringing about the changes he wanted at the school as if, he told her, he was already dead. Nevertheless, he said that he was going to live another ten years.

It had been arranged for K to go again to Sri Lanka that winter but this visit was canclled on Pupul Jayakar's advice because of the troubles there with the Tamils. K followed his usual programme, therefore—giving talks in Delhi, Rajghat, Madras (after a month at Rishi Valley) and Bombay in February 1984.

It was not only at Brockwood that K had difficulties. At Rajghat there were troubles both inside the school and outside with a neighbouring village. The latter trouble was long-standing. The Rajghat Education Centre comprises the school and a college for women occupying 140 acres on the west side of the Varuna river, at the point where it enters the Ganges. In addition to this there are 110 acres on the other side of the river which now contain a small hospital, a village primary school for 150 children and a rural centre with a number of training activities. Between this centre and the Ganges is a village which has gradually grown in population since the land surrounding it became part of the centre. The villagers have been given free education for their children and medical treatment as well as some five acres of Foundation land for their houses, but they still resent the presence of the centre on land which they feel should be theirs. The situation is complicated by the fact that the road leading to the village and the rural centre goes through the college campus and crosses the Varuna river by a small bridge which breaks down during the rainy season; the rural centre can then only be reached by boats operated by the villagers. It will be seen that much tact and some firmness are demanded of those in charge of the rural centre for a working relationship to be preserved.

There were difficulties too at Vasanta Vihar at Adyar which K felt did not have the truly religious atmosphere he expected. Did he spread himself too thin? He could usually change the atmosphere of a place when he was there, put people on their toes, but when he went away he took so much of this spirit with him. There was no one in his entourage in India, America or England who could act as his deputy; nor did he want such a person, for that would lead to authority. What he asked was that every person who worked for him should be a light unto himself—a light that would burn as brightly whether he was there or not.

*   *   *   *

In 1984, before K arrived in England on February 15, Mary Zimbalist had returned to Brockwood to make sure that his room was ready for him. Rita Zampese, from Lufthansa, flew to Bombay for the sole purpose of accompanying him back to Heathrow. She has told me that just sitting beside him during the flight, hardly talking, had a profound effect on her. Afterwards she felt utterly committed to him and his teaching.

Friedrich Grohe went to Brockwood again on the evening of K's arrival, and for the next two days, while K and Mary remained there before flying to Los Angeles, they discussed what was soon to be called simply the Centre which K was going to build with Mr Grohe's financial help, and chose the site for it. This was to be the old apple orchard, south of the main building and separated from it by the long lawn and a high yew hedge, with uninterrupted views to the south over fields that could never be built on. None of the big trees would have to be cut down and there would be a separate entrance from a lane which would make the building quite independent of the school. The first step was to obtain outline planning permission.

At Ojai K was at first exhausted by having to deal with problems arising from opening a secondary day school with some boarders, adjoining the primary Oak Grove School. The parents of the primary school pupils, who had moved to the Valley in order to send their children to a Krishnamurti school, had been pressing for this. All the same, K's annual medical check-up was very satisfactory and he was full of enthusiasm when, on March 19, he drove with Mary and Alan Kishbaugh to Albuquerque where they stayed at the Los Alamos Inn. Dr M. R. Raju had invited K to take part in a symposium at the National Laboratory Research Center at Los Alamos, New Mexico, on the subject of 'Creativity in Science'. On March 20, K gave a talk on the subject and next day he answered questions.

Los Alamos is situated at 7,000 feet on a plateau. When Dr Robert Oppenheimer, the celebrated physicist, discovered the site it was empty apart from a small private boys' school, but having been chosen soon after America entered the Second World War to be the centre of atomic research in the U.S., it has grown into a town of some 20,000 inhabitants.

K spoke for over an hour at 8 a.m. in an overflowing hall that held about 700 people, mostly scientists, though the talk was open to the public. His main theme was that knowledge could never be creative because it was incomplete. He asked:

Can we, as human beings, look at the world as we have made it? I wonder if we ever ask ourselves whether we are individuals at all. Our consciousness is made up of our reactions, our beliefs, our faith, all the prejudices that we have, the multiplication of opinions, the fears, the insecurity, the pain, the pleasure, and all the suffering that human beings have borne for thousands of years—all that is our consciousness. Our consciousness is what we are. And in this confusion, this contradiction, can there be creativity? . . . So, if thought is not the ground of creation, then what is creation? When does it take place? Surely creation can take place only when thought is silent. . . . Science is the movement of knowledge gathering more and more and more. The 'more' is the measurement, and thought can be measured because thought is a material process. Knowledge has its own limited insight, its own limited creation, but this brings conflict. We are talking about holistic perception in which the ego, the 'me', the personality, does not enter at all. Then only is there this thing called creativity. That is it.

The following morning he answered questions in a much smaller auditorium for an audience confined to Fellows of the Los Alamos National Laboratory. Of the fifteen questions handed to him on behalf of the scientists present, he answered only the first and the

last. The first question was, 'What is creativity? What is meditation?' His answer to this took up most of the hour and a half
allotted time and he repeated much of what he had said in his talk
the day before. The last question was, 'If you were the Director of
the Laboratory with the responsibility for the defence of the
country and recognizing the way things are, how would you direct the
activities of the Laboratory and the research?' To this K replied in part:

We have divided the world. You are a Christian, I am black, you are
white, you are a Caucasian, and I am Chinese—whatever the beastly thing
is. We are divided, we have fought each other from the beginning of time.
. . . Sir, a group of people like you at Los Alamos—you have given your
time for destruction. You are doing a great deal of benefit, and on the other
hand you are destroying every human on earth, because you have
recognised *my* country, *my* responsibilities, *my* defence. And the Russians
are saying exactly the same thing on the other side. India, which has
immense poverty, is saying the same thing. Building up arms. So what is the
answer to this? If I have a group of people who say, let's forget all
nationalism, all religions, let's, as human beings, solve this problem—try to
live together without destruction; if we gave time to all that as a group of
absolutely dedicated people who have gathered together at Los Alamos for
one purpose and are concerned with all the things we have been talking
about, then perhaps there is something new that can take place. . . . I am not
asking you to do anything. I am not a propagandist, but the world is like
this now. Nobody is thinking about it. Nobody has a global outlook—a
global feeling for all humanity—not *my* country—for God's sake. If you
went around the world, as the speaker does, you would cry for the rest of
your life. Pacifism is a reaction to militarism, that's all. The speaker is not a
pacifist. Instead, let's look at the cause of all this—if we all seek together the
causation, then the thing is solved. But each one has different opinions about the
causation and sticks to his opinions, his historical directories. So, sir, there it is.
Member of audience: Sir, if I may say so—I think you have convinced us.
Krishnamurti: I'm not convincing anything.
Member of audience: What I mean is, that when once we really try to
understand this and do something in that direction, somehow we seem to
lack the necessary energy . . . what is it that is really holding us back? We
can see the house is on fire, but still we are not able to do anything about
stopping the fire.
Krishnamurti: The house on fire, which we think is over there, is here. We
have to put our house in order first, sir.[49]

*　　　*　　　*　　　*

On K's return to Ojai from Los Alamos he dictated three more pieces into his tape-recorder while quietly alone in his bedroom— on March 27, 28 and 30. These were the last we were ever to have of his reflections when alone and, ironically, the last piece of all was about death. He described how while walking on a beautiful sunny morning in spring, he saw a dead leaf, 'yellow and bright red', lying on the path. 'How beautiful that leaf was,' he wrote, 'so simple in its death, so lively, full of the beauty and vitality of the whole tree and the summer. Strange that it had not withered. . . . That leaf was all the tree.' He went on:

Why do human beings die so miserably, so unhappily, with a disease, old age, senility, the body shrunk, ugly? Why can't they die naturally and as beautifully as this leaf? What is wrong with us? In spite of all the doctors, medicines and hospitals, operations and all the agony of life, and the pleasures too, we don't seem able to die with dignity, simplicity, and with a smile. . . . As you teach children mathematics, writing, reading and all the business of acquiring knowledge, they should also be taught the great dignity of death, not as a morbid unhappy thing that one has to face eventually, but as something of daily life—the daily life of looking at the blue sky and the grasshopper on a leaf. It is part of learning, as you grow teeth and have all the discomforts of childish illnesses. Children have extraordinary curiosity. If you see the nature of death, you don't explain that everything dies, dust to dust and so on, but without any fear you explain it to them gently and make them feel that the living and the dying are one—not at the end of one's life after fifty, sixty or ninety years, but that death is like that leaf. Look at the old men and women, how decrepit, how lost, how unhappy and how ugly they look. Is it because they have not really understood either the living or the dying? They have used life, they waste away their life with incessant conflict which only exercises and gives strength to the self, the 'me', the ego. We spend our days in such varieties of conflict and unhappiness, with some joy and pleasure, drinking, smoking, late nights and work, work, work. And at the end of one's life one faces that thing called death and is frightened of it. One thinks it can always be understood, felt deeply. The child with his curiosity can be helped to understand that death is not merely the wasting of the body through disease, old age and some unexpected accident, but that the ending of every day is also the ending of oneself every day.

There is no resurrection, that is superstition, a dogmatic belief. Everything on earth, on this beautiful earth, lives, dies, comes into being and withers away. To grasp this whole movement of life requires intelligence, not the intelligence of thought, or books, or knowledge, but the intelligence of love and compassion with its sensitivity . . . . As one looked at that dead leaf with all its beauty and colour, maybe one would very deeply comprehend, be aware of, what one's own death must be, not at the very end but at the very beginning. Death isn't some horrific thing, something to be avoided, something to be postponed, but rather something to be with day and day out. And out of that comes an extraordinary sense of immensity.[50]

Asit Chandmal came to Ojai for ten days on April 1 and showed K the dummy of a book of beautiful coloured photographs he had taken of him throughout his eighty-fifth year, in India, Ojai, Brockwood and Saanen, which he hoped to have published in time to present to K on his ninetieth birthday the following year.[51] Asit flew with K, Mary and the Lilliefelts on April 11 to New York for another two talks at the Felt Forum where K had spoken the year before. K and Mary stayed again at the Dorset Hotel and had most of their meals at a little Italian restaurant, Il Nido. K had the pleasant relaxation one afternoon while they were there of going to see a Tarzan film.

After the talks, on the 17th, K was the guest speaker of the Pacem in Terris Society in the Dag Hammarskjöld Library Auditorium of the United Nations. The invitation to speak there had been conveyed through Dr Patricia Hunt-Perry. Part of his talk is given below:

There have been many organisations including this one to bring about peace in the world, but there has been no peace for various obvious reasons: nationalism, tribalism, opposing religions, divisions of classes, races, and so on. . . . Why is it that after all these millions of years human beings don't live in peace? Do we realise that we are responsible for this horror that is going on in the world? Every form of violence, terrorism, wars—we are responsible for it. War is not in Beirut. It is in our hearts and minds. We have created this society in which we live. We are this society, and until each one of us radically transforms himself, we will have perpetual wars.

Man is conditioned, his brain has been moulded according to a particular tradition, religion. . . . Is it possible for human beings to be free of their conditioning? Why are human beings so conditioned? Is it because we want security—both external and inward? Is there any kind of security inwardly? If we are not sure about that, we try to seek security outwardly, externally, through nations, through religious organisations . . . it seems that we should talk over together now and discover for ourselves if there is security in our relationships with each other, however intimate they may be. If there is security, why is there such contention between man and woman, such conflict in their relationship—each one pursuing his own ambition, his own fulfilment, his own desires and so on? To go very far, we must begin very near, and the nearest is man and woman, wife and husband. In that relationship, if there is conflict, as there is now, then that conflict is spread—ultimately to war. We have never given thought to this, that while our house is burning—which is that society is burning, degenerating—we are also degenerating. If we don't alter our lives, how can we bring about peace on earth? It seems so logical, so rational, sane, but we don't do it. Unless the psychological world is quiet, sane, peaceful, that psychological state will always overcome every kind of organisation. The psyche is far more important than the external legislation, governments, and so on.

We have been conditioned from the beginning by religion, by society, by culture that each one is separate, individual, and therefore he must seek his own salvation, his own expression, his own fulfilment. And this so-called separate individuality is creating havoc in the world—which does not mean that we should all become the same, turned out in the same mould. On the contrary. Freedom is the highest form of existence. It's the greatest art to live free. But we are not free. One thinks one is free to do what one likes. Especially in this country, each individual thinks he is supreme to do what he wants. But when you travel around and observe very closely, every human being, whether he has great position, a great deal of money, status, power, is like the rest of the world. He goes through great pain, desperate loneliness and all the rest of the psychological world of uncertainty, confusion; we are the rest of humanity. We are not Africans and Europeans and all that nonsense. We are humanity. Unless we realise that one major factor in our life, that psychologically we are one, we are going to be eternally in conflict. And no organisation in the world is going to change that fact. So what is a human being to do if he is seriously concerned with the world? Form another group, another religion, another institution? Or become aware of his condition and radically change, bring about a deep mutation? Otherwise, there will be no peace on earth in spite of all the religions, in spite of every institution. It must begin with us, not with somebody else out there.[52]

*　　　*　　　*　　　*

K had little rest at Ojai that year because a few days after returning from New York he was off to San Francisco again with Mary for two more talks and another hour-long interview with 'New Dimensions' radio. The same interviewer drew from him as good a talk as the year before. He was hardly back at Ojai before the Oak Grove talks started in a temperature of 106°. Friedrich Grohe was at Ojai for the Gathering and flew to London with K and Mary on June 1. K found that a compact-disc-player had been installed in his newly decorated bedroom at Brockwood which became a great joy to him.

A few days later Iris Murdoch lunched at Brockwood. Afterwards she and K talked for some time about the possibility of recording a videotaped dialogue in October. This meeting had been arranged through a friend of mine, Harold Carlton, who had boldly written to Iris Murdoch, whom he admired but had never met, suggesting it. After meeting K she seemed anxious to talk to him again, and he liked the idea too. He was always looking out for people with whom to have deep discussions, and she seemed an ideal person. He had never read any of her novels and had heard of her only as a philosopher. The date of a further meeting was arranged.

Scott Forbes was in hospital in Winchester at this time with acute appendicitis. He was determined not to have an operation until after the Saanen Gathering in spite of the danger, and was eventually discharged after a course of antibiotics. While he was still in hospital K suddenly had the idea of putting him in charge of the Brockwood Centre, to oversee both the building of it and the running of it when it was opened. Scott and his wife Kathy accepted this charge after thinking it over carefully. Scott was a dynamic young American who had been working at Brockwood for about ten years, first on maintenance and then in charge of the video. He was widely travelled, had lived for a time in Paris and had run a successful small antique business in Geneva before coming across K. He had gone to Saanen one summer almost by chance, had listened to one of K's talks and had been utterly captivated. In going to work for K at Brockwood he completely changed his style of living while retaining all his energy. His youth, enthusiasm, vitality, knowledge of the world, fluent French and cosmopolitan ease of manner appealed to K, who enjoyed his company—he was someone he could laugh with—as well as appreciating his usefulness.

Scott approached one of the leading British architects. The specification for the Centre was for twenty simple bedrooms, each with its own shower and W.C., and each facing the view; a living-room, library, video-room, dining-room with its own kitchen, staff rooms and a flat for Mr Grohe. But K also envisaged what he called 'the quiet room' as the most important room in the building, rather difficult of access, perhaps approached by a winding staircase that would shut it away from the communal rooms. Here the people staying in the Centre would come for the sole purpose of sitting quietly, not talking or doing anything.

Friedrich Grohe and Scott were now asked to become trustees of the English Foundation. Dorothy Simmons was to remain Principal of the school while Harsh Tankha and Stephen Smith became co-directors of studies, Ingrid Porter school manager, and Gary Primrose and Christina West, who looked after the garden together, were given the special responsibility of seeing that K's teaching did not get swamped by the academic curriculum. When K announced all these new appointments to the assembled school there was a great deal of dissension. The students were critical and K was disturbed by the feeling that he had no real contact with the staff.

On June 18 I went to Brockwood to record a talk with K about his wish that no one should claim to represent him after his death. It was not a satisfactory recording because he was too occupied with school difficulties. He soon broke off and said that he must go and lie down because his head was bad. Later that afternoon he talked for two and a half hours at a school meeting. He spoke most intensely and was almost in tears at the end.

He was thankful to escape to Switzerland at the end of June. Tannegg had now been sold so another house, Chalet Horner at Schönried, had been rented, and there K and Mary found Vanda and Fosca. K, missing Tannegg after so many years, continued to take his usual afternoon walk through a wood to the river, but this now meant driving to Tannegg to begin the walk. Each time they came to the wood, K would ask aloud, 'May we come in?'. He did not much like Chalet Horner; therefore, for the following year Friedrich Grohe offered to lend him his own small flat at Rougemont while Vanda and Mary arranged for the lease of a larger flat in the same building. K said that next year he would come earlier to Switzerland and rest before the talks.

Although there was a larger tent this year for the Gathering it hardly held the crowds who came to Saanen. When K returned to

Brockwood on August 14 he found an angry, divided staff. He said he could not live with such discord and that unless there was agreement he would close the door between the school and the west wing. It seemed that those who were close to K in their different ways were no nearer to living his teaching than those who had only read his books and listened to his tapes. Indeed, the closer we were to the sun the more likely we were to get burnt.

*   *   *   *

The Lilliefelts, the Patwardhans and Friedrich Grohe went to Brockwood for the Gathering held between August 25 and September 3 and stayed on for a six-day international meeting of the Foundations. Pupul Jayakar, Radhika Herzberger and Asit Chandmal came from India; Alan Kishbaugh and Evelyne Blau from America, and Alfonso Colón, with two of his colleagues, represented the Spanish Foundation from Puerto Rico. (Mary Zimbalist was a trustee of both the English and American Foundations.) Mary Cadogan, Jane Hammond and Scott Forbes were there as well as Jean-Michel Maroger and Count Hugues van der Straten, who had been a trustee of the English Foundation from the beginning.

I went for the one day set aside to discuss publications. This was a difficult meeting at which K was present, though taking little part. Pupul was not satisfied with the three-year publication cycle which had been legally agreed in 1980. She again asked to share the copyright in K's work. We believed that it would not be legally possible for the English Foundation, as a charitable trust, to give away one of its assets even if K had wanted to. (On later consultation with the Foundation's solicitor this was found to be the case.) We decided as a compromise to form an international publications committee with two representatives from each of the three English-speaking Foundations who would consult together on all publication matters. Mary Zimbalist and Alan Kishbaugh became the members for America, Sunanda Patwardhan and Asit Chandmal for India, and Mary Cadogan and I for England. Pupul declined to join this committee, yet we knew that the Indian representatives would not be empowered to make any decisions without the consent of the Indian Foundation, so really the meeting had achieved nothing. (In the event this International Committee never had an opportunity to act.) At the end of a tiring day we felt very despondent. Almost in tears, I had burst out emotionally at one moment against the terrible way we were wasting K with our squabbles, using up his energy which should have been going into his teaching.

Mary Zimbalist had to go to Rome for two nights at the end of October to see an old Italian maid who had worked for her at Malibu. On her return K told her, 'When you are away it is much more work for me. You must hurry to understand everything. I may live another ten years but you must understand.' Mary was not young, though she was not old, hence the need for her to hurry. But so many of those who had served K devotedly for years were old; he had demanded a great deal of them but never for himself, only for his work. He naturally felt an urgency now to bring forward and train young people to carry on after his death. The most we old ones could do for him was to try to help the young.

*　　　*　　　*　　　*

Iris Murdoch went to Brockwood on October 18 and a discussion between her and K was recorded on video[53] before a small audience in another room, including Joe and me and Harold Carlton who had been instrumental in bringing them together. Alas, the conversation was disappointing. They never managed to get on the same wavelength. Irish Murdoch seemed unable to approach K with a mind uncluttered by the mass of philosophy she had read. One could almost see her trying to pigeon-hole him as they talked. At last he said something which reminded her of Plato, after which she seemed more relaxed; she appeared to have dropped him neatly into the Plato slot.

The architect had now not only produced his plans for the Centre but a model because K could not understand plans. When K saw it, he did not like it; it looked to him too much like a motel. Scott Forbes, who felt that the firm of architects was not taking the project enough to heart, decided that it was best to cut losses and look for another architect.

8

First Talks in Washington

Mary Zimbalist flew to Delhi with K on October 28. Pama Patwardhan met them in a car at the aircraft steps, a great convenience arranged for K by Pupul Jayakar who was waiting for them in the lounge with her male secretary to see to the passports and luggage. K went to stay with her in Safdarjang Road while Mary was taken to the Taj Mahal Hotel, though she was to have her main meals at Pupul's. K was most insistent that Mary should take nothing in the hotel except tea; he was very concerned for her health in India. Nandini Mehta, Asit Chandmal and the Patwardhans were also staying with Pupul.

On the 30th, K, Mary, Pupul and the Patwardhans went to lunch with the Vice-President, Mr. Venkataraman, whom K knew quite well, at Rashtrapati Bhavan, as Viceroy's House, designed by my father, had been called since Indpendence. (When K first went there he had written to me to say how much he liked the palace. I had first been to Raisina, as New Delhi was then called, in 1923. It was still partly desert then and I had helped to plant some of the trees there. When I went back in 1957 and was shown over the palace and its marvellous garden, I experienced one of the most moving moments of my life: whereas all the statues of Kings and Queens and portraits of Viceroys had been relegated to some boneyard, I suddenly saw a bust of my father in a niche on the stairs, bearing the simple inscription 'Architect of this House'.)

Next morning came the horror of Mrs Gandhi's assassination. Mary did not know of it until she arrived at Pupul's at 11.30. Pupul had rushed to Mrs Gandhi's house close by with Asit who had returned with a message for K to say that Mrs Gandhi was dead. K and all the others in the house watched television for the rest of the day. It was not until 6 p.m. that the news of Mrs Gandhi's death and

Rajiv Gandhi's election as Prime Minister was announced. Pupul did not get home until ten. She had been at the hospital with Sonia, Rajiv's wife. Asit took Mary back to the hotel through empty streets but the attacks on Sikhs had begun and the glare of fires could be seen in the outer districts.

The next day Pupul accompanied Mrs Gandhi's body to where it was to lie in state until the funeral. The violence made it possibly unsafe for K to stay in Delhi, and his planned departure for Varanasi was brought forward from the 5th to the 3rd. K, Mary and Nandini drove that afternoon with Asit through the empty streets of that part of the city round Safdarjang Road, which was closely guarded by the police, to an almost empty Lodi Park where they took a walk. K's ultrasensitive system was greatly affected by the disturbed atmosphere so Mary was relieved when on the 3rd they flew with the Patwardhans and Dr Parchure to the peace of Madras instead of to Varanasi which was considered dangerous on account of riots there. This was the day on which Mrs Gandhi's funeral took place in Delhi.

After six days at Vasanta Vihar, K insisted on going to Varanasi, although it meant flying there via Delhi, because a two-day camp had been planned at Rajghat for some 200 people who would be arriving on the 10th in spite of the danger of travelling by train at a time when the fever of revenge was running high.

K spoke to the campers on both days and stayed on at Rajghat afterwards for nearly three weeks, talking to the teachers and students and planning a study centre like the one at Brockwood, though on a much smaller scale, which Friedrich Grohe had undertaken to build. K also held discussions with several distinguished pandits. On November 30 he and Mary flew back to Madras, via Delhi again, and three days later they drove to Rishi Valley.

Narayan, Radhika Herzberger and Dr Parchure and his wife (who worked at Rishi Valley) were at the school when K arrived, and in the course of the three weeks he remained there the Patwardhans, Nandini, Pupul, Asit, Dorothy Simmons, Friedrich Grohe and Rita Zampese came to stay. K had specially asked Dorothy to come and be with him in India this year and she had gone, most gallantly, although she had been very ill when she had been there in 1980, and she hated the heat. Teachers from the

Rajghat, Bangalore and Madras schools also came. For three days running K spoke to all the assembled teachers. He also spoke several times to the younger children and was exhilarated by their interest. He talked to them about mediocrity as he had talked to us at Pergine in 1924. He explained to them the meaning of the word and told them to avoid mediocrity above all things. You could rise to the highest position in the land and still be mediocre, he told them. To be mediocre was to have a mechanical, second-hand mind.

On one of his afternoon walks with friends, K went to choose a site where Friedrich had offered to build bungalows for a study centre as at Rajghat. On another afternoon, with Nandini, Radhika and Mary, K went along the road as far as a small temple at Tetu. On the way back, K told Mary that he had felt 'something following' him. He had 'done something' and said to it, 'That's enough', and it had stopped immediately. A few days later when they walked again to Tetu, K said that he 'did something at the temple and told it to stay in its place'.

When on December 26 they returned to Madras and Mary felt ill in the car, K put his hands on her to help her throughout the long drive. Since she did not feel at all well in Madras and both she and K were afraid of her falling really ill, she decided not to wait for K but to fly back to England with Dorothy and Rita Zampese in the middle of January.

*   *   *   *

K went to Bombay on January 25, 1985, and after giving four talks there to larger audiences than ever he flew to London on February 12, accompanied by Asit Chandmal. Mary had already returned to Ojai. I went to Brockwood two days later to see K and as soon as we were alone he started telling me in a rather confused way about a talk he had recently had in Madras with a Brahmin pandit, Jagannath Upadhyaya, a well-known Buddhist scholar. The Pandit, it seems, was studying some very early Tibetan manuscripts (K could not remember whether it was AD 600 or 900) which predicted the coming of the Lord Maitreya and actually gave the name of Krishnamurti as the human vehicle the Lord would inhabit when he came. K seemed excited and impressed by this revelation, though sceptical of it at the same time. I said that if it were true it would bear out the Theosophical conception of Krishnamurti as the vehicle for the World Teacher and dispel any mystery as to who and what he was. This K would not accept. He said it was 'too concrete'. He spoke to others about the Pandit's revelation but always in a shy, hesitant way.

Nine months later Mary Zimbalist and Scott Forbes asked him to record on tape what the Pandit had said to him and what he felt about it. This he did with reluctance, not allowing the Pandit to be identified by name. K said that he was a great scholar whom he had been talking to for years in Benares, and who sometimes came to Madras to see him. One evening in Madras, he could not remember how it came about—Achuyt Patwardhan was there and Sunanda Patwardhan who took notes—the Pandit began to speak. (His words must have been translated from Hindi since he could speak no English.) The Pandit began with 'great hesitancy, a great sense of reverence, a feeling of non-verbal communication, a certain sense of awe, a quality of utter secrecy; he was very, very reserved about it', in K's words. When Mary and Scott tried to question him he told them quite crossly not to interrupt; he could not allow them to ask questions about it. *He* had listened to the Pandit and never said a word to him, he told them. He then repeated that the Pandit had 'said all this with the utmost reluctance and sense of holiness, a sense of not wanting to tell others, or commit himself. What he was talking about was sacred, not to be bandied about.' At the end, K had asked the Pandit, 'Do you really believe all this, sir?' The Pandit had answered, 'Perhaps a little, perhaps not.'[54]

It is curious that K was so intrigued by this story, and seemed himself to regard it as something sacred. It was as if he was becoming more and more interested in his own mystery.

*   *   *   *

When K flew to Los Angeles with Asit on February 17, he had one more year to live to the very day. He felt a need to rest when he reached Ojai but after only a few days he started holding discussions with the staff of the Oak Grove schools. (Friedrich Grohe had become interested in the American Foundation as well as in the English and Indian Foundations.)

In March K had his annual check-up from a new doctor—Dr Gary Deutsch, at Santa Paula, only sixteen miles from Ojai. This doctor had been recommended by a friend of Mary's when it was considered wise by K's doctor in Los Angeles for him to have a practitioner nearer Ojai. K took at once to Dr Deutsch who was quite a young man. This was the doctor who was to attend him in his last illness.

It had been arranged by the author, Milton Friedman, at one time special assistant to President Ford and White House speechwriter, for K to talk in Washington this year instead of in New York. His subject was to be 'Do we really want peace?'. Friedman had met K the year before at Ojai after which he had written a long article about him in the July/August 1984 number of *New Realities*, with the title 'Is Washington Ready for Krishnamurti?' 'Albert Einstein would have been delighted by the prospect of Krishnamurti coming to Washington,' Friedman had written. 'Einstein maintained that issues like nuclear war could not be resolved at the same level of understanding at which such problems evolved. A higher level of awareness was essential.' He continued:

Krishnamurti has no desire to provide Washington with a spectacle. . . . There will be no flower-adorned puja in the Kennedy Center. No incense will waft down the aisles. No chanting nor the strains of the harmonium and sitar. Just Krishnamurti sitting, erect and serious, on a straight-backed chair all alone on the vast stage of the concert hall.

Krishnamurti renounces the role of guru. He is coming to Washington simply because he has been asked to come at a time when it is becoming apparent that old concepts of human existence are no longer credible—even to some who still espouse them. . . . Krishnamurti said recently that, 'Whether it's the Buddha, Christ, the Pope, or Mr Reagan telling me what to do . . . I won't. This means we have to be extraordinarily capable of standing alone. And nobody wants to do that.' . . . He abhors those who self-righteously try to transform others. His credo is change yourself . . . you are the world. . . . Krishnamurti refers endlessly to 'choiceless awareness'. Choice implies direction, the action of the will involving egoism. In Krishnamurti's view it was awareness from moment to moment of all that has taken place inside oneself without any effort to direct or change it—a matter of pure observation, perception, which would result in change without effort. . . .

Who in Washington will be open to the Krishnamurti philosophy? Certainly not those devoted to conservative dogmas. . . . Krishnamurti emphasizes that he is no authority. He has made certain discoveries; he is simply doing his best to make those discoveries accessible to all who are able to listen. He does not offer a body of doctrine nor a method of obtaining a silent mind.

He is not concerned with establishing any new system of religious belief. Rather, it is up to each person to see if he can discover for himself that to which Krishnamurti is calling attention, and to proceed from there to make new discoveries on his own.

Before going to Washington, where he would be speaking publicly for the first time, K went with Mary to New York early in April and stayed again at the Dorset Hotel. On April 11 he spoke for a second time at the United Nations at the invitation of Pacem in Terris, on 'Peace', a subject suggested as part of the U.N. fortieth-birthday celebrations. At the end of his talk he was presented with a small silver peace medal which he forgot to take with him when he left the platform. There had been some muddle as to the hall he was to speak in and he was kept waiting half an hour. The audience was small and not much interested. As he left the building he said to Mary, 'No more United Nations.'

Next day he and Mary flew to Washington where they were met by Milton Friedman, taken to the Watergate Hotel to drop their luggage and then driven round the city and to the Kennedy Center to see the hall where K was to speak in a week's time. During that week he visited the Lincoln Memorial and was deeply moved by the statue. He wanted to see the new Vietnam War Memorial but there was too long a queue. He was interviewed by Michael Kernan for the *Washington Post*, gave a radio interview for 'The Voice of America', and an interview on education for the Washington radio, had tea with Senator Clairborne Pell at his office in the Senate Building and answered questions on thought and the origin of conflict by members of Congress.

Kernan's long article appeared in a prominent position two days before the first talk. It told a little of K's early life but consisted mostly of short quotations from his books, such as, 'It's terrible what gurus have done in America. People want to be helped. Look, this idea of being helped, asking for help, is a destructive way of living. We make ourselves helpless by asking for help, handing yourself over to someone else,' and, 'Thought has created God, thought has created ideology, created wars, murdered in the name of God millions of people. God was invented by man, it's so obvious, so clear. He is our image projected, what we want to be, wiser, more poweful.' And, 'Unless one is completely free from belief, from emotional attachment, one is a slave. . . . When you end

95

attachment completely, then love is.' And again, 'To learn about, to understand, oneself, all authority must be set aside. Obviously, authority is part of oneself. . . . There is nothing to be learnt from anybody, including the speaker; especially one must not be influenced by the speaker. . . . The speaker has nothing to teach you. The speaker is merely acting as a mirror in which you can see yourself. Then when you can see yourself clearly you can discard the mirror.'

He was asked in another interview: 'What if a listener takes your suggestions to heart and does indeed change, what can one person do? What use will that be in Washington, this citadel of power and fear?', to which K replied, 'I was speaking the other day at the United Nations and somebody asked the same question: what if one person changed? That is a wrong question. Change . . . and see what happens.'

In a radio broadcast for 'The Voice of America' on April 18, K was asked his opinion of the religious revival taking place in America. A growing number of Americans wanted their children to pray in public schools. K's answer was predictable:

It's not religious revival at all. What's revival? To revive something that's gone, that's dead, isn't it? I mean, you can revive a half-dying body. Pump a lot of religious medicine into it, but the body, after it's revived, will be the same old body. That's not religion. Religion is essentially not to belong to a single organisation, because then you are free to observe, free to find out, what is truth. But you can't find out what is truth if you are anchored, tethered to a post and say, 'I'm free.' That's what's happening in the world.

Later in the interview he said:

If man doesn't radically change, fundamentally bring about a mutation in himself, not through God, not through prayers—all that stuff is too infantile, too immature—we will destroy ourselves. A psychological revolution is possible now, not a thousand years later. We've already lived thousands of years and we're still barbarians. So if we don't change now we'll still be barbarians tomorrow or a thousand tomorrows. . . . If I don't stop war today I'll go to war tomorrow. So the future is now, very simply put.

There was a good audience for the first talk on April 20, but the second talk on Sunday morning was a triumph. The hall was sold out and so were all the 500 Krishnamurti books sent from Ojai. In the afternoon Milton Friedman brought reporters from the United Press International to interview K for an hour and a half.

In the two talks, K covered almost every aspect of his teaching. Towards the beginning of his first talk he said, 'Though we don't know each other we are going to have a conversation which is much more important than being lectured at, told what to do, what to believe. We are going to observe together dispassionately, impersonally, not anchored to any particular problem or theory, what mankind has done to the world and what we have done to each other. . . . The society in which we live is put together by man. Whatever that society be, each one of us has contributed to it.'

In this talk he went into the question of fear:

What is fear? Humanity has put up with fear, has never been able to solve fear. Never. There are various forms of fear; you may have your own particular fear: fear of death, fear of gods, fear of the devil, fear of your wife, fear of your husband, fear of the politicians—god knows how many fears humanity has. What is fear? Not the mere experience of fear in its multiple forms, but the reality, the actuality of fear? How is it brought about? Why has humanity, which is each one of us, accepted fear as a way of life: violence on the television, violence in our daily life and the ultimate violence of organised killing, which is called war? Why do we accept violence?

Is not fear related to violence? We are enquiring into fear—the actual truth of fear, not the idea of fear—you understand the difference? The idea of fear is different from the actuality of fear. Right? So what is fear? How has it come about?

What is the relationship of fear to time, to thought? One may be frightened of tomorrow, or of many tomorrows; the fear of death—the ultimate fear—or fear of what has happened before in the past, or fear of what is actually going on now. So we must enquire together—please, the speaker keeps on repeating together; it's no fun talking to myself. Is fear brought about by time? Someone has done something in the past, hurt you, and the past is time. The future is time. The present is time. So we are asking, is time a central factor of fear? Fear has many, many branches, many leaves, but it's no good trimming the branches; we are asking, what is the root of fear? Not the multiple forms of fear, because fear is fear. Out of fear you have invented God, saviours. If you have absolutely no fear psychologically, then there is tremendous relief, a great sense of freedom. You have dropped all the burdens of life. So we must enquire very seriously, hesitantly, into this question: is time a factor? Obviously. I have a good job now, I may lose it tomorrow so I am frightened. When there is fear there is jealousy, anxiety, hatred, violence. So time is a factor of fear.

Time is a factor and thought is a factor: thinking about what has happened, what might happen; thinking. Has thinking brought about fear? As one sees, time has brought about fear, right? Time: not only time by the clock, but psychological time, the inward time: 'I am going to be', 'I am not good but I will be', 'I will get rid of my violence', which is again the future.

Are you prepared for all this? Do you want to go into all this? Really? I'm rather surprised because you've all been instructed, you've all been informed, you've been told what to do by the psychologists, by the priests, by your leaders; always seeking help and finding new ways of being helped. So one has become a slave to others. One is never free to enquire, to stand psychologically completely by oneself.

At the end of this first talk the audience started to applaud. 'I don't know why you clap,' K said. 'Perhaps you are clapping for yourself. You are not encouraging the speaker or discouraging him. He doesn't want a thing from you. When you yourself become the teacher and the disciple—disciple being a man who is learning, learning, learning, not accumulating knowledge—then you are an extraordinary human being.'

In the second talk he spoke of sorrow and whether sorrow could ever end. He said:

When there is sorrow there is no love. When you are suffering, concerned with your own suffering, how can there be love? . . . What is sorrow? Is sorrow self-pity? Please investigate. We are not saying it is or it is not. . . . Is sorrow brought about by loneliness—feeling desperately alone—isolated? . . . Can we look at sorrow as it actually is in us, and remain with it, hold it, and not move away from it? Sorrow is not different from the one who suffers. The person who suffers wants to run away, escape, do all kinds of things. But to look at it as you look at a child, a beautiful child, to hold it, never escape from it—then you will see for yourself, if you really look deeply, that there is an end to sorrow. And when there is an end to sorrow there is passion; not lust, not sensory stimulation, but passion.

He also went into the questions of love and death. 'We use the word love so loosely . . . to find that perfume one must go into the question of what is not love. Through negation you come to the positive, not the other way round . . . love is not hate: that's obvious. Love is not vanity, arrrogance. Love is not in the hands of power. . . . Love is not pleasure, love is not desire. . . . Love is certainly not thought. . . . So love is something that cannot be invited or cultivated. It comes about naturally, easily, when the other things are not.' About death he said in part:

What does it mean to die? . . . Death comes through accident, through disease, through old age, senility. (Is senility only for the old? Is it not senility when we act mechanically, thoughtlessly? Isn't that a form of senility?) . . . Because we are frightened of death, we never see the greatness of it. . . . I ask myself, is it possible to live with death all the time—not at the end of one's life, but with all my energy and vitality live with death all the time? Not commit suicide—that's too silly. But live with death, which means the ending every day of everything I have collected. . . . Ending is more important than continuity. The ending means the beginning of something new.[55]

The next day K returned to Ojai. The Washington trip had been altogether highly successful. K considered that he had never before had such a responsive audience for a public talk.

*   *   *   *

Pupul Jayakar arrived at Ojai in time for K's ninetieth birthday on May 11 which coincided with the first Oak Grove talk on a lovely clear morning. It so happened that the Saanen and Brockwood Gatherings in this last year of K's life, as well as the Ojai one, took place in perfect weather.

At supper at Pine Cottage that evening with K and Mary, Pupul talked of Jagannath Upadhyaya's revelation about the Lord Maitreya taking the body of Krishnamurti. She also spoke of a long letter from Nitya to Mrs Besant, found in the Adyar archives, about the agonising pain K had suffered when 'the process' had first started at Ojai in 1922.[56] On one occasion during 'the process', according to Nitya's letter, K had felt that someone was lurking round the house. Semi-conscious, he had insisted on walking to the low wall surrounding the cottage and had said in a loud voice, 'Go away. What do you mean by coming here?' When Pupul told them this, K seemed to understand what it meant and admonished Pupul and Mary not to enquire too far into esoteric matters because 'if you open the door to "that", you also open the door to what is beyond the wall.' After Pupul had left the cottage that evening, K told Mary severely, 'You must have no disorder because of that beyond the wall.' He was concerned at this time about the amount of secretarial work Mary had to do. 'You must not wear yourself out,' he told her. 'As long as I live you are with me. You must be able to look after me.' And a few days later he told her again, 'You must outlive me so that you can look after me. After that you can follow me.' To understand these apparently heartless remarks to Mary, one should translate the word 'me' into 'this body'. It was 'the body' that was important to carry on his work. While he was well he could look after his body himself; if he fell ill someone else would have to look after it and the only person he wanted to do this was Mary.

His sense of dissociation from his body was a phenomenon beyond one's understanding. He obviously knew more about himself than he had ever yet divulged to anyone, yet there appears to have been a great deal that he did not know. And if he had known, could he have put it into words? He could feel 'the other' but he did not seem to know what it was. 'The other' was limitless, as he had often said. If it could be expressed in words it would be limited, it would be part of thought and, as he had emphasised over and over again, thought could never be anything but limited; therefore anything expressed by a process of thought in words could not be 'the other'. Did 'the other' inhabit him? When talking to me at Brockwood about it he had said, it may be remembered, that if Mary and I 'sat down and said, "Let us enquire", I am quite sure you could find out. I can never find out. Water can never find out what water is.' From this it would appear that 'the other' *was* him, that he was not separate from it. But it also seems that although it was always part of him, it was at times more present than at others. When he was in a state of meditation it was fully present; if he spoke seriously about it he said he could feel it in the room as if it were something that came from outside—'always from the left'. But was it from outside? Or was it something in him made more palpable? Was it a form of energy? Shortly before he died he was to make an illuminating statement about the energy that had passed through his body.

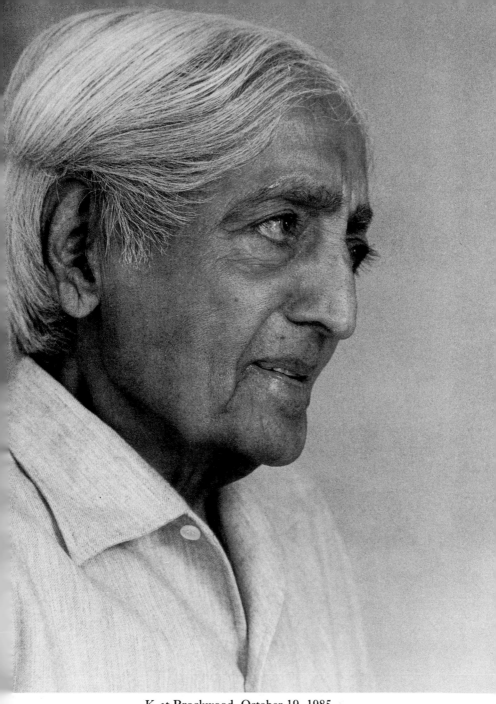

K at Brockwood, October 19, 1985

Walking at Rishi Valley, December 1985. *From left:* Lakshman Rasiah, Christina West, Mahesh Saxena, Friedrich Grohe, K, Stephen Smith, Gary Primrose, Michael Krohnen

Walking on the beach at Adyar, December 24, 1985. *From left:* Radha Burnier, Pama Patwardhan, Jayant Sathaye, K, Radha Burnier's niece, Scott Forbes, Mahesh Saxena

9

Dilemma

Friedrich Grohe and Rita Zampesi were at the Ojai Gathering that year. K had a stomach ache on and off during the Oak Grove talks which he attributed to the food in Washington. At the last talk on May 19, which was to be his last talk of all in California, he spoke among other things about attachment:

What is attachment? Why are we attached to something or other, to property, money, wife, husband, to some foolish conclusion, to some ideological concept? The consequences of attachment are fear of loss, and out of that fear there is jealousy; from jealousy there is hatred. Of course. Jealousy is hatred. And can you, if you are attached to something, some idea or some person, end that attachment now? That is death. Can you live with death all the day long? Ah, think of it, go into it, you will see the greatness, the immensity of it, living with that ending of all sense of attachment, all sense of fear, which means having a brain that is acting but never acting with preconceived direction and purpose. That is, to live with death every second, never collecting, never gathering or giving anything a continuity. If you do, you will see what it means. It is real freedom. And from that freedom there is love. Love is not attachment, pleasure, desire or fulfilment.

He ended this talk:

The brain, which has its own rhythm, is everlastingly chattering, praying, demanding help—you follow? It is tremendously active. Now, can that activity calm down, become very quiet, still, without any movement? Not an induced or cultivated silence. There is a great deal to be said about silence; the silence between two wars, peace, the silence between two notes, between two words, between two thoughts—yet all that is not the still, quiet, utterly peaceful brain which is empty of everything which man has collected and which man has always sought from the beginning, which is nameless.[57]

Dilemma

K was still feeling far from well when he flew to London on May 24 with Mary and Friedrich. Daily massage, however, from Dr Parchure, who was awaiting him at Brockwood, and injections of Vitamin B greatly helped him.

On June 1 Duncan Fallowell, novelist and travel writer, went to Brockwood to interview him for *Harpers and Queen*. It was a good article which came out in the December number. After giving a résumé of K's career, the author described him:

He is tiny and fragile and walks at a slow pace into the large, pale drawing-room, picking up his feet like a small wading bird, twinkling as he comes. He is dressed in blue jeans, soft slip-on shoes and a greenish-blue shirt open at the neck, and he sits on a hard, straight-backed chair because he doesn't like to sit on soft ones. His voice is tiny but carries and impresses itself very clearly on the magnetic tapes (sometimes bigger voices fail to do this, for no clear reason). He doesn't drawl but speaks precisely, clipping many words. He also giggles and laughs a great deal. Generally his talk is not smooth but full of gaps, switches, exclamations, changes of tempo. He uses his body a lot and has a number of characteristic gestures; the eyes roll up into the head showing their whites when he is thinking or embarking on a long statement; when horrified (by the Bomb, by over-population, for example) he throws his hands up to his face and throws his body forward; and he is constantly grabbing one's elbow or shaking one's knee to emphasise a point.

The conversation that followed, though extremely well reported, was not remarkable to anyone who had already heard K speak. Duncan Fallowell found some of it irritating, for it raised as many questions as it answered. 'Krishnamurti is not in the business of customer satisfaction,' he truly remarked.

While K had been in India and Ojai, Scott Forbes had been looking for another architect for the Brockwood Centre. Having consulted several, he asked five of them to make rough drawings. Two or three of these, eager to secure the commission for a million-pound private building on a glorious site, sent in quite finished plans. None of them was wholly approved of. Then, by reading an article given to him by chance, Scott heard of Keith Critchlow, an expert on Islamic architecture, and immediately got in touch with him. There was no building of his in England but he showed Scott photographs of his work abroad, mostly religious buildings, which convinced Scott that he had found the right man at last. On June 5

Critchlow went to Brockwood, spoke of his ideas to K and showed him his first rough drawings. The van der Stratens and Jean-Michel Maroger as well as Friedrich Grohe happened to be there and they all liked his sketches and ideas. He was given the commission there and then. K himself was more impressed by the man than his designs (it turned out afterwards that Critchlow had had a long-standing interest in K's teaching). K felt that Critchlow understood perfectly what he wanted the Centre to be, especially the quiet room. 'There should be a room . . . where you go to be quiet,' K had written. 'That room is only used for that and not for anything else . . . It should be like a fountain filling the whole place. . . . That room should be the central flame, . . . It is like a furnace that heats the whole place. . . . If you don't have that, the Centre becomes just a passage, people coming and going, work and activity.' K was insistent that all the materials used for the building should be of the very best. He wanted the highest standard of excellence throughout. Since Critchlow, although an Englishman and a fellow of the Royal College of Art, was not qualified to practise in England, the English firm of Triad was brought in to act as technical architects. At the end of June planning permission was granted.

Dorothy Simmons had now decided to retire and it had been proposed by the staff that Scott Forbes should become the new Principal. K agreed to this, but did not relieve Scott of responsibility for the new Centre. Many administrative matters in the school had still to be settled and K spoke every day to the staff or to the students. He said urgently to Mary one evening after he had been in bed all day with a cold and sore throat: 'You must listen—do you feel it? It—that thing has been with me all day. It is with me most of the time now that I am older. You must pay attention. You must outlive me, but not as an old person—not living in memories as people do; you must be alive, alert. I think I will live another ten years and you must take care of me. Do you understand?'

On the day before K and Mary flew to Geneva on June 23, he spoke to the whole school—for the last time, as it happened.

*   *   *   *

That summer in Switzerland K and Mary stayed at Rougemont in the flat Friedrich Grohe had lent K, as had been planned. In a larger flat in the same chalet Vanda and Dr Parchure stayed and also

Raman Patel who was in charge of the kitchen at Brockwood and who cooked for K that summer since Fosca, now aged ninety, had at last been obliged to give up work. It was sad that she was not there for the last summer at Saanen. She died in August. From Rougemont, as from Schönried the year before, K had to drive to Tannegg for his favourite walk. On his first walk that year he went ahead alone into the wood 'to see if we are welcome'.

On July 1 Pupul Jayakar came to stay at Rougemont for three nights and again brought up the subject of the copyright in K's works. She said that only two alternatives were acceptable to the Indian Foundation—either sharing the copyright with England or for the Indian Foundation to bring out an international book every third year with any publisher of their own choosing without submitting it to the English Publications Committee. Failing either of these alternatives K must himself decide the issue. (It was of course entirely to avoid this that we had been appointed and, presumably in both countries, had agreed to serve.) Mary Zimbalist telephoned to Mary Cadogan in London so that Pupul could put the position to her; Pupul wanted an answer next day. Mary Cadogan naturally said that she could make no decision until she had put the matter to the other members of the Publications Committee, particularly to me who happened to be the chairman. She also pointed out, what Pupul knew already, that we could not legally share the copyright. My immediate reaction when hearing of Pupul's request was 'anything for peace, anything to save K from involvement in our disputes'. I then wondered whether we had any right to shirk the responsibility K had laid upon us.

When Mary Cadogan arrived at Saanen for the Gathering she told K that the difficulties with India over publications had been going on for over thirteen years. K said it was ridiculous and that he was going to take the matter into his own hands since Pupul had given him that option, and settle it once and for all as soon as he got to India. He wanted no advice from anyone, only a memorandum of facts.

*   *   *   *

There was a sense of euphoria that summer at the Saanen Gathering, perhaps because of the beauty of the weather; the crowds were larger than they had ever been. It so happened that Mark Edwards was there at the request of the English Foundation to photograph the Gathering from the putting up of the tents to the ending of the last talk.[58] Mark was a sought-after free-lance photographer, best known for his work on the Third World. He had first become interested in K in 1968 when a friend of his had insisted on his reading one of K's books. In September '68, after taking his degree, he had got in touch with Mary Cadogan to ask to be allowed to photograph K. Having for many years refused to have any photographs taken, K had recently relented, so Mark's request was well timed and Mary Cadogan made an appointment for him one afternoon. This was his first professional assignment. Since then he has done a great deal of photographic work for the Foundation, rarely charging more than his bare expenses.

During the Saanen talks an international meeting was held of the three Foundations. The Lilliefelts were there representing America, Dr Parchure and J. Y Sathaye, the Principal of the Rajghat School, represented India and all the English trustees were there. These now included Jane Hammond. (Jane had been doing the transcripts at Saanen ever since a tape-recorder had been used. She would transcribe a talk immediately it was finished to give to the translators into French, German and Dutch. Later on, when video came into use, there would be video showings of the morning talk in these three languages by the late afternoon.) K brought up at the meeting the idea of having only one set of talks a year in Europe in order to cut down his travelling. He suggested one more year at Saanen, after which the international annual Gathering should be held at Brockwood.

At a later and larger meeting Dorothy Simmons's retirement was announced. K spoke very warmly of all she had done in creating the Brockwood School; this drew loud and genuine applause, for Dorothy was very much loved. It was then announced that Scott Forbes was to be the new Principal of the School. Dorothy would remain a trustee, and a much nicer flat at Brockwood would be made for her and Montague than the one they had occupied all the time she was Principal.

K was not at all well during the talks. One evening he had felt so ill that he had said to Mary, 'I wondered if my time had come.' The fourth talk on July 17 was a special one. Mary wrote in her diary, 'He began in a remote voice which deepened and strengthened as he went to greater depths. It was the pure essential K teaching coming from that fragile, gentle, utterly commanding figure, as it had all these many, so many, years. There was complete stillness of the audience at the end, then he made a gesture that he would get up only when they did.' In this talk he spoke of beauty among other things:

What is beauty? Is beauty in a person, in a face? Is beauty in museums, in painting. . . . Is beauty in music? . . . Is beauty in a poem? In literature? Dancing? Is all that beauty? Or is beauty something entirely different? . . . When you look at those mountains, those immense rocks jutting into the sky—if you look at them quietly you feel the immensity of it, the enormous majesty of it, and for the moment, for the second, the tremendous dignity of it, the solidity of it, puts away all your thoughts, your problems—right? And you say, 'How marvellous that is.' So what has taken place there? The majesty of those mountains, the very immensity of the sky and the blue and the snow-clad mountains, drives away for a second all your problems. It makes you totally forget yourself for a second. . . .

Is that beauty? To be absorbed by the mountains, the river, or the green fields, means that you are like a child absorbed by a toy, and for the moment you are quiet, taken over, surrendering yourself to something. Is that beauty? . . . Is there beauty where there is self-conscious endeavour? Or is there beauty only when the self is not—when the 'me', the observer, is not? So is it possible, without being absorbed, taken over, surrendering, to be in that state without the self, without the ego, without the 'me' always thinking about itself? Is that at all possible, living in this modern world with all its specialisations, its vulgarity, its immense noise—not the noise of running water, of the song of a bird? Is it possible to live in this world without the self, the 'me', the ego, the persona, the assertion of the individual? In that state, when there is really freedom from all this, only then is there beauty.

After this talk, on the way back to Rougemont in a car driven by Mary, K fell against her shoulder in a faint, something that had not happened for some years. She drove on very slowly and he soon recovered.

The day before the fifth and last talk, on July 21, Hugues van der Straten, Jean-Michel Maroger and Mary Cadogan went to Rougemont and urged K not to hold even one more Gathering at Saanen but to start his new programme of having the international talks at Brockwood the following year. K listened carefully and then agreed. Dr Parchure and Dr Dagmar Liechti, who was again at

Saanen, very much approved of this decision on medical grounds. At the end of the last talk, therefore, it was announced that after twenty-five years there were to be no more Gatherings at Saanen.

Two days later K began the first Question and Answer meeting characteristically: 'I have been told that there are so many people who are sad leaving, ending Saanen. If one is sad it is about time that we left.' But at the last meeting he spoke with intense feeling: 'We have had the most marvellous days, lovely mornings, beautiful evenings, long shadows and deep blue valleys and clear blue sky and snow. A whole summer has never been like this. So the mountains, the valleys, the trees and the river, tell us good-bye.'

*   *   *   *

K was tired and disturbed after the Gathering, pondering his future programme. He intended to give only one series of talks in America in 1986 and cut down his Indian programme; he would go to Rajghat and Bombay one year and the next year to Rishi Valley and Madras. He did not intend, though, to shorten the time he stayed in India. Mary pointed out how unhealthy Bombay had become, so he said he would spend only a fortnight there just for the talks. Mary then asked him if he intended to spend three months at Rajghat where it got very cold in the winter. He said no, he could not do that. He was in a dilemma. Travelling had become too tiring, yet he could not stay too long in one place. He had become so hypersensitive that he felt people were focusing on him if he stayed too long; it was a pressure he could no longer stand. And he must go on talking; he was there to talk. He needed someone to challenge him. No one he knew could do it any longer. He needed someone new with whom to go much deeper. Mary foresaw great difficulties with this paradox of his needing to rest more yet not being able to stay long in one place. He was not at ease in new surroundings. He missed Tannegg.

He talked at length to Mary, trying for himself to find the answer to his dilemma. Mary was learning to let him talk without interruption in the way he liked to do, stating well-known things as if 'laying a ground work of the known in order to come upon the new'. A letter had just come from a Greek couple asking him and Mary to visit them on a Greek island. K was tempted and enjoyed looking up the island on the map but wondered whether there would be enough shade in Greece. (He had once had sunstroke and could not bear sitting or walking in the sun.)

He said one day, 'It is watching.' Mary noted, 'He speaks as if that something is deciding what happens to him; "it" will decide when his work is done and hence by implication his life.' On another day at Rougemont, Mary jotted down an exchange she had with him when discussing travel plans:

K: It is not the physical effect of the brain. It is something else. My life has been planned. It will tell me when to die, say it is over. That will settle my life. But I must be careful that 'that' is not interfered with by saying, 'I will give only two more talks.'
M: Do you feel how much more time it gives?
K: I think ten years more.
M: Do you mean ten years of talking?
K: When I don't talk it will be over. But I don't want to strain the body. Also too long a holiday is bad. I need a certain amount of rest but no more. A quiet place where nobody knows me. But unfortunately people get to know me.

He told Mary once again at this time that she should write a book about him—'even if only 100 pages. What it was like being with him, what he said.' He also asked her to make some notes as to what he wanted the Centre at Brockwood to be: '1) Look at trees, nature, be aware of everything. 2) Study K's teaching to know (even intellectually) all he has said. 3) Are you interested in all this? If not, do your job as well as you can but ease out.' He also asked her to make a separate note: 'If anyone gets hurt by what I am about to say they haven't listened to the teaching.'

Before Erna Lilliefelt left to return to California, K told her and Mary that they must see that he had things to do while he was at Ojai. He wasn't just going to sit there, but they mustn't arrange things just to please him: 'It must be something you think is necessary.' Walking in the woods the next afternoon he said, 'The spirit has left Saanen, probably that's why I feel so uncomfortable. It has moved to Brockwood.'

Vanda Scaravelli, who had been back to Florence, returned to Rougemont on August 9. She advised K to have a long rest and suggested his going to Cortina d'Ampezzo next summer instead of to Switzerland. K suddenly became cheerful and enthusiastic. 'We can go to the French Alps or the Italian mountains,' he said to

Mary. 'When we are in Ojai let's study French and Italian one hour a day.' Two days later he said he would like to go to Florence, Venice and Rome.

He was leaving next morning for England and said to the trees on his last walk, 'Good-bye, we'll see you in two or three years.' He also spoke that day about using the apartment that was to be built on the Saanen land where the tent had stood when the land was sold—something that could not exist for at least five years. 'All this is music to me,' Mary wrote in her diary, 'and lets in a blessed sense of ease and summer light.'

On August 12, K said good-bye to Vanda at Rougemont. It was their last good-bye.

*   *   *   *

Three days later Joe and I went to Brockwood and sat with K and Mary in the kitchen catching up on all the summer news. K told me among other things that he was going to settle the publication matter himself, and he repeated what he had said to Mary Cadogan that all he wanted from me was a memorandum of facts. I said it would be best to get that from Mary Cadogan who had all the correspondence. We then turned to a pleasanter subject: ever since he had moved back to Pine Cottage from Malibu, K had been inviting us to go and stay at Ojai in the spring in the flat next to the cottage which Mary had done up for guests. We had been going this year but then we suddenly had to move from our flat after thirty years, so it had not been possible. Now, however, the visit was fixed for April, 1986. Mary had most thoughtfully and generously put a sitz-bath into the guest flat, knowing how I hated showers, and during this day at Brockwood K told us that he was going to hire a car for us with Miss Dodge's money. How he loved to give—not only presents but himself. I think he was quite excited at the idea of our visit but not, of course, nearly as much so as I was.

The next day he was too tired to do his exercises—a very rare occurrence. He mentioned to Mary that day that since the end of the Saanen Gathering (July 25) 'something had been going on in him'. He said, 'If something decides everything that happens to K it is something extraordinary.' Mary asked whether he considered as true what had been told to him by Pandit Jagannath Upadhyaya. 'I am sceptical,' he replied. Mary pointed out that he had seemed impressed by it. 'I don't know,' he said. Mary then asked him if he was aware of certain changes in himself. 'What changes?' he asked. 'In manner. A roughness that is unlike you.' 'I am rough to others?' 'No.' 'Just to you?' 'Yes.' He said that he never did anything unawares, but that she had to hasten to change and therefore he had been rough. He was bothered by the situation in India. He felt that Brockwood had at last been pulled together but that India was unsettled. He wanted 'to end discord and set all right' before he was 'gathered to his fathers'. Mary felt he was 'burning' with impatience to settle everything in India. The next day he was sick several times. In the evening when he was better he said, 'I mustn't be seriously ill; no accident or it will be nip and tuck [a close-run thing]. I have to hold on to it. Death is always so close.' Mary sat with him while he slept in the afternoon. She noted, 'He is so frail, so extraordinarily beautiful. There is no age on his face, only total beauty.' In spite of his impatience to get to India, he was thankful to have time to rest at Brockwood. His physical strength was waning. His walks were getting shorter. 'No one in all these years has changed,' he said to Mary. 'I want to give you a new brain.'

A fortnight later, in the middle of the Brockwood Gathering, he told Mary one evening that he had been looking at his irritability: 'Either I'm getting old or I've fallen into a habit [of picking on her] and it is my fault and it must stop. My body has become hypersensitive. Most of the time I want to go away and I mustn't do that. I'm going to deal with this. It is unforgivable.' On the same day he told Mary and Dr Parchure that 'the body exists to talk'. He thought little of discussions any more because no one could be found to challenge him sufficiently. He considered having talks the following year at Boston or Toronto, but if such talks were arranged he was not sure whether he would be able to fulfil the engagements after a heavy Indian tour. He had not attempted to cut down his usual programme in India that winter.

*   *   *   *

The talks at Brockwood had begun on August 24 in superb weather—hot, sunny and windless. A camera crew was there for the third talk to make a film. They had a crane so that they could take pictures of the whole scene. The film, called *The Role of the Flower*, was shown on Thames Television on January 19, 1986. It could not have been a better film of the Gathering as a whole, though the interview with K at the end was too short.

After the talks, K and Mary lunched with us for the first time in our new little house near the Regent's Canal. It was the only time K came there, for we still usually lunched at Fortnum and Mason. K always went to Huntsman in Savile Row when he came to London if only to take in a pair of trousers to be altered. The evening before coming to London he would carefully choose the suit he was to wear and lay out the shirt and tie to go with it and polish his shoes, even the insteps. His suit would always look pristine, yet he took pride in showing one how old they were by looking inside the inside pocket of the jacket where a good tailor always inscribed the date. London-tailored gentlemen vied with each other over the longevity of their suits. But on this occasion K ordered a new suit and a new pair of trousers, very heartening to Mary and me because it showed a confidence that he did not expect to die soon. So little pleasure did he have in his life that it was a joy to see him at Huntsman. Strangely enough he looked more at home in this masculine English shrine than when speaking on a platform.

On his way to London a few days later he told Mary, while they were waiting on the station platform at Petersfield, that Scott had asked him how long he was going to live. He had answered that he did know but would not tell him. 'Do you really know?' Mary asked.

K: I think I know. I have intimations.
M: Are you willing to tell me?
K: No, that would not be right. I can't tell anyone.
M: Could one at least have some vague idea of time?
K: Scott asked me if I would still be here when the Centre was built at Brockwood. I said I would. [The Centre could not be completed before September 1987.]
M: Is one to live thinking that at any moment K might leave?
K: No, it's not like that; it won't happen for quite a while.
M: How long have you known?
K: About two years.

At lunch that day at Fortnum's he told me also that he knew when he was going to die but could not tell anyone. I gathered that it might be within two or three years. There no longer seemed a possibility of ten years. He also talked about India that day at lunch and said that he must 'put the house in order there'. He refused any comment or opinion from me or Mary. It was as if talking aloud helped him to explore his own mind. He said that he found it insulting the way people said he had been 'influenced', maintaining that it was not his own opinion when he said or wrote something they did not like to hear.

This accusation of being 'influenced' had dogged him most of his life. As early as 1916 Nitya had written to Mrs Besant: 'He [K] has a great deal of insight into character and he is able to judge for himself . . . and although he is not aggressive and never will be, some people are irritated by what they call his sudden firmness and attribute it to the influence of the person who happens to be nearest to him. I think they forget his judgement is not likely to be far wrong.'[59]

K also spoke at lunch that day of wanting to find someone with whom he could go deeper into his teaching. He said surprisingly that the only person he would like to hold a discussion with was Jonathan Miller whom he had seen in some television programme.

*　　　　*　　　　*　　　　*

At this time K started teaching Scott Forbes some of his yoga exercises. He was a severe and exacting teacher. Scott would have found K's suppleness extraordinary even in a much younger man.

K also had a long tape-recorded talk with Scott this autumn at Brockwood about the school and about Scott himself. He asked if the group of teachers chiefly responsible for the school knew, even intellectually, what he was talking about? Scott replied that they responded to 'the otherness' which was there. Then K wanted to know what was taking place in Scott: what was his feeling about K? What was his attitude to K's teaching and to all the work that was going on in America, India and Brockwood? Why was he, Scott, at Brockwood? Was his contact with the teaching only because of K himself? Was he dependent on K? Supposing K died tomorrow? Having come in contact with K, 'with that whiff, that breath, or that feeling, will that die after K's death or will that flower grow, multiply? . . . Will it flower by itself? Not be dependent on circumstances? Nothing can corrupt it once it is there. It may pass through different circumstances but it is always there.' Scott replied that it was 'not solid yet'.

'Don't use the word "yet",' K admonished him. 'Yet means time. Will you allow it to become solid, strong and take deep roots, and flower? Or will it depend on circumstances?' They went on:

S: No, sir. One would do everything . . .

K: No, no, no, sir. Not you do anything. The thing itself, the seed itself—like in a womb, you have nothing to do. It grows. It is there. It is bound to grow. It is bound to flourish—that is a better word. . . . Is Scott aware that the seed is there? Is Scott preventing the flowering of it by too much activity, too much organisation, not giving it sufficient care? Sufficient air to flower? What generally happens is that organisations smother that thing. . . . You must be quite sure that the seed is there, not invented by thought. If the seed is strong you really have nothing to do with it. But you can smother it. . . . Wash away any sense of power, position, all that stuff. . . . There can be no conflict at all in you. They [the students] can have conflict but you cannot. . . . They may offer opinions. You can't have opinions. That's very difficult. You have to listen to them, see what they are saying, listen to each one, not react to it as Scott or from your background, but listen to them very, very carefully . . . let them come out so that they feel you are not blocking them. Can you be free of your background? That's very difficult. . . . That really demands all your energy. . . . Background being all your American training, your American education and so-called culture. Freeing all that is a deliberation, not just saying, 'I must leave it'. Discuss with it, weigh it, take counsel together. Not say, 'Well, I must get rid of my background'—that you can never do. . . . You can be aware of the background and not let it react, not let it interfere. I think there [for that] a deliberate act is necessary because you are going to run this place. You have got the energy, you have got the drive. Keep it. Don't let it gradually wither because of this burden.

S: Sir, if one is doing the things here you are describing, and if the seed is there, is that enough to keep the school absolutely . . .?

K: Yes, yes. If the seed is there and it is active, living.

S: Sir, if all that is brought about then what will happen when I die?

K: Oh, don't bother about that. You have to find somebody. That is part of it. No apostolic succession.[60]

The idea that the organisation and busy-ness of the schools might be swamping the teaching was very present with K at this time. It was not organisation that would keep the Foundations together. 'The unifying factor should be intelligence,' he told Mary and Scott. 'To be free in the real sense and that freedom is intelligence. Intelligence is common to all of us and that will bring us together, not organisation. If you see the importance that each one of us is free and that freedom implies love, consideration, attention, co-operation, compassion—that intelligence is the factor to keep us together.' He also asked Mary to note down: 'Independence without freedom is meaningless. If you have freedom you don't need independence.'[61]

On September 21 he asked at a staff meeting: 'How do you instantly, without time, make the students see that self-interest is the root of conflict? Not only see it but instantly be transformed?' He went on to say that of all the hundreds of students who had passed through Rishi Valley not one had been changed. After the meeting, when they were alone, Mary asked him what was the point of having students if no students in all these years had changed? If, with all his influence, no student had been transformed, how could the rest of us, who had apparently not changed either, bring about change in the students? 'If you haven't done it, is there any likelihood that we can?' she asked. 'I don't know,' he replied, but he said it rather jokingly, evidently not wanting to continue with a serious subject.

K had what he called 'remarkable meditations' at this time, as he told Mary, which meant that 'the other' was very much a part of him.

*   *   *   *

Pupul Jayakar went to Brockwood for two nights on September 28. According to what K told me, she repeated the request she had made at Rougemont about publishing. He said that he was going to decide the question himself. He would make his decision after talking to everyone concerned in India, including all the Trustees of the Indian Foundation, at the Foundation's meeting in Madras. From Pupul's own account, he also told her during this visit, as he had told Mary, Scott, the Lilliefelts, me and probably others as well, that he knew when he was going to die but could not tell anyone.[62]

Pupul saw Mary Cadogan in London after leaving Brockwood and stated her position again over the Indian books. According to Mary she insisted that the administration was separate from the teachings and that we ought to be able to settle this publication matter without involving K. Mary could only say that K had taken it out of our hands and was determined to make the decision himself as Pupul had suggested.

Keith Critchlow was at Brockwood again on October 23 with detailed plans for the Centre and samples of the two different coloured bricks he wanted to use, and of the roof tiles. These met with general approval. K, Mary and Scott had just held a video discussion on what the Centre was intended to be. After some false starts and hesitations, as in all such discussions, K had said ultimately:

It should be a religious centre, a centre where people feel there is something not cooked-up, not imaginative, not some kind of 'holy' atmosphere. A religious centre, not in the orthodox sense of the word; a centre where a flame is living, not the ashes of it. A flame is alive, and if you come to that house you might take light, the flame, with you, or you might light your candle or be the most extraordinary human being, not broken up, a person who is really whole, has no shadow of sorrow, pain, all that kind of thing. So, that is a religious centre.[63]

During Critchlow's October visit, details of the building were discussed at length. K told Critchlow at one moment that he did not want it to look '*nouveau riche*' or like 'a country hotel'. 'Will it make me want to dress properly—clean?' he asked. 'Not dirty clothes. Make me feel I must be very careful in my dress—in my walk?' Critchlow replied that if the building was 'respectful to the people, the people would be respectful to the building'.

*   *   *   *

K would not allow Mary to go with him to India that year for fear of her falling ill. She wondered whether she would ever see him again after he left Brockwood, it was so evident that he was growing physically more frail. 'If I'm going to die, I'll telephone to you right away,' he assured her. 'I won't die all of a sudden. I'm in good health, my heart, everything is all right. It is all decided by someone else. I can't talk about it. I'm not allowed to, do you understand? It is much more serious. There are things you don't know. Enormous, and I can't tell you. It is very hard to find a brain like this and it must keep on as long as the body can; until something says enough. If I die you mustn't mourn as you would have in the past.'

The last time I saw K before he went to India was on October 21. Joe and I met him and Mary at Waterloo as usual—then Huntsman, a haircut at Truefitt in Bond Street where he had been for years, lunch at Fortnum's, Hatchard's bookshop and home. It was what Mary called in her diary 'a happy day in the familiar and cherished ways'. He talked as he so often did now about what would happen when he was gone. He seemed reluctant to go to India and yet eager to put 'the house in order' there as soon as possible. I asked him if he would wear my turquoise and diamond ring at lunch as he sometimes did. He put it on his little finger. He knew it well because my mother had worn it. When he gave it back the diamonds sparkled as if they had just been cleaned by a jeweller as they always did after he had worn it. All the time he was talking he was looking round alertly at the people within view, noticing what they wore, what they ate, how they ate. He had an extraordinary awareness of his surroundings. I have never known anyone with such keen powers of observation. He looked so ageless and beautiful that day that talking about his death seemed hypothetical.

K's last talk, Vasanta Vihar, January 4, 1986

Outside the Ranch House Restaurant, Ojai, February 1986. *From left, back row:* Helen Hooker, Theodore Lilliefelt, Alan Hooker, Dr Krishna, R. Morali, Mary Cadogan, Joe Links, Dorothy Simmons, Evelyne Blau. *Front row:* Asit Chandmal, Radhika Herzberger, Mary Links, Pupul Jayakar, Erna Lilliefelt, Jane Hammond

'A jewel on a silver plate'

Friedrich Grohe, who had been at Brockwood for a few days, accompanied K to Delhi on October 24. Mary drove K to Heathrow. 'I will be back,' he told her as they left the house.

K spent a week with Pupul Jayakar in Delhi, eating and sleeping very little. In the course of those days he saw Mr Venkataraman again, and Rajiv Gandhi twice. Friedrich was staying at an hotel but he walked with K every afternoon in Lodi Park. Friedrich has recorded that one day in the Park a man approached K and asked, 'Are you Krishnamurti? You should stay in India; here is your source.' K replied: 'I am nobody.' Afterwards he lifted his hands and said to Friedrich, 'You see, they have a fixed idea and they stick to it.' 'He was always friendly.' Friedrich wrote 'especially to the poor people. At the entrance to the Park there was an ice-vendor he used to greet and to whom he gave much attention.'[64]

On November 2, K flew with Friedrich to Varanasi where Dr Parchure, who had returned to India from Brockwood some weeks before, was awaiting him. From that day until K's death the doctor never left him and kept a record of his state of health. The doctor believed that K's frequent abdominal pains in 1980, before his hernia operation, could have been 'preparation for his chronic pancreatitis and late-aged diabetes'. Dr Parchure had seen his growing tiredness and drop in energy at Saanen and Brockwood. When he arrived at Rajghat he seemed very weak but caught up on his sleep, ate more and went for walks to fit himself for the small Gathering there of some 300 campers. There was no actual illness but on two occasions his legs were so weak that he had difficulty in climbing a staircase. This disturbed him very much; nevertheless, he refused to be helped, saying, 'If I fall on the steps that is my affair.'

He gave four public talks while he was there and conducted discussions with a group of Buddhist scholars, including Pandit Jagannath Upadhyaya.

Friedrich was very struck by how beautifully the grounds were kept at Rajghat. This was the responsibility of R. Upasani, the Principal of the Agricultural College in the compound, who had worked for K for thirty years and to whom K was devoted. One afternoon Upasani and Friedrich, with Radhika Herzberger and Nandini Mehta, who had joined K at Rajghat, went with him to look at the site near the old British cemetery where a small Centre was to be built, financed by Friedrich.

One of the first tasks K had to perform in India was to choose a new Head for the Rajghat School (or Rector, as he was called) after trouble among the staff and students had resulted in J. Y. Sathaye's resignation, much to K's regret. K's choice fell, by what seems pure chance, on Dr P. Krishna. Dr Krishna was Professor of Physics at the Benares Hindu University; he had worked in the U.S.A. and Europe and had such an impressive record that he could have commanded a professorship anywhere. His father was a brother of Sri Ram, former President of the Theosophical Society, and of Rukmini Arundale. His wife was a gynaecologist working at the Hindu University. He had first met K in Delhi in 1958 with Shiva Rao, an old family friend. Thereafter he had read all K's books, had gone to his talks at Rajghat, had been to Brockwood in 1977 and taken part in a discussion there with David Bohm and Asit Chandmal, but apart from that he had had very little personal contact with K. Now, in November 1985, he had been asked by his cousin, Radha Burnier, to bring his parents, who were staying with him, to meet K at Mrs Besant's old house, Shanti Kunja, in the Theosophical compound at Benares. That evening Dr Krishna was surprised to receive a telephone call inviting him and his wife to lunch at Rajghat next day. They went, and after the meal Dr Krishna was 'overwhelmed' when K asked him to take charge of the Rajghat School. Dr Krishna said that he did not know anything about the place nor what K expected him to do. K replied: 'I will tell you. I want you to come and live here, make this your home for life. You understand, I mean for life. It is yours to build, to do what you like with. It is being offered to you like a jewel on a silver plate. And I am asking you, will you take it?'

A dialogue followed, part of which is given below:

PK: Sir, I am not sure you should trust me so much. You hardly know me.

K: Don't say that. I know you enough and I trust you completely.

PK: But, sir, I am a very ordinary man. I don't know if I can do as you want.

K: Sir, sir, I am also a very ordinary man. Don't say all this. The son does not say all this to his father when he is dying and wants to leave him something. He doesn't say no, he accepts it.

PK: Sir, I am not saying no. I am saying I would like to do it for you, but I am not sure if I can, if I am the right person for it. I am so young and inexperienced. Don't you think you should consult someone like Radha Burnier who knows both me and the Foundation?

K: No, sir, I don't need advice. I don't do things that way. I have never lived that way. I go by what I feel here [points to his heart] and that's it.

PK: Sir, give me time to consider it. Let me see all that there is here, what needs to be done, whether I can do it. I don't want to accept something I cannot do well. I would be letting you down.

K: No, sir, I don't want you to do it that way. Look, sir, when you fell in love with your wife and wanted to marry her, did you say, 'I will consider, I will decide it tomorrow, I will think it over?' No, you didn't. So I want you to tell me 'Yes' from here [pointing to his heart]. Then if it is all right with you we will sort out all the other problems together. I want you to say yes before you go today, but I am not persuading you, sir, if you understand what I mean.

PK: Yes, sir, I understand you are not persuading me and I have told you that I would very much like to do it but I want some time to consider all the implications of it for my family, for myself and above all whether I can make a success of it. I am not looking at it as a job offer and I am not trying to bargain with you but I have never taken decisions in life this way. I have always considered things carefully and planned my life, so I want to have some time to consider all aspects of it and then give you my final acceptance.

K: Wait, sir, let me ask your wife [takes her hand into his and looks at her intensely]. My dear darling, will you do this for me? Will you make this your home?

MK [in tears]: Yes, sir, we will do anything for you. We will come and live here.

K: Right. It's done. That's all, now you can come another time and we will sort out all the details of how to do it and the rest.

PK: Yes, sir. I will come tomorrow and we will discuss the details. You must rest now.

K: No, sir, I am all right. Are you accepting?

PK: Yes, sir I very much want to but I do not feel confident if I am the right person.

K: Sir, don't worry. Come here and it will come to you. You know, sir, all this intelligence up here [points to his head], I must park it some place before I go. I want you to know that I trust you completely.

PK: That's what makes it so difficult, sir, but thank you and I will come again tomorrow and we will work it out together. I want to do it together with you, because if it is good for you it is good for me. I am not looking at my good as separate from yours.

K: Yes, sir, I like that. We will do it together. Together.

The next day, when all the trustees of the Indian Foundation who were at Rajghat had agreed to the appointment, Dr Krishna's hesitation was swept aside. He had to cancel the agreement he had made to spend a year a Birkbeck College, London University, as a visiting professor from September 1986. He then suggested that he should come to Rajghat after the current session at the Hindu University ended in May 1986. 'No,' said K, 'that is too late for me.' 'When would you like me to join?' 'Tomorrow.' Eventually it was decided, after Dr Krishna had spoken to the Vice-Chancellor of his University, that he should take over Rajghat on February 1, 1986. K was concerned that Dr Krishna and his wife and two teen-aged daughters should be happy living at Rajghat and that they should not lose financially by their new life. A house at Rajghat was put at their disposal.[65]

It had been K's habit to write diary letters to Mary Zimbalist from India. This year he dictated his letters to her on to a cassette which he posted weekly. This was an unexpected joy to her.

*   *   *   *

At the end of November K went, with Friedrich among others, to Rishi Valley where, according to Dr Parchure, 'though there was no actual illness [in K], his feebleness showed when he dragged while returning from evening walks and leaned on the right side so much that he might fall.' He was also feeling the cold as he had never done before, probably because he had lost so much weight. True, it did get quite cold at night at Rishi Valley but now K could not get warm however many blankets were piled on him. He was considering cancelling his Bombay talks because his strength was rapidly failing.

In the middle of December, at K's request, teachers gathered at Rishi Valley from all the Krishnamurti schools for a conference. David Moody, now the Director of the Oak Grove School, and his wife, Vivienne, and Michael Krohnen came from Ojai. Six teachers came from Brockwood, including Scott Forbes and Stephen Smith, second in charge there. All the Rishi Valley teachers were there, of course, as well as teachers from Rajghat and the three other Indian schools. K regarded all the schools as one, as he did the Foundations.

When Scott, on his arrival on December 12, saw K, he was struck by his weakness and the amount of weight he had lost. By that time he was already having some fever which persisted in spite of Dr Parchure's efforts to bring down his temperature. His mind, however, seemed very much alive and he was continuing his afternoon walks almost every day. Different people from Ojai and Brockwood were invited to accompany him on these walks on a rota basis so that no one should be left out. His walks were much shorter now and seemed to be taken more as a form of therapy than for pleasure. Radhika Herzberger always accompanied him on these walks, as did Scott as soon as he arrived.

There was a great deal of talk about a small study centre that was to be built at Rishi Valley, financed again by Friedrich Grohe as at Rajghat. There was, in addition, to be a retreat and centre at Uttar Kashi in the Himalayas near Dehradoon, on a piece of land presented to the Foundation, very difficult of access, the last two miles from the nearest village having to be covered on foot and not accessible in winter. (Friedrich was financing this building also.)*

On December 19 a very long discussion took place in K's room between Radhika, Scott, Friedrich, Dr Parchure and one or two others as to the purpose of the study centres. Scott started, at K's request, to outline what the Centre was to be at Brockwood. 'In general,' Scott said, 'we are building a place which is dedicated and designed exclusively for people to study the teachings. And so we have included everything that is necessary for that.' He added that the architect was sending plans to Madras so that they could be shown to all the Indian Trustees. K then turned to Radhika and

* The Uttar Kashi retreat with twelve bedrooms was opened in 1986 when the Rajghat Centre, consisting of two bungalows, was also opened. At the time of writing, the Rishi Valley Centre is in process of being built.

asked for her opinion. She felt that Scott's definition was too narrow; that the Centre should be open to anything sacred, that people should be allowed to come there if they seemed likely to become interested in K's teaching, even if they had no knowledge of it when they arrived. Scott maintained that that was 'too loose', at any rate for Brockwood. The danger would be that people would say, 'This is sacred and that is sacred and the other is sacred.' They might feel that Jesus or the Buddha had said the same things as Krishnamurti so why should they not go and stay at the Brockwood Centre, in that wonderful environment, to study Jesus or the Buddha? The argument went on for a very long time with Radhika and Scott both ably and firmly putting their points of view without influencing the other while K kept a balance between them.[66] It became obvious that the different centres would be run in accordance with the sentiments of those in charge of them and that no definition was possible which would be acceptable to both sides. The meeting ended amicably with them all going off to look at the site, suggested by Radhika, where the Rishi Valley Centre might be built. K had already made clear what he wanted the Brockwood Centre to be but he seemed equally sympathetic to Radhika's view. The year before he had said publicly:

If I went to the Study, first of all I would want to be quiet, not bring my problems there; not my household problems, business preoccupations and so on. And also I think I would want what K says to be entirely part of my life, not just that I have studied K and I repeat what he says. Rather, in the very studying of it I am really absorbing it; not bits of it here and there, not only just what suits me. . . . If I went there to study what K is saying, I would want to investigate it, question it, doubt it: not just read something and then go away. I would be reading not just to memorise; I would be reading to learn to see what he is saying and my reactions to it, whether it corresponds or contradicts, whether he is right or I am right, so that there is a constant communication and interchange between what I am reading and what I am feeling. I would want to establish a relationship between what I am reading, seeing, hearing and myself with my reactions, conditioning, and so on; a dialogue between him and me. Such a dialogue must inevitably bring about a fundamental change.

Let us say that a man like you comes to this new Study. You take all the trouble to come to this place, and for the first few days you may want to be quiet. If you are sensitive you realise there is something here which is different from your home, totally different from going to a discussion somewhere. Then you begin to study, and not only you but all the people living here are studying, seeing, questioning. And everyone actually listening with their whole being will naturally bring about a religious atmosphere.

That is what I would want if I went there. I would be sensitive enough to quickly capture what K is saying. And at lunch, or walking or sitting around together in the sitting-room, I might like to discuss. I might say, 'Look, I didn't understand what he meant by that, let's talk about it'—not, you tell me about it, or I know better—'let's go into it'; so it will be a living thing. And in the afternoon I might go out for a walk, or do some other physical activity.

The Study will be a place for all serious people who have left behind them their nationality, their sectarian beliefs and all the other things that divide human beings.[67]

K was not expected to take part in the teachers' conference because by then it was generally recognised that he was ill and should conserve his strength for the Madras talks. He did take part, however. According to Stephen Smith, 'Krishnaji seemed to be looking to us (to Scott in particular) to give some kind of lead to the Conference and not let it centre merely around curriculum and the day to day functioning of a school. He spoke three times at the Conference. On the first occasion he came in as an "observer", and really, as was his wont, set the whole thing on a different footing. The third talk was particularly eloquent and intimate. He spoke of and radiated greatness.'[68] Scott wrote:

> The people at Rishi Valley were very conscious of his frailty, and all the students and staff were very gentle and cautious with him. There was a sense of foreboding in the air. People were not openly speaking about it— at least not to me—but there were lots of broad hints that they did not expect Krishnaji ever to come back to Rishi Valley. Krishnaji must have been preparing the people for this because gradually it became accepted that he would probably not come back to India.
>
> Radhika was playing hostess to everyone, running this conference and trying to take care of Krishnaji as well as meeting her continuing responsibilities in the school. I remember several times thinking to myself that she did this very well and was handling a very, very difficult situation as well as it could be done.[69]

At Rishi Valley, a Hoopoe bird, rather like a woodpecker, with a short tail, very long beak and high crest, would sit on the windowsill of K's bedroom, pecking at the glass, wanting to get in. Once, when it had managed to get in, K had said to it, 'I don't mind sharing a room with you but when I leave, the room will be closed and you won't like being shut up in it.' K never fed it and it seemed to have no reason for wanting to get in, yet it was nearly always there, pecking at the glass. K said they were friends; he talked to it and it liked the sound of his voice. (It tried to get in three times during the discussion about the Centre. One can hear it on the cassette.)

K now had all his meals in bed instead of eating as he had always done before in the dining-room of the old guest house where his room was situated. The devoted Parameswaran did his utmost to tempt his appetite, though K himself was most anxious not to have any food that the rest of the school was not having.

Before K left Rishi Valley for Madras on December 22 he had cancelled the Bombay talks and had asked Scott to go with him to Ojai instead of returning to England with the other Brockwood teachers. K had also asked Scott to change his and Dr Parchure's tickets and get one for himself in order to fly across the Pacific to Los Angeles without stopping anywhere en route. He could not face the cold of Europe in January. He wanted to leave as soon as the Madras talks, and the Trustees' meetings which were to follow them, were over.

Radhika knew he would not be returning to Rishi Valley and probably everyone else there at least suspected it. She wrote, 'Even though I was to say good-bye to Krishnaji three more times, I found this parting was the most painful. The thought that he would never again set eyes on those ancient hills continues to be difficult to bear.'[70]

*   *   *   *

Dr Parchure, alarmed by K's loss of weight at Rishi Valley, arranged for him to have a check-up, as soon as he got to Madras, by a distinguished doctor, Thiru Venkadam. The doctor wanted to make further investigations, for he suspected some malignancy, but K refused to have any tests done which would disturb him during the period of the talks.

It had been arranged for K to give two talks on December 28 and 29, to hold Question and Answer meetings on the 31st and January

2 and to give the last two talks on the 4th and 5th, after which there were to be several days of Trustees' meetings. Dr Thiru Venkadam advised, though, that K should have at least two days' rest between talks. K did not like to disappoint people by changing his schedule so it was decided that he should give the first talk and then see how he felt. If he needed to make a change it could be announced at the meeting.

Scott found there were only three flights a week considered direct to Los Angeles, with a change of planes at Singapore and a stop at Tokyo. K chose to leave on January 17 and refused to stop over on the way, so Scott procured three first-class tickets for that day. Fortunately he had an American Express card. Some members of the Indian Foundation felt that this was the most tiring route to take; they wanted him to give at least one talk in Bombay and leave from there. But K was adamant. He could not get warm even in Madras; he was running a temperature and wanted to get to Ojai as soon as possible. He must have known better than anyone how limited his strength was.

Before the talks at Vasanta Vihar started, people would come and see K in his bedroom in the mornings, and Nandini Mehta would have lunch with him there and sometimes supper. After lunch he would have a short rest; then more people would come to see him until his walk in the late afternoon. Nandini and Scott would drive with him through the Theosophical compound to Radha Burnier's house on the beach, almost opposite the place where it was said that K had been 'discovered'. Tired as he was, K would sometimes go into Radha's house for a few moments to put his hands on the eyes of Radha's niece who was in danger of losing her sight. (I understand it has now stabilised. Two years before, he had treated Radha's brother, who had already lost the sight of one eye, for threatened blindness as the result of a detached retina in the other eye. His sight was saved after K had put his hands on him every evening for a month.)[71]

K's talks coincided with the annual Theosophical Convention, so there were thousands of Theosophists in the T.S. compound waiting to greet him as he drove through. Usually, after leaving Radha's house, he would walk south along the beach as far as the fishermen's village, then turn and walk north to the Adyar river and to the end of the unfinished footbridge that jutted out a short way across the river. Then he would turn again and walk back to Radha's house where the car awaited him. Radha, with others, would always accompany him on these walks. K would now hold on to Scott's shoulder when they walked along the bridge which had no parapet. He said that if he fell he was afraid he would hurt his watch! (He had a watch pocket in his *bundi*, a waistcoat worn over his *kurta*, a long shirt.)

Before the first talk K asked Scott to bring forward the day of their departure to an earlier flight; he intended to cancel some of the Trustees' meetings. The first direct flight before the 17th was the 12th. K decided to leave on that day.

*   *   *   *

Mark Edwards had arrived in Madras on December 22 to photograph the talks. He had been in India for over a month, taking pictures for the United Nations of some of the poorest parts of Bombay and Delhi, and he was feeling mentally drained. The next afternoon he went from his hotel to Vasanta Vihar in a bicycle rickshaw. He found Pupul and Sunanda just starting out in a car for Radha Burnier's house to fetch K after his walk and they took him with them. He went out on to the beach and turned right to meet K and his friends who were just returning from the fishermen's village. Mark was reassured when he saw the tracks of K's footsteps in the sand (unmistakable from their narrowness even though he was wearing sports shoes) and noticed that he was walking with his usual long strides. It was all the more of a shock, therefore, to find how thin and frail he had become since he had photographed him at Brockwood in October when, according to Mark, he had 'radiated good health and had seemed always on the point of laughter'. Nevertheless, when K greeted him, taking his hand in both of his, 'all the strain of the previous month emptied out of' Mark: 'That healing touch he had for others was not affected.' K asked Sunanda to invite Mark to have his meals at Vasanta Vihar.[72]

K now weighed only 97 lb. and continued to have fever all through the talks which were held in the evenings in the large garden of Vasanta Vihar. People closely surrounded on all sides the dais on which he sat cross-legged. At the Saanen and Brockwood Gatherings he had been able to slip out of the tent through an opening behind the platform.

At 4 p.m., before the first talk on December 28 which was to start at 5.30, K complained to Dr Parchure that he was feeling very low. It was found that he had a temperature of over 100°. This was no doubt the reason why the first talk was a poor one. He sounded rather truculent with his audience. When he tried to leave the dais at the end of the talk the crowds pressed around him so closely, trying to touch him or his clothes to receive his blessing, that he had great difficulty in making his way back to the house although Narayan, Parameswaran, Scott and Mark endeavoured to clear a way for him. While he was being mobbed, he kept saying, 'I don't want all this', giving the impression to Mark that not only did he not want the crowd pressing on him but he did not want people holding back the crowd either.

As soon as he regained the house, Dr Parchure persuaded him not to talk next day. An announcement was made, therefore, before the crowd dispersed, that he would be giving only two more talks, on January 1 and 4.

During the night before the second talk K got out of bed, fell and dashed his head against the wall, hurting himself quite badly. After this fall, Parameswaran slept outside K's screen door so that he would be able to hear K if he moved. K refused to have a bell rigged up with which to summon Parameswaran from where he normally slept because it would, he said, be treating his old friend like a servant.

Stephen Smith who, with the other Brockwood teachers, had come to Madras for the talks, has written:

It was obvious the talks were taking their toll of his health, physically. (He had to run the gauntlet of the crowd both to get to the platform and get back to his room.) His voice was sometimes strident; he looked mortal like the rest of us. (Among groups of intimates he remained peerless, unimpaired.) The last time I saw him was the day we left Madras. All the Brockwood people—apart from Scott—were leaving. We went up to his room; he was sitting upright on his bed. He asked Alan Rowlandson [the piano teacher] about the concerts he was giving. The sparkle was in his eyes and he seemed relaxed. Throughout the Madras period I had a strong sense of the presence of death. It was in the air as a tangible presence but unrelated—as far as I could tell—to anyone in particular. Obviously, with hindsight, it had come from Krishnaji.

Mark too felt very strongly, and quite independently of Stephen, the presence of death at Vasanta Vihar, but he felt it in connection with K.

At some time between the first and last talks, K asked Scott to move his departure forward again to the 10th. This was the earliest he could leave if he was to talk to the Indian Trustees at all. ('He was almost rushing back to Ojai to hand over himself to Dr Deutsch's care,' Dr Parchure recorded.) It was generally understood by then that he intended never to return to India, for he was giving away all his Indian clothes, yet none of those around him seems to have suspected that his death was so close. When Mark left after the talks K said in good-bye, 'See you in London.' But when Scott begged him to conserve his energy so that he would be there when the Brockwood Centre opened he said, 'Old boy . . .' and shook his head as though it was most uncertain. (K would sometimes use old-fashioned English expressions like this; the most frequent was 'By Jove'.)

It seems probable that K expected to recover sufficiently at Ojai to talk at the Oak Grove Gathering, at the first International Gathering at Brockwood, to lay the foundation stone of the Centre and then to return to Ojai, perhaps to die. There is little doubt in my mind that he intended to die when the time came in his bed at Pine Cottage.

      *   *   *   *

At the end of the second talk K spoke about death:

We are trying to find out what it means to die, while living—not committing suicide; I am not talking that kind of nonsense. I want to find out for myself what it means to die, which means, can I be totally free from everything that man has created, including myself?

What does it mean to die? To give up everything. Death cuts you off with a very, very, very sharp razor from your attachments, from your gods, from your superstitions, from your desire for comfort—next life and so on. I'm going to find out what death means because it's as important as living. So how can I find out, actually, not theoretically, what it means to die? I actually want to find out, as you want to find out. I am speaking for you, so don't go to sleep. What does it mean to die? Put that question to yourself. While we are young, or when we are very old, this question is always there. It means to be totally free, to be totally unattached to everything that man has put together, or what you have put together—totally free. No attachments, no gods, no future, no past. You don't see the beauty of it, the greatness of it, the extraordinary strength of it—while living to be dying. You understand what that means? While you are living, every moment you are dying, so that throughout life you are not attached to *anything*. That is what death means.

So living is dying. You understand? Living means that every day you are abandoning everything that you are attached to. Can you do this? A very simple fact, but it has got tremendous implications. So that each day is a new day. Each day you are dying and incarnating. There is a tremendous vitality, energy there because there is nothing that you are afraid of. There is nothing that can hurt. Being hurt doesn't exist.

All the things that man has put together have to be totally abandoned. That's what it means to die. So can you do it? Will you try it? Will you experiment with it? Not for just a day; every day. No, sir, you can't do it; your brains are not trained for this. Your brains have been conditioned so heavily, by your education, by your tradition, by your books, by your professors. It requires finding out what love is. Love and death go together. Death says be free, non-attached, you can carry nothing with you. And love says, love says—there is no word for it. Love can exist only when there is freedom, not from your wife, from a new girl, or a new husband, but the feeling, the enormous strength, the vitality, the energy of complete freedom.[73]

In the last talk on January 4, the last talk K ever gave, he covered many of the subjects he had gone into so often before—the origin of life, religion, computer technology and genetic engineering, the difference between the mind and the brain, creativity, meditation, knowledge, thought, conditioning, and back to the origin of life. He asked at the end:

Is there a brain, your brain, which is not muddied up, muddied by environment, by tradition, by society and all the rest of it? So what is the origin of life? Are you waiting for me to answer? This is much too serious a subject for you to play with, because we are trying to enquire into something that has no name, no end. I can kill that bird; there is another bird. I can't kill all birds; there are too many of them in the world. So, we are enquiring into what makes a bird. What is creation behind all this? Are you waiting for me to describe it, go into it? You want me to go into it? Why?

[*From the audience*]: To understand what creation is.

K: Why do you ask that? Because I asked? No description can ever describe the origin. The origin is nameless; the origin is absolutely quiet; it's not whirring about making noise. Creation is something that is most holy. That's the most sacred thing in life and if you have made a mess of your life, change it. Change it today, not tomorrow. If you are uncertain find out why and be *certain*. If your thinking is not straight, think straight, logically. Unless all that is prepared, all that is settled, you can't enter into this world, into the world of creation.

It ends. [These two words are hardly audible, breathed rather than spoken. They can just be heard on the cassette. They could not have been heard by his audience.][74]

Then, after a long pause, he added: 'This is the last talk. Do you want to sit together quietly for a while? All right, sirs, sit quietly for a while.'

*   *   *   *

The Indian Government had given an Arts grant for G. Aravindan, a well-known producer, to make a film about K, *The Seer Who Walks Alone*. The end of this film had been shot at Rajghat during K's last visit. (This was no doubt the documentary that Anita Desai had seen (p. 54). Friedrich Grohe has written about the film: 'K crossed the river and walked up the path that the Buddha had walked to Sarnath, the place of his Enlightenment. K said to the producer, "I'll do everything you want me to." Once, at sunset, on a hill above the Varanasi river, K stood against the setting sun, like one of the ancient sculptures.' On January 4, everyone at Vasanta Vihar, except K, went to the premier of this film which had been completed in a remarkably short time. The photography, according to Scott, was 'absolutely stunning'.

The Trustees' meetings that followed the talks were not happy ones. K had certain things to say, some changes to make which he had been dreading for months. One result was the appointment of a new secretary for the Foundation—Mahesh Saxena, a comparative newcomer among K's associates. Mahesh had had an interesting career. He had resigned from his job as head of the central police in Delhi, put on a sannyasi's robe and lived in the Himalayas for several years. He then started wandering until he came to Rajghat and found in Krishnamurti what he had been seeking.

The question of publications was evidently gone into at one meeting because Scott telephoned to us in London to ask whether cheap, paperback editions of K's books could be made available in India. India already had the paperback rights in several of K's books which they had not yet published. The paperback rights in other books had already been sold, but we were able to tell Scott that there was no reason why India should not be given the Indian rights in all future books. This telephone call from Scott left us as much in the dark as ever as to what decision K had come to over publications.

Also during the meetings K 'had insisted that the houses where he had lived should not become places of pilgrimage, that no cult should grow around him'.[75] And he asked for the following memorandum to be inserted in the rules and regulations of the Foundation:

Under no circumstances will the Foundation or any of the institutions under its auspices, or any of its members set themselves up as authorities on Krishnamurti's teachings. This is in accordance with Krishnamurti's declaration that no one anywhere should set himself up as an authority on him or his teachings.[76]

The flight to Los Angeles on January 10 was scheduled for midnight. This last day, people were continually coming to say good-bye. K went for his usual walk on the beach that evening, having previously driven through the grounds of the Madras School to say good-bye. He went to bed at an early hour, the plan being that he should be woken in time to be taken by car to the steps of the aircraft as had been arranged for him. Scott and Dr Parchure went ahead to check in the luggage and go through the controls. Asit, who would be going with them as far as Singapore where he had an apartment, would go later with K. When Scott got to the airport, almost an hour's drive away, he found that the plane was to be two hours late. This would still leave forty-five minutes to change planes in Singapore. Not wanting to remain at the airport, he and Dr Parchure, having checked in the luggage, returned to Vasanta Vihar to find that those in charge there, having heard that the plane was to be late, thought it wiser for K to postpone his journey until the 12th in order not to risk missing his connection and having to wait two days in Singapore; therefore they had not disturbed his sleep. Scott felt that K should be woken so as to make his own decision. This was done and after being informed of the situation he decided to go.

'I am still the Teacher'

K had been driving himself so hard in Madras that once relaxed on the aircraft all his exhaustion was released. In Singapore, where they had just enough time to change planes after a four-hour flight, K complained of acute stomach ache. He was given pills and the pain gradually subsided so that he was able to sleep on and off during the six-hour flight to Tokyo, but he had great difficulty in keeping warm because of the air-conditioning.

At Tokyo, where he wanted to stretch his legs, he needed Scott's help in walking. As they were going out of the departure lounge to continue the flight, a middle-aged Japanese gentleman came up and asked, 'Are you Mr Krishnamurti?' This turned out to be Mr S. Takahashi who had given us much good advice on the translation of K's books into Japanese. Having heard from a friend in Madras that K would be on this flight, he had taken a return ticket to Los Angeles simply in order to travel with him. He sensitively realised at once that K was too ill to talk to anyone. He felt, though, that merely sitting with him in the same aircraft had been fully worth the journey. From the Los Angeles airport he flew straight back to Tokyo.

They arrived at Los Angeles at 9.30 a.m. after a twenty-four-hour journey. Mary Zimbalist was there to meet them and drove K back to Ojai, leaving the others to deal with the luggage. As soon as they were alone K told her that for the next two or three days she must not leave him or he might 'slip away'. He said, '*It* doesn't want to inhabit a sick body, one that couldn't function. We must not have an accident, because if I were hurt that would be the end.'

When he arrived at Pine Cottage all his friends were there to greet him. He seemed delighted to be back in his own room. That evening he had a temperature of 101° and was very drowsy from jet lag.

Mary slept that night on a mattress on the floor of his room. Scott slept all the time he was there on the sofa in the living-room while Dr Parchure slept at Arya Vihara but spent his waking hours at Pine Cottage. It was Mary, though, who looked after K at night.

I have three independent accounts of K's last illness—Mary Zimbalist's daily diary notes, Dr Parchure's daily report, couched for the most part in medical terms, and Scott's recollections written after K's death. In essentials all three accounts tally exactly. A combination of the three will be given here, using layman's language and omitting the brand names of the particular medications K received.

Mary had made an appointment for K to see Dr Deutsch at 10 a.m. on the 13th; she and Dr Parchure accompanied him to the doctor's office at Santa Paula, and went afterwards to the Santa Paula Community Hospital for a full range of blood tests. The results showed an inflammation of the liver and a very high blood-sugar count. K was given an antibiotic, a sleeping pill, and his dose of anti-diabetes medicine was doubled. Dr Deutsch wanted a sonogram done of the liver, gall bladder and pancreas. This was arranged for the 20th at the Ojai Hospital.

K was now finding it very difficult to eat. All food seemed to him too rich, however carefully it was prepared. Mary gave him breakfast and supper while his main meal was cooked in the kitchen at Arya Vihara where the Moodys lived. Michael Krohnen, who had cooked devotedly for him for a long time at Ojai, used all his art to tempt his appetite just as Parameswaran had done in India.

On the 19th, K felt stronger and wanted to go out for the first time since his arrival. He walked slowly down the length of the drive, about a quarter of a mile, with Mary and Scott on either side of him in case he needed support. The drive sloped downwards, so unfortunately it was up hill all the way back. When he reached the pepper tree outside Pine Cottage he sat down to rest for five minutes on the low stone wall that surrounded it before continuing the short distance to the house.

The sonogram next day showed 'a mass' on the liver, and Dr Miller of the Ojai Hospital asked for a CAT scan to be done on the 22nd. K's weight had dropped to 94 lb.

On the 21st he went for what was to be his last walk. It was a longer one than two days before, down the drive, round by Arya

Vihára, and back through the orange grove to the pepper tree where he again sat and rested before returning to the cottage.

At 1 a.m. on the 22nd he began to have bad pain which could not be relieved. Three hours later it had become almost unbearable. K had suffered some agonising pain in his life and he never complained until it was really intolerable. At 8.45 he started to vomit. Mary called Dr Deutsch who said that he needed the facilities of a hospital to be able to deal with the case. Years ago, K had told Mary never to put him in hospital; he would rather die at home. When he had gone into hospital for his two operations it was he who had taken the decision. When Mary told him now, in the presence of Dr Parchure, the Lilliefelts and Scott, what Dr Deutsch had said, he looked at them for a few moments and then said, 'All right.' The CAT scan for that afternoon was cancelled and K, in his dressing-gown and wrapped in blankets, was driven the sixteen miles to Santa Paula Community Hospital where he was admitted to a private room in the intensive care unit.

Dr Deutsch met them there. An immediate X-ray showed an obstruction of the bowel. K agreed to have a tube passed through his nose to pump out the fluid and relieve the pressure, and hyper-alimentation was given intravenously when he was found to be seriously undernourished. He said to Scott when all these unpleasant things had been done to him, 'I must accept. I have accepted so much.' But what he accepted gratefully were the injections of morphine which were given after the pain-killers had failed to act.

Dr Deutsch asked for a reclining chair to be put in K's room, and, during the eight nights he remained in the hospital, Mary, Dr Parchure and Scott took it in turns to stay with him at night while the Lilliefelts spent every day there.

On the 23rd K was examined by a surgeon and an oncologist (a specialist in tumours). After the examination K, according to Scott, 'began to tell Dr Deutsch [who had been to some of the Ojai talks] something of what he was. He seemed to need to do this in order to help the doctor know how to take care of him, i.e., that it was not an ordinary body, that something extraordinary used the body, that the body was extraordinarily sensitive, that somehow, regardless of how experienced the doctor was, he had no experience of dealing with what he was now going to deal with.' K then gave the doctor 'the most wonderful brief sketch of his life'. He also talked to him about 'Patek Philippe watches, Huntsman suits and Jacquet ties'.

This was a critical day, Dr Parchure noted in his report, because of the danger of K's falling into a coma from hepatitis. Injections of morphine were given to him every two hours as well as other medication. At 5 p.m. Dr Parchure 'explained to him the nature of the crisis'. In fact Dr Parchure had told him that he probably had cancer for which there was no treatment. This upset Mary and Scott who felt that the diagnosis was not yet definite. They understood, however, when Dr Parchure explained to them that a long time ago he had promised K to tell him immediately if he ever saw any danger of death and, because of the fear of a coma, he felt it right to fulfil his promise.

When Mary and Scott next went into K's room, K said, 'It seems I am going to die,' as if he had not expected it so soon but accepted the fact. Later he said, 'I wonder why "the other" doesn't let the body go.' He was to wonder this often in the succeeding three weeks. On another occasion he said to Mary, 'I'm watching it. It's most curious.' And at another time, he remarked, '"The other" and death are having a struggle.' Once after he knew definitely that he had cancer he said to Mary in a faraway voice, 'What have I done wrong?', as if he had somehow failed to look after the body as he should have done.

The 23rd was the day on which Mary telephoned to Vanda Scaravelli in Florence and to me in London to warn us of how ill K was. A final diagnosis would not be made, she said, until he had had a CAT scan on the 27th. Erna Lilliefelt was keeping Pupul Jayakar in Delhi fully informed, and Erna and Scott were in constant touch with Mary Cadogan in London.

On the 24th there was an improvement. The bowel obstruction was dispersing and the signs of jaundice were receding. The surgeon changed the intravenous connection from a vein in K's hand to a larger tube inserted under the collarbone so that more fluid could go through. This released both his hands which was a relief to him. Dr Deutsch asked him if he would accept a transfusion of a pint of blood to give him strength. He said he would if the donor was a vegetarian who did not drink alcohol. Any of his friends at Ojai would, of course, have been happy to give their blood but it was not whole blood that was needed, only some part of it which would take too long to process from fresh blood. K therefore accepted what he was given. That evening he asked Mary and Scott not to leave him until the end because he wanted the body looked after as he had looked after it himself. There was nothing at all sentimental or pathetic in the way he put this request.

The next day the nose tube was removed which made him feel 'like a new man'. This day he asked that three people should be requested to come to Ojai as soon as possible. These were all Indians—Radhika Herzberger, Dr Krishna and Mahesh Saxena, and 'possibly Upasani'. K wanted to see his old friend Upasani because he had not had a chance to say good-bye to him in India. He wanted to see the other three because they were the young ones whom he trusted to carry on his work in India in a non-authoritarian spirit. These were the only people he did ask to see. In the event, Upasani could not go because it took so long to get a passport.

K also asked Scott that day to make a recording of what should be done with his ashes. He wanted them divided into three—one part to stay in Ojai, the other parts to go to India and Brockwood. He did not want any ceremonies and 'all that nonense', and the ground where his ashes were buried 'shouldn't become a holy place where people came and worshipped and all that rot'.[77]

After spending the night of the 25th in K's room, Mary wrote in her diary:

K had many awakenings in the night but spoke of meditation having been present. I barely doze and become immediately alert if he makes the smallest movement. It is as if there is some invisible connection to him. For hours I watch the pattern of his heartbeat on the monitor. Life becomes the beat, the rise and fall of his breathing. He is alive and so all the ugliness, the violence, the wretchedness of the world is held at bay by that small body and vastness of spirit. He is, as always, infinitely beautiful. He turned his head this morning to look out of the window where he can just see the hills, and his face seemed suddenly 30 years old.

On the 27th K had a CAT scan in a large van that went round the local hospitals. He was wheeled out on a stretcher and a fork-lift raised him into the van. Dr Parchure sat with the doctor while the scan was being done. K was intensely interested in the machinery of the proceedings as he always was in anything mechanical. The scan confirmed that there was a three-inch mass in the liver with calcification in the pancreas, suggesting that the latter was the primary seat of the malignancy. When these findings were conveyed to K by Dr Deutsch, K asked to be allowed to return to Pine Cottage; he did not want to die in hospital. But he was put through one more ordeal the next day—a liver biopsy which was so painful, in spite of a local anaesthetic, that it set him back for twenty-four hours without achieving its object of reaching the growth. That day Mary telephoned to Vanda and to me again.

On the 29th the result came through of a new and highly specialised blood test. As Dr Parchure reported: 'This almost clinched the diagnosis of malignancy of the head of the pancreas with secondaries in the liver.' That day K had to have morphine again. He asked Dr Deutsch if he could last until the three Indians arrived. The doctor wanted to know what his wishes were. K replied that he wanted to be clear in his mind until the end but that he did not want to suffer great pain; 'the other' could not get through when there was too much pain.

The next morning, free from pain, and having gained weight as a result of the hyper-alimentation, K returned to Pine Cottage. A hospital bed, lent by Mark Lee, had been put in his room and arrangements made for round-the-clock nurses. He was still almost entirely relying on nourishment from the intravenous drip, but at the relief of getting home he asked for something to eat—a tomato sandwich and some ice cream. It was not a success; after a mouthful or two he was sick. His spirits, though, were still high and he asked Mary to put on a record of Pavarotti singing Neapolitan songs. But in the evening the pain returned and he was given morphine again.

*   *   *   *

The moment I heard from Mary on the 24th how ill K was, I longed to fly to Ojai, yet I hesitated because I knew that if I went it would be for my own sake, not for his. He had not asked for me. Mary Cadogan went at once but then she had been invited by Erna Lilliefelt with whom she stayed. She arrived on the 26th and was taken next morning to see K in hospital. He looked weak but appeared cheerful and pleased to see her. He enquired courteously about the details of her journey. It was after Mary Cadogan arrived that he asked someone to find out from Pandit Upadhyaya in India what the Indian tradition was with regard to the treatment after death of a holy man, not, he said, that he intended to follow the tradition.[78]

If I went to Ojai, Joe would go with me, so we applied for visas. After Mary Zimbalist's second call on the 28th I found it impossible not to go. We left on the 30th, the day K returned to Pine Cottage, and were delighted to find Dorothy Simmons and Jane Hammond on the same flight. We arrived next day on a pouring wet afternoon (Californian time is eight hours behind English time) to be met at the Los Angeles airport by Evelyne Blau. The traffic congestion on a wet Friday afternoon was appalling and the eighty-mile drive to Ojai seemed longer than the twelve-hour flight. Evelyne was charming but one realised what an ordeal it must be for those at Ojai to have to do that journey to and from the airport to meet people coming to see K on his deathbed. Thank goodness we four had arrived together. Dorothy was staying with Alan Hooker and his wife Helen, and Jane with Evelyne. We were to stay in the guest flat next to Pine Cottage where we would have stayed if our happy April plan had materialised. The flat was over the Krishnamurti office, approached by an outside flight of stone steps.

We had hardly entered the flat when Mary Zimbalist appeared. We hugged silently and she then asked me to come and see K at once. I had not expected to be able to see him that day and could not possibly go to him without at least washing my hands and cleaning my teeth after that long journey. Mary went back to the house and I followed in five minutes.

K was lying flat on his back in the hospital bed, his hair spread out wildly on the pillow. He said in a weak voice, ' This is not my usual style,' and he indicated the bed and the drip-bottle on the stand above him. I felt strongly at that moment how right my first instinct had been not to come, what an imposition it was on him. I felt sure he did not want to be seen like that. I stayed only a few minutes but they were minutes in which he had to make the effort to ask after our journey and how Joe was and to hope we would be comfortable in the flat.

Because it was still pouring, Evelyne came to fetch us that first evening for dinner at Arya Vihara where long tables had been placed end to end to accommodate all the guests. We were introduced to Michael Krohnen whom we were fortunate to have to cook for us (he also did some teaching at the Oak Grove School), and to his young Finnish assistant. David and Vivienne Moody I had already met at Brockwood as well as the Hookers, and the Lilliefelts I knew well. (Erna, in addition to all her other work, and seeing K daily, took responsibility for the visitors.) I met Mark Lee and his Indian wife Asha, and K's niece Indira (Narayan's sister), who was there with her husband from the school in Connecticut where they both worked. Friedrich Grohe and his new wife Magda, whom he had first met at Ojai and had married the year before, were also there; he now had a house at Ojai. Dr Krishna, a tall, handsome man, looking more like a soldier than a professor, had arrived before us as had also R. Morali, a trustee of the Indian Foundation. Pupul Jayakar, with Radhika Herzberger and Asit Chandmal, was expected later that evening. They came in a chauffeur-driven car. Mahesh Saxena was waiting for a visa and did not arrive until February 5. The Indians stayed at Arya Vihara. Radhika has recorded that when she saw K next morning one of the first questions he asked her was, 'Has it rained in Rishi Valley?' He was happy when she told him that it had rained nearly three inches at the time he left Madras.[79]

The next morning, February 1, the rain had stopped. Some kind person, I never discovered who, had stocked our kitchenette-cupboard with everything conceivable one could want for breakfast. Directly after breakfast I went across to Pine Cottage, past the black granite *nandis* I had heard about and some flower beds, and through the Pompeian-red front door into the new house. I noticed in time that shoes were left outside which I had not noticed the evening before. The house was on one floor—a large living-room with a high, raftered ceiling and a great fireplace for burning logs, a dining-room, a small office for Mary, and a beautifully fitted, spacious kitchen with laundry room beyond. To the right of the entrance a short passage connected the house with the old cottage* where two bedrooms, two bathrooms and a small sitting-room for K were situated. The floors throughout the new house were underfloor-heated and laid with white, flower-patterned tiles. All the fittings, furniture, curtains and covers showed Mary's (to my mind) perfect taste.

I felt worried about Mary who was evidently suffering from

---

* The cottage was painted white. When my mother and I had stayed at Ojai with K for four months in 1926–7 it was of dark pinewood.

strain and lack of sleep. (She did not sleep more than two hours a night the whole time K was ill.) It was easy to see that her entire being was concentrated exclusively on caring for him; she was not really aware of anyone else. Scott also looked strained. K was shy of the nurses and wanted either Scott, Mary or Dr Parchure to help him with intimate functions. Mary continued to be the one who ministered to him at night. Since he refused to have the discomfort of a catheter he was disturbed very frequently in the night and sometimes in the daytime too. Because of this he asked Scott to stay in the room when he saw people for more than a few minutes. He would catch Scott's eye and Scott would ask whoever was with him to go out for a little while. This was hard on Scott, for it tended to make him unpopular with those who did not understand the reason for his being in the room when they wanted to be left alone with K.

I talked with Mary and Scott in the kitchen for a while that morning and then went in to see K. He was propped up a little and his hair had been neatly combed so that he looked more himself. He was weak and sleepy, though. Later he saw Joe for a moment and, of course, he saw all the Indians who were there. When Dr Deutsch came that afternoon he was fully awake and free from pain. The doctor spoke to the Indians afterwards and answered questions from Asit. All agreed that K should be given what he wanted to relieve the pain and enable him to sleep.

That night he slept without morphine or sleeping pills and, according to Dr Parchure, looked alert and fresh next morning. He talked to Mary about being strong after he was gone; she must live in the way she had lived with him. He told Dr Deutsch, when he came that afternoon, that he had woken up in meditation and that the pain, jaundice, morphine and other drugs had left no effect on his brain. In the course of the day he saw everyone from India and England.

Six years before, K had tried to describe what this night meditation was like:

For a long time he [K was referring to himself] has been awakening in the middle of the night with the peculiar meditation which has been pursuing him for very many years. This has been a normal thing in his life. It is not a conscious, deliberate pursuit of meditation or an unconscious desire to achieve something. It is very clearly uninvited and unsought. He has been adroitly watchful of thought [not] making a memory of these meditations. And so each meditation has a quality of something new and fresh in it.[80]

I had now discovered by chance that Radhika Herzberger and Dr Krishna had been made the two Indian members of the International Publications Committee in place of Sunanda Patwardhan and Asit. I asked them, therefore, whether they would come and have a talk that afternoon with me, Mary Cadogan and Jane Hammond in our flat. We liked them both enormously and had a very friendly conversation. It transpired that they had only been appointed by the Indian Foundation on January 13, after K had left India, and that they knew next to nothing of our publishing difficulties with India. As far as I remember, most of the meeting was taken up with filling in the background for them. We English did not yet know what K's decision over publications was. They did know, it turned out, but they did not tell us. No doubt they thought we knew already. We also discovered to our disappointment that they were no more empowered to make decisions on their own than their predecessors had been.

The next morning, February 3, K called together into his room all those concerned with publications. He had not slept well but had had no pain or sickness and had spoken to Mary of having had a 'marvellous meditation'. Dr Parchure confirmed this and added that he was 'fresh and strong'. The meeting was tape-recorded. Those present were Mary Zimbalist, Radhika, Dr Krishna, Mary Cadogan, Jane Hammond, Scott and I. Scott had nothing to do with publications; he was there because he had to stand by the bed holding the tape-recorder. (In the middle of the meeting he had to turn us all out of the room for a little while.)

K began by saying that since England and India had been quarrelling over publications for thirteen years he had decided to 'take charge of it'. 'You have nothing more to do with it,' he said. In future he wanted India to be concerned only with translating his books into the many vernacular languages. All his talks and discussions in India were in future to go to England to be edited. The Indian Foundation would be given the paperback rights of our edited manuscripts for distribution in India.

It was with dismay that I heard this. K was taking away from the Indian Foundation the right it had been given in perpetuity to edit and publish for the Indian market all K's talks and discussions in India without any reference to England. Besides, it would put an extra burden on our small team of editors. K's wishes were paramount, however, and we said we would carry them out although it would involve much more work.

K asked Dr Krishna whether he agreed to this decision. Dr Krishna replied that, although he would personally agree and could put K's wishes to the Indian Foundation, he did not represent the Foundation so he could not say whether the Foundation would agree. He said that 'Pupulji' was 'not agreeable' to what K wanted; she was his President and he could not overrule her. (It appeared from this that the matter had already been thoroughly discussed by the Indian Foundation.) And again, when K repeated what his wishes were, Dr Krishna said, 'If Pupulji agrees to this, sir, there is no problem,' to which K replied, 'I don't see why should she agree, or why you all say "yes" to what she agrees.'

This to-ing and fro-ing went on for some time, Mary Zimbalist insisting that K's wishes superseded every other argument, K asking for agreement and Dr Krishna explaining that he had no authority to agree to anything. I asked K at one point whether this decision was really his own since it might be said afterwards that he had been influenced when he was ill. 'I understand,' he said. 'Just listen: you're not enforcing this on me, you're not trying to convince me, you're not saying, be on this side and not on that side. You have nothing to do with it. Right?'

K said towards the end of the meeting that the Indian Foundation felt they were separate—they felt they understood him better than others because he had been born in India. 'You see, Dr Krishna,' he said, 'I am not an Indian.' 'Nor are we Indians,' Radhika interposed; 'in that sense I don't think I am an Indian either.' 'Nor am I English,' Mary Cadogan put in.

Radhika told K that we had had a very good meeting the day before, and I twice assured him that we had established a very good relationship with Radhika and Dr Krishna. In the end we reached a compromise, which was that anyone in any part of the world who knew English really well might do the editing for the Indian editions.* (I did not want to point out at this stage that there was more to editing K than just speaking or writing good English.)

K seemed very relieved that the discussion was over. 'May I say

---

* G. Mohan, the man who had edited so well the book *Mind Without Measure* for the Indian market (see p. 73), is now helping the Indian Foundation again with the editing.

something?' he asked. 'You have finished the discussion—right? This is over?' He went on:

My brain is very clear. I had a very good—I won't go into it—I couldn't sleep last night but marvellous meditation was going on for me. And I would like to go away as quickly as possible. According to the doctor the thing is increasing very rapidly. I can go through the cycle of stopping the pain by morphine. A few days quiet and then begin again. I don't want to go through all that. I am going to find out from the doctor whether there is a way of getting the whole thing out [over?], finished. I doubt if he can tell me but that is what I want to say. While my brain is clear as it is this morning I can talk, you know, easily, but when the pain begins and all that I won't be able to talk freely, openly, easily. That's all.[80]

Jane Hammond, Mary Cadogan and I had two more friendly talks with Radhika and Dr Krishna in the course of which we worked out an arrangement which we hoped would fulfil K's wishes and be acceptable to Pupul: the material for the Indian international book should be selected in India, given a first editing there, and then sent to England for a final revision which might well not be necessary.

* * * *

In the afternoon after this morning meeting K felt well enough to go out in a wheel-chair. Unfortunately the chair turned out to be a wheel-walker with a seat on it. Scott raised the seat as high as it would go and K sat on it cross-legged. With his bottle of fluid suspended above him, he was wheeled out of the door of his sitting-room on to the verandah and carried down the few steps to the path. Mary, Scott, Dr Parchure and Mark Lee went with him. It was a sunny day and he asked to be left alone in the shade of the pepper tree from where he could see across the valley to the hills. Scott, afraid that he might fall backwards, remained a few paces behind him. K sat there perfectly still for some time before being wheeled back to the cottage. It was the last time he went out.

That evening Scott's wife Kathy arrived from Brockwood with revised plans for the Centre which Scott had to discuss with the architect over the telephone and which K, with his unabated interest in the new building, was pleased to see. Kathy's presence was a blessing for she undertook unobtrusively many of the chores in the house.

Next day, the 4th, K was so well that Dr Deutsch, when he came to see him in the afternoon, spoke of a possible remission. K asked the doctor whether he would be able to travel again and give talks. The doctor said, not as before but he might be able to write or dictate or hold discussions with individuals. The doctor also promised him that if the pain returned he would not let him suffer. Before he left, after over an hour, the doctor suggested that K should go into the living-room in the wheel-chair.

Scott built up the log fire in the living-room which had been kept going since K's return from hospital, and K sat there, delightedly watching the flames. At first he asked to be left alone (there were usually a few people sitting quietly in the room as if in some holy place) but consented to Scott remaining behind the chair in case he fell backwards, for he was again perched cross-legged on the seat. Mary noted, 'I guessed that he wanted to do whatever it is he does to cleanse rooms from all evil and bring about that extraordinary atmosphere that is his.' (He had always done this in any new room he was to occupy.) Scott wrote, 'He did something to the room. One could see him doing it, and the room was not the same afterwards. He had all the power and magnificence he had always had. Though he was sitting in his wheeled walker, covered up in blankets, being fed intravenously from these bottles, yet he was immense and majestic, and he absolutely filled the room and made the whole thing vibrate. And he glowed.'

When after half an hour he wanted to return to bed he amazed everyone by walking back unaided to his room. It was impossible not to hope that a miracle had occurred.

*   *   *   *

The next morning, the 5th, K called a meeting and asked Scott to record it. Those who attended were the Lilliefelts, Pupul, Radhika, Dr Krishna, Mahesh Saxena (who had only just arrived), Mary Zimbalist, Mark Lee, David Moody, Dr Parchure, Mary Cadogan, Jane Hammond and I. It was a very painful meeting because K kept breaking down and apologising for it. 'I don't want to cry in front of you,' he said. 'It is not pleasant to see a man crying.' He was obviously crying from sheer physical weakness, and our concern for him was not helping him. It was impossible to keep back one's own tears (for me at any rate; the others may have been more self-controlled, though they would have felt it just as much. I did not notice anyone but him and Scott standing by the bed with the tape-recorder).

K started by telling us what Dr Deutsch had told him the day before that the body could go on in that condition for a month, two months, but there would be no more travels, no more talks. At the moment he had no pain, he said, and his brain was 'very, very, very clear. . . . As long as this body is living . . . I am still the teacher. K is here as he is on the platform. . . . I am still the head of everything, the schools, the Foundations . . . I am still the *head* of it. I want to make this very, very clear. As long as the body is living K is there. I know it because I have marvellous dreams all the time—not dreams, whatever happens.' He wanted, he said, to be informed in detail of what was happening in India and Brockwood. 'Don't tell me everything is all right.'

He then asked all the visitors, as politely as possible, to leave. 'Please don't waste your time sitting here. You can't help me, I'm sorry to say. You can't keep the body alive.' The only exceptions he made were of Mahesh, because he had only just arrived and he wanted to talk to him quietly—he could stay as long as he liked and go when he liked—and perhaps Dr Krishna for a while, though he had his family and Rajghat to get back to. He repeated, 'I would request you most earnestly, don't waste your time here.'

He went on to say that he had lived without any hierarchy. 'I like to talk to lots of people, not that they influence me.' Nobody, not even Mrs Besant, had ever told him what to say. When he dissolved the Order of the Star, he did it; when Saanen came to an end it was *his* decision. 'So please be good enough, generous enough, not to the body, [but] to that teaching, not to bring hierarchy into this: no priests, no temples, no rituals.' When he was dead he did not want people to come and 'salute the body'. He did not want 'any of that business—sandalwood and all that put over the body'. He did not want good shawls destroyed by putting them round the body. He repeated that it was a waste of time our staying there, and then he asked Scott not to change the words that were being recorded. 'Tell them, sir, that you promise.'

'None of the recordings will ever be altered and things won't be erased,' Scott said.

'No, you must be more firm. Say, I swear it will never be altered.'

Scott turned to us. 'I swear nothing will be altered on any of the tapes. Nothing ever has been and nothing will be.'[82]

*   *   *   *

I had been sitting on the far side of the room, out of K's vision, I would have thought, but with his extraordinary powers of observation he had evidently noticed everything, for when I went in next morning to see him, he said, 'I'm sorry I upset you yesterday.' Joe and I decided to leave that day in accordance with his wishes, though it was agony leaving him. I heard afterwards that he was grateful to us for leading the way.

Everyone at Ojai had been wonderfully kind to us. I had been delighted to meet Mahesh who was very warm. He and Dr Krishna were like the close Indian friends I had made when I first went to India at fifteen and had fallen in love with the country. They had the great gift of showing immediate affection.

Vivienne Moody had taken us round the Oak Grove Schools which occupied several disparate buildings of arrestingly successful modern architecture, and one day the Hookers had asked us all to lunch at their well-known Ranch House Restaurant. They gave us a delicious meal and afterwards a group photograph was taken for which we all succeeded in looking cheerful. Mary Cadogan, Dorothy Simmons and Jane Hammond went to see K that afternoon. He seemed in excellent spirits, Mary Cadogan has recorded, and was anxious to know every detail of what we had had to eat at the restaurant. He said after they had told him, 'You obviously had a better lunch than I did,' indicating his feeding bottle, and he laughed naturally and easily. Dorothy asked him whether the scent of the orange blossom brought on his hay fever. He replied that he did not get hay fever until June; he then added, 'It won't bother the poor chap this year.' His laughter at this was so infectious that they could not help joining in.

On the afternoon of the 6th I said good-bye to K. I asked him if there was anything I could do for him and he said no. So then there was nothing left but to embrace him and leave as quickly as possible. We had hired a car to take us to the airport and characteristically K sent Mary out afer we had said good-bye to her to see what make of car it was. He was satisfied to hear it was a good car.

Dorothy Simmons, Jane Hammond, Dr Krishna, Radhika and Asit left within the next few days, but the last two were to return. Mary Cadogan remained until the 15th since she had promised to give a talk to the school, and Pupul, who moved from Arya Vihara to the Grohes' house, stayed until the 16th. K found visitors very trying. One day, when a couple came to see him in the living-room where he was sitting, he started to cry. When they left he turned to Scott and said, 'Too much emotion, too much devotion. Not good for me.'

What he did look forward to were the visits of Dr Deutsch although he was worried by the amount of time he was taking from the doctor's other patients. But Dr Deutsch came now more as a friend than as a doctor. K had given him his beautiful Patek-Philippe clock which we had brought with us from Brockwood at his request, and it was as a friend, not as a doctor, that Dr Deutsch accepted it. K also gave him a Huntsman suit and some Jacquet ties from Geneva. (Dr Deutsch never sent in a bill.) K was giving away all his clothes as fast as he could; he also gave instructions that all his clothes at Brockwood should be given away. Apart from the Patek-Philippe clock, and his clothes, his only possessions were two Patek-Philippe watches, one of which, with a Greek coin attached to it on a short chain, he had worn for years.

'. . . if they live the teachings'

On February 5 Mary Cadogan had written a letter of appreciation to Mary Zimbalist for all she had done and was doing for K. At the end of it she wrote:

Although I don't want to bother Krishnaji with anything just now, there is one question I would dearly like to put to him. Perhaps if you or Scott feel that the moment is right, you might be able to put it to him? I know the traditional answer to it, of course, but would so much like to hear what K says about it. The question is: When Krishnaji dies what *really* happens to that extraordinary focus of understanding and energy that is K?

On the morning of the 7th, when K seemed to be feeling fairly strong, Mary Zimbalist told him that Mary Cadogan had given her a question for him to answer but only if he felt like it. 'Bring it,' he said, so Mary read it aloud to him and scribbled down on the side of the letter his immediate reply: 'It is gone. But if someone goes wholly into the teachings perhaps they might touch that; but one cannot *try* to touch it.' Then after a moment he added, 'If you all only knew what you have missed—that vast emptiness.'

It seems that Mary Cadogan's question may still have been in his mind when in the middle of the morning he sent for Scott and asked him to record something he wanted to say. 'His voice was weak,' Mary noted, 'but he spoke with intent emphasis.' There were pauses between most of his words as if it was an effort for him to bring them out:

I was telling them this morning—for seventy years that super energy—no—that immense energy, immense intelligence, has been using this body. I don't think people realise what tremendous energy and intelligence went through this body—there's twelve-cylinder engine. And for seventy years—was a pretty long time—and now the body can't stand any more.

Nobody, unless the body has been prepared, very carefully, protected and so on—nobody can understand what went through this body. Nobody. Don't anybody pretend. Nobody. I repeat this: nobody amongst us or the public, know what went on. I know they don't. And now after seventy years it has come to an end. Not that that intelligence and energy—it's somewhat here, every day, and especially at night. And after seventy years the body can't stand it—can't stand any more. It can't. The Indians have a lot of damned superstitions about this—that you will and the body goes—and all that kind of nonsense. You won't find another body like this, or that supreme intelligence operating in a body for many hundred years. You won't see it again. When he goes, it goes. There is no consciousness left behind of *that* consciousness, of *that* state. They'll all pretend or try to imagine they can get into touch with that. Perhaps they will somewhat if they live the teachings. But nobody has done it. Nobody. And so that's that.[83]

When Scott asked him to clarify some of what he had said in this statement for fear it might be misunderstood he became 'very upset' with him and said, 'You have no right to interfere in this.'

As I said earlier, K knew far more than anyone else can ever hope to know about who and what he was, and in this last recording he ever made was he not sharing with us all something of what he did know which he had never revealed before? This sharing is surely an ineffable privilege. Did he not intend this message to be for all of us? Is he not telling us that the work is done, that it will not, and does not need to, be done again—at any rate not for a very long time? Nor is he taking away hope from us, for he tells us again, as he had maintained most of his life, that if we live the teachings we may be able to touch 'that'. *If.* The teachings are there. The rest is up to us.

*   *   *   *

After this last tape K had nine more days to live. On February 8, Dr Deutsch ordered a higher alimentation with a pump instead of a drip to give him more strength. K allowed this although he did not want to go on living, having now said all he had to say. He asked what would happen if the feeding-tube was withdrawn; he was told that the body would quickly dehydrate. He knew that he had a legal right to ask for the drip-feed to be removed, nevertheless he felt that nothing must be done that might cause difficulties for the doctor or for Mary Zimbalist in whose house he was. (Mary did not consider it to be her house. She always looked upon it as K's.) He also felt that it was very important not to precipitate the ending of the body. That night he seemed to feel some special danger and asked Mary and Scott to be near him, so they brought cushions and spent the night on the floor on either side of his bed.

The next day K at last agreed to have a catheter which he did not find uncomfortable and which enabled him to sleep without constant interruptions. That afternoon he went into the living-room where he lay on the sofa watching the fire. It was a welcome change from his bedroom. Mary sat beside him for a time and 'felt emanating from him and filling the room such a sense of peace and power and stillness that all life seemed contained in that room. All that he is was there, all that mattered in the world.'

Throughout his illness K continued to look after his body as he had always done. He cleaned his teeth as regularly as ever (he would clean the roof of his mouth as well as his tongue) and even asked for something to chew because, he said, 'if I don't my teeth will go bad.' His hair was shampooed and almond oil was rubbed into his scalp. He was no longer shy of the nurses giving him a bed bath. He continued to do his Bates's eye exercises every day and to put drops against glaucoma into his left eye. As a result of lying in bed, a little fluid had collected in the base of his lungs. When Dr Deutsch suggested that blowing into a surgical glove would help to clear this, K inflated the glove every hour until he no longer had the strength to blow. It seemed that 'the body' about which he had spoken in his last recording had been given into his charge to care for and that he was determined to fulfil his responsibility towards it to the very end.

He was worried that he had put Mary into a position where she would grieve at his death. He made her go out walking again with Erna Lilliefelt in the early mornings as she used to do. (She had not wanted to leave the house for an instant.) He wanted her to enjoy herself after he was gone, to travel, to go to Venice with Joe and me (where we went every year) and to the Dordogne with Scott and Kathy. He asked her, 'Who will you go to Huntsman with? Will you go on lunching with Mary at Fortnum's?' (We have frequently lunched together there since his death—a precious place to us—still full of his presence.)

On the 10th, Pupul brought to K the answer from Pandit Jagannath Upadhyaya to his enquiry about the traditional Indian treatment of the body of a religious man after death. On hearing it, K said that he did not want any of it. He did not want any ceremony, any flowers, any lying in state; he did not want anybody to see his body after death and there should be as few people as possible at his cremation.

He spent the whole of that day in the living-room and was able to stand to get in and out of the wheel-chair, but in the evening the pain came on and he needed morphine. Patrick Linville, a male nurse who was now on the nursing rota, was amazed that he was able to stand alone even for a moment. Patrick was French and K liked him very much. He enjoyed talking French to him.

K spent also the whole of the 11th in the living-room and saw a few people, but on the 12th he had acute pain and his temperature went up to 104°. Dr Deutsch, who had come for the fourth day running, believed that he had had an internal haemorrhage. He was too weak to see anyone that day. Mary sat with him holding his hand for a long time in the evening and he asked her, as he often did now, to press with her hand on his stomach as hard as she could. He would also ask Scott to do this. It seemed to give him some relief. All the same, he was anxious to know 'what the gossip was', and he listened to the evening news.

By the 13th K was too weak to get into the wheel-chair, so Scott, Dr Parchure and Patrick carried him to the sofa in the living-room in a hammock of his sheet. Their progress made him laugh. At 4 a.m. on the 14th the pain came on. He was given morphine and during the ten minutes it took to work he said to Mary, 'Too good to be true—sorrow I thought I'd lost you,' meaning, 'I thought I had lost suffering, but this was too good to be true.' Mary noted, 'The high voice groaned with pain and the low voice came in— "Don't make such a fuss about it".' He was again carried into the living-room that day in a hammock of bedclothes.

On the 15th K began talking to Scott about the state of the world; he then asked, 'Do you think Dr Deutsch knows about all this? Do you think he sees it? I will have to talk to him about it.' This he did when the doctor came that afternoon. Scott has written:

What Krishnaji said to Dr Deutsch on that occasion was an extraordinary ten- or fifteen-minute encapsulation of so much of what he says about the nature of the world. It was eloquent and concise and complete, and I stood there astonished and impressed, listening at the foot of the bed with Dr Deutsch sitting next to him by the side of the bed. The one thing I do remember Krishnaji saying to Dr Deutsch was, 'I am not afraid of dying because I have lived with death all my life. I have never carried any memories.' Later the doctor was to say, 'I feel like I was Krishnaji's last pupil.' It was really lovely. It was also extraordinarily impressive that Krishnaji, as weak as he was and also as close to death as he was, could have summoned up the strength to make that encapsulation that he did, and it's also an indication of the affection he felt for the doctor.

Dr Deutsch had discovered that K was a Clint Eastwood fan, as he was himself, and he had brought him some Eastwood films which he had videoed and also some slides of the Yosemite, knowing how much K loved trees and mountains. Someone had sent K a postcard of an eagle in flight which had been selotaped to the blank white cupboard door opposite his bed. He asked Scott to get him a picture of a bear or a deer to stick beside it. Scott was deeply regretful that he neglected to do this.

K was so weak that day, the 15th, that he could hardly lift his arms and he did not go into the living-room, yet he asked Scott to tell him any news he had heard about the Brockwood school. He also talked about the new Centre. As he knew, there was not enough money to finish it, and efforts might be made to cut it down or abandon the project altogether. He implored Scott, 'Don't diminish it. Don't reduce it. Make it first class. (The Foundation Stone was laid in September 1986.)

On the same day Mary Cadogan left for London, and Radhika and Asit, who had never left the States, returned. Radhika had been to see her daughter in Philadelphia. She was to leave with Pupul on the afternoon of the 16th but Asit asked Mary Zimbalist if he might stay on until the end. He said he could no more leave than if his father were dying. Mary said that of course he could stay if he wished and that he was welcome to come to the house whenever he liked. She also put a car at his disposal since the Grohes' house, where he was staying, was some way from Pine Cottage. When Mary told K that Asit was staying on he said again that he did not want anyone to see him after he was dead. When she pointed out, however, how hard this was on people who had been close to him, he agreed that 'after he had been bathed and his body wrapped, his face might be uncovered for a while'.

That evening Mary massaged almond oil into his scalp after cleaning his hair with a hot flannel and brushing it carefully. Afterwards she wrote in her diary, 'I stood doing this behind the top of his bed, holding in my hands this warm and beautiful head that holds the brain that is the light of the world. It is there, alive, marvellous beyond any knowing, the source of his teaching, his endless giving.'

On the morning of Sunday the 16th, K was woken at 3 a.m. by pain which continued in spite of repeated doses of morphine. Dr Deutsch was on weekend leave but when contacted he ordered a separate drip of morphine to be started. In spite of the morphine and pain, 'Krishnaji was looking clear,' Dr Parchure reported, 'talked without slur, even his eyes did not look droopy.'

Pupul and Radhika came to say good-bye in the morning. They were leaving after lunch. Mary assured Pupul that she would do everything she could for K. Neither of them had any idea that death was quite so near.

Towards evening the pain gradually subsided. At 7 p.m. K took a sleeping pill. The end comes in Mary's words:

Parchure, Scott and I were there as usual and as usual K was thinking of others' welfare. He urged me, 'Go to bed, good-night, go to bed, go to sleep.' [He repeated this several times.] I said I would but that I would be close by. He fell asleep and when I moved to sit on his left and hold his hand it did not disturb him. The upper part of his bed was raised as he had been more comfortable with it that way and his eyes were half open. We sat with him, Scott on his right and I on his left, Dr Parchure quietly keeping watch and coming and going, the male nurse, Patrick Linville, in the next room. Slowly Krishnaji's sleep deepened into a coma, his breath slowed. Dr Deutsch suddenly and quietly arrived around eleven. Somewhere in the night one's desperate wanting him to be better had to change to wanting him to be free at last of his suffering. Dr Deutsch, Scott and I were there when Krishnaji's heart stopped beating at ten minutes past midnight.

Mary, Dr Parchure and Scott washed him and wrapped him in a length of unused *khadi* silk given by Mark Lee. Then they laid him on his own bed which had been moved into his sitting-room when he returned from hospital and covered him with a woolly cover he had often used. Only a few people came in to see him. Asit put a white camellia at his feet.

'The hours until eight o'clock [a.m.] when the funeral people were to come,' Mary wrote, 'gave a blessed space of time to sit quietly near Krishnaji, seeing that face, that infinite beauty. When the time grew shorter I held his feet, his child's feet, pliable as ever. Just before eight, when Scott came in, I said we would cover his face from the strangers coming.' (Mark Lee had made all the arrangements for the early cremation.)

Only Mary, the Lilliefelts, Asit, Mark Lee, Mahesh, Dr Parchure and Scott attended the cremation at Ventura. Mary went with him in the hearse, faithful to her promise that she would stay with him to the end.

Krishnamurti's body has gone—the spark has entered into the flame. But the teaching which is the treasure he gave us remains immaculate and uncorrupted for anyone in the world to draw upon.

Source Notes

Page Note

3   1   *Krishnamurti: The Years of Awakening*, p. 275 (Murray, 1975 & Rider, 1984)

4   2   *Krishnamurti's Journal*, pp. 23, 26, 44 (Gollancz, 1982)

4   3   *The Years of Awakening*, pp. 5, 22, 28–9, 41

6   4   *Krishnamurti* by Pupul Jayakar, p. 27 (Harper & Row, 1986)

6   5   *The Last Four Lives of Annie Besant* by A. H. Nethercote, p. 193n (Hart-Davis, 1961)

7   6   *Freedom from the Known*, p. 85 (Gollancz, 1969)

7   7   English Foundation Bulletin, No. 3. K had set this question himself when asked to write something for the Bulletin about falling in love

8   8   *Krishnamurti: The Years of Fulfilment*, p. 119 (Murray, 1983 & Rider, 1985)

10   9   English Foundation Bulletin, No. 3, 1969

10   10   From the transcript of a discussion between K and some members of the American Foundation, March 1, 1972 (Ojai Archives)

14   11   Part of an article K wrote for the *Herald of the Star*, January 1926, quoted more fully in *The Years of Awakening*, p. 220.

15   12   *The Years of Fulfilment*, p. 237, where the account is given in full

16   13   From same transcript as Note 10

18   14   Gollancz, 1985

18   15   Her books include *You're a Brick, Angela!* and a biography of Richmal Crompton

20   16   *The Future of Humanity* (Mirananda, Holland, 1986)

20   17   English Foundation Bulletin, No. 41, 1981

21   18   *Freedom from the Known*, p. 81

22   19   *Letters to the Schools*, p. 7 (Krishnamurti Foundation Trust, 1981)

27   20   *Questions and Answers*, p. 47 (Krishnamurti Foundation Trust, 1982)

29   21   Ibid., p. 101

30   22   Ojai Archives

31   23   *The Years of Fulfilment*, pp. 224–31

34   24   *Krishnamurti* by Pupul Jayakar, p. 132

37   25   From tape-recording (Brockwood Archives)

Source Notes

40	26	From a letter to me from Mary Zimbalist
40	27	From another letter to me from Mary Zimbalist
42	28	*Krishnamurti* by Pupul Jayakar, p. 441
42	29	*The Network of Thought*, p. 104 (Mirananda, 1982)
43	30	English Foundation Bulletin, No. 42, 1982
45	31	*Letters to the Schools*, pp. 33–4
46	32	*The Network of Thought*
46	33	English Foundation Bulletin, No. 43, 1982
49	34	*The Network of Thought*, pp. 99–110
56	35	*The Years of Fulfilment*, p. 230
56	36	English Foundation Bulletin, No. 42, 1982
60	37	*The Flame of Attention* (Mirananda, 1983)
61	38	Ojai Archives
62	39	Ibid.
63	40	*Krishnamurti's Notebook*, p. 121 (Gollancz, 1976)
63	41	English Foundation Bulletin, No. 41, 1981
63	42	*Meditations*, p. 41 (Gollancz, 1980)
63	43	Ibid. Foreword
65	44	English Foundation Bulletin, No. 44, 1983
67	45	Indian Foundation Bulletin, No. 1, 1983
68	46	*Krishnamurti to Himself* (Gollancz, 1987)
70	47	Ojai Archives
76	48	These dialogues under the same title as the conference were published as a booklet (Krishnamurti Foundation Trust England, 1985)
82	49	*Los Alamos*, a booklet (Krishnamurti Foundation Trust England, 1983)
84	50	*Krishnamurti to Himself*
84	51	This sumptuous book, entitled *The Thousand Moons*, was published by Abrams, New York, 1985
85	52	*UN Secretarial News*, May 16, 1984, and English Foundation Bulletin, No. 47, 1984
89	53	Brockwood Archives
93	54	Ibid. Pupul Jayakar in her *Krishnamurti* gives a full account of the Pandit's revelation (pp. 30–31) and Mrs Besant's supposed involvement in the story at Benares in 1909. Mrs Jayakar asks why Mrs Besant was in Benares at this time. The answer is that she was presiding over the annual Theosophical Convention there. The Conventions were held on alternate years at Adyar and Benares.
99	55	These Washington talks are being prepared for publication.
99	56	This harrowing account of K's suffering is given in Pupul Jayakar's *Krishnamurti*, pp. 50–57.
101	57	American Foundation Bulletin, No. 55, 1987
105	58	70 of these excellent photographs are published in *Last Talks at Saanen* (Gollancz, 1986)
112	59	*The Years of Awakening*, pp. 95–6

Source Notes

113	60	Brockwood Archives
114	61	Ibid.
114	62	*Krishnamurti* by Pupul Jayakar, p. 498
115	63	Brockwood Archives
117	64	From an account by Friedrich Grohe of K in India in 1985, written after his death
120	65	From a typescript by Dr Krishna
122	66	Brockwood Archives
123	67	English Foundation Bulletin, No. 47, 1984
123	68	From a letter to me from Stephen Smith, written after K's death
123	69	From a long account by Scott Forbes of K's last illness, written after his death
124	70	American Foundation Bulletin, No. 54, 1986
125	71	From a letter to me from Radha Burnier
126	72	From an account of K in Madras by Mark Edwards, written to me after his death
129	73	English Foundation Special Bulletin, 1986
130	74	Ibid.
131	75	Indian Foundation Bulletin, 1986/3
131	76	Ibid.
136	77	Brockwood Archives
138	78	From Mary Cadogan's account of K's last illness, written to me after his death
139	79	American Foundation Bulletin, No. 54, 1986
140	80	*The Years of Fulfilment*, p. 237
143	81	From tape-recording. Brockwood Archives
146	82	Ibid.
149	83	Ibid. Verbatim transcription

Available books by J. Krishnamurti

PUBLISHED BY GOLLANCZ AND HARPER & ROW
The First and Last Freedom (1954)
Education and the Significance of Life (1955)
Commentaries on Living (1956)
Commentaries on Living, Second Series (1959)
Commentaries on Living, Third Series (1960)
This Matter of Culture (1964)
Freedom from the Known (1969)
The Only Revolution (1970)
The Urgency of Change (1971)
The Impossible Question (1972)
Beyond Violence, paperback (1973)
The Awakening of Intelligence, illustrated (1973)
The Beginnings of Learning, illustrated (1975)
Krishnamurti's Notebook (1976)
Truth and Actuality, paperback(1977)
The Wholeness of Life (1978)
Exploration into Insight (1979)
Mediations (1979)
Poems and Parables (1981) (American title, *From Darkness to Light*)
Krishnamurti's Journal (1982)
The Ending of Time (1985)
Last Talks at Saanen, illustrated (1986)
Krishnamurti to Himself (1987)
PUBLISHED BY PENGUIN
The Penguin Krishnamurti Reader (1970)
The Second Penguin Krishnamurti Reader (1973)
The Beginnings of Learning (1978)
The Impossible Question (1978)

Index

Index

Index

KING PENGUIN

THE VENDOR OF SWEETS

R. K. Narayan was born in Madras, South India and educated there and at Maharaja's College in Mysore. His first novel *Swami and Friends* (1935) and its successor *The Bachelor of Arts* (1937) are both set in the enchanting fictional territory of Malgudi. Other 'Malgudi' novels are *The Dark Room* (1938), *The English Teacher* (1945), *Mr Sampath* (1949), *The Financial Expert* (1952), *The Man-Eater of Malgudi* (1961), *The Vendor of Sweets* (1967) and *The Painter of Signs* (1977). His novel *The Guide* (1958) won him the National Prize of the Indian Literary Academy, his country's highest literary honour. As well as three collections of short stories, *A Horse and Two Goats*, *An Astrologer's Day and Other Stories* and *Lawley Road*, he has published a travelogue, *My Dateless Diary*, two collections of essays, *Next Saturday* and *Reluctant Guru*, and a volume of memoirs *My Days*. He is currently working on a novel to be published in 1983. In 1982 he was made an honorary member of the American Academy of Arts and Letters.

R. K. Narayan

THE VENDOR OF SWEETS

A KING PENGUIN
PUBLISHED BY PENGUIN BOOKS

Penguin Books Ltd, Harmondsworth, Middlesex, England
Penguin Books, 625 Madison Avenue, New York, New York 10022, U.S.A.
Penguin Books Australia Ltd, Ringwood, Victoria, Australia
Penguin Books Canada Ltd, 2801 John Street, Markham, Ontario, Canada L3R 1B4
Penguin Books (N.Z.) Ltd, 182–190 Wairau Road, Auckland 10, New Zealand

First published in the U.S.A. by The Viking Press 1967
First published in Great Britain by The Bodley Head 1967
Published by William Heinemann Ltd 1980
Published in Penguin Books 1983

Filmset, printed and bound in Great Britain by
Hazell Watson & Viney Ltd, Aylesbury, Bucks
Set in VIP Baskerville

Chapter One

'Conquer taste, and you will have conquered the self,' said Jagan to his listener, who asked, 'Why conquer the self?' Jagan said, 'I do not know, but all our sages advise us so.'

The listener lost interest in the question; his aim was only to stimulate conversation, while he occupied a low wooden stool next to Jagan's chair. Jagan sat under the framed picture of the goddess Lakshmi hanging on the wall, and offered prayers first thing in the day by reverently placing a string of jasmine on top of the frame; he also lit an incense stick and stuck it in a crevice in the wall. The air was charged with the scent of jasmine and incense and imperceptibly blended with the fragrance of sweetmeats frying in ghee, in the kitchen across the hall.

The listener was a cousin, though how he came to be called so could not be explained, since he claimed cousin-hood with many others in the town (total incompatibles, at times), but if challenged he could always overwhelm the sceptic with genealogy. He was a man-about-town and visited many places and houses from morning till night, and invariably every day at about four-thirty he arrived, threw a brief glance and a nod at Jagan, passed straight into the kitchen, and came out ten minutes later wiping his mouth with the end of a towel on his shoulder, commenting, 'The sugar situation may need watching. I hear the government are going to raise the price. Wheat-flour is all right today. I gave that supplier a bit of my mind yesterday when I passed Godown Street. Don't ask me what took me there. I have friends and relations all over this city and everyone wants me to attend to this or that. I do not grudge serving others. What is life worth unless we serve and help each other?'

Jagan asked, 'Did you try the new sweet the cook experimented with today?'

'Yes, of course. It is tasty.'

'Oh, I think it is only an old recipe in a new shape. All sweetmeats after all are the same. Don't you agree?'

'No, sir,' said the cousin, 'I still see a lot of difference between one sweet and another. I hope I shall not become a *yogi* and lose the taste for all.'

It was then that Jagan pronounced his philosophy, 'Conquer taste and you will have conquered the self.' They chattered thus for half an hour more, and then Jagan asked, 'Do you know what I eat nowadays?'

'Anything new?' asked the cousin.

'I have given up salt since this morning.' Jagan said it with a glow of triumph. He felt satisfied with the effect produced and expanded his theory. 'One must eat only natural salt.'

'What is natural salt?' asked the cousin, and added, 'The salt that dries on one's back when one has run a mile in the sun?'

Jagan made a wry face at the coarse reference. He had the outlook of a soul disembodied, floating above the grime of this earth. At fifty-five his appearance was slight and elfish, his brown skin was translucent, his brow receded gently into a walnut-shade of baldness, and beyond the fringe his hair fell in a couple of speckled waves on his nape. His chin was covered with whitening bristles as he shaved only at certain intervals, feeling that to view oneself daily in a mirror was an intolerable European habit. He wore a loose *jibba* over his *dhoti*, both made of material spun with his own hand; every day he spun for an hour, and produced enough yarn for his sartorial requirements. He never possessed more than two sets of clothes at any one time and he delivered all the excess yarn in neat bundles to the local handloom committee in exchange for cash; although the cash he thus earned was less than five rupees a month, he felt a sentimental thrill in receiving it, as he had begun the habit when Gandhi visited the town over twenty years ago and had been commended for it. He wore a narrow almond-shaped pair of glasses set in a yellowish frame, and peeped at the world over their pale rim. He draped his shoulders in a *khaddar* shawl with gaudy, yellow patterns on it, and he shod his feet with thick sandals made out of the leather of an animal which had died of old age. Being a follower of Gandhi, he explained, 'I do not like to think that a living creature should have its throat cut for the comfort of my feet,' and this occasionally involved him in excursions to remote villages where a cow or calf was reported to be dying. When he secured the hide he soaked it in some solution, and then turned it over to an old cobbler he

6

knew, who had his little repair-shop under a tree in the Albert Mission compound.

When his son was six years old he was a happy supporter of Jagan's tanning activities in the back verandah of the house, but as he grew older he began to complain of the stench whenever his father brought home leather. Jagan's wife proved even less tolerant than the son; she shut herself in a room and refused to come out until the tanning ended. Since it was a prolonged process, carried on over several days, one can understand the dislocation into which the household was thrown whenever Jagan attempted to renew his footwear. It was a difficult and hazardous operation. The presence of the leather at home threatened to blast his domestic life; he had to preserve it, in the early stages of tanning, out of his wife's reach in the fuel shed, where there was danger of rats nibbling it. When she lay dying, she summoned Jagan to come closer to her and mumbled something. He could not make out her words, but was harrowed by the thought that probably she was saying, 'Throw away the leather.' In deference to what was possibly her last wish, he did give away the last bit of leather at home to a mission and felt happy that he was enabling someone else to take to non-violent footwear. Afterwards he just trusted the cobbler at the Albert Mission to supply his rather complicated footwear.

Now his cousin's reference to natural salt upset his delicate balance and he reddened in the face. The cousin, satisfied with the effect he had produced, tried to restore his mood with a pleasing remark, 'You have simplified your life so completely, and made yourself absolutely self-dependent, as I was saying to the Co-operative Registrar the other day . . .' This had the desired effect and Jagan said, 'I have discontinued sugar, as you know. I find twenty drops of honey in hot water quite adequate, and this is the natural way of taking in the sugar we need.'

'You have perfected the art of living on nothing,' said the cousin.

Encouraged, Jagan added, 'I have given up rice too. I cook a little stone-ground wheat and take it with honey and greens.'

'And yet' said the cousin, 'I cannot understand why you go on working and earning, taking all this trouble!' He waved his hands in the direction of the sweets displayed on trays at the window, but stopped short of asking why Jagan should expect others to eat sweets and keep him flourishing. He felt he had said enough, and stirred in his seat. Jagan's counting hour was approaching, and the cousin knew he should move, as Jagan did not like his cash to be watched.

The time was six, the peak sales were over and the front-stall boy would be bringing in the main collection for the day. At this moment Jagan almost fancied himself a monarch on a throne surveying his people (consisting of the four cooks in the kitchen and the front-stall boy) and accepting their tributes. The throne was a flat-bottomed wooden chair covered with a thin cushion hoisted on a platform, strategically placed so that he could keep an eye on all sides of his world of confections. The chair was nearly a century old, with shining brass strips on the arms and back and carved legs, especially made by his father when he built his house behind the Lawley statue. Normally he would not have bothered to design a piece of furniture, as the family always sat on the polished floor, but he had frequent visits from a Mr Noble, an Englishman, the District Collector, who came for lessons in astrology, and found it painful to sit on the floor, and even more painful to extricate himself from the sitting posture at the end of the lessons. A signed portrait ripening yellow with time was among the prized possessions dumped in the loft; but at some point in the history of the family the photograph was brought down, the children played with it for a while, and then substituted in its glassed frame the picture of a god and hung it up, while the photograph in the bare mount was tossed about as the children gazed on Mr Noble's side whiskers and giggled all the afternoon. They fanned themselves with it, too, when the summer became too hot; finally it disappeared back to the loft amidst old account-books and other obscure family junk.

Sitting there, Jagan was filled with a sense of fulfilment. On one side he could hear, see and smell whatever was happening in the kitchen whence a constant traffic of trays laden with colourful sweetmeats passed to the front counter. As long as the frying and sizzling noise in the kitchen continued and the trays passed, Jagan noticed nothing, his gaze unflinchingly fixed on the Sanskrit lines in a red bound copy of the *Bhagavad Gita*, but if there was the slightest pause in the sizzling, he cried out, without lifting his eyes from the sacred text, 'What is happening?' The head cook would give a routine reply, 'Nothing,' and that would quicten Jagan's mind and enable it to return to the Lord's sayings until again some slackness was noticed at the front stall and he would shout, 'Captain! – that little girl in the yellow skirt, ask her what she wants. She has been standing there so long!' His shout would alert the counter-attendant as well as the watchman at the door, an ex-army man in khaki, who had a tendency to doze off on his dealwood seat. Or Jagan would cry, 'Captain, that beggar should not be seen here except on Fridays. This is not a charity home.'

The surroundings were hushed when the master counted his earnings for the day. Although the boy at the front stall received all the cash, he was not supposed to know the total. He just dropped every paisa he received into a long-necked bronze jug, and brought it in at six o'clock, returned to his seat and brought in another instalment in a smaller container at seven, when the shutters were drawn. Jagan would not count the cash yet, but continued to read the Lord's sayings. Without looking up he was aware that the frying had stopped, he noticed the hissing of the oven when the fire died out, the clinking of pans and ladles being washed, and then the foot-steps approaching him, four pairs of feet from the kitchen, and one pair from the front stall, as trays of left-overs were brought in as the last act for the day. Then, when he knew that all of them were assembled at his desk, he addressed in a general way a routine question, 'How much is left over?'

'Not much.'

'Be exact.'

'Two seers of Mysore Pak.'

'That we can sell tomorrow.'

'*Jilebi*, half a seer.'

'Won't be so good tomorrow. All right, go.'

The front-stall boy carried in the left-over trays and unobtrusively made his exit. The cooks still awaited his permission to leave. Jagan asked, 'Are all the windows shut?'

'Yes.'

Jagan now addressed himself to the head cook, 'Tomorrow no *jilebi*. What is wrong with it?' It bothered him to think of the left-overs. They rankled in his mind as if he had a splinter in his skull. He loved to see clean shining trays return to the kitchen at the end of a day. A babble of argument followed. Jagan asked, 'What do we do with the left-overs?'

The head cook said soothingly as usual, 'We will try a new

sweet tomorrow, if you will let me do it. There will be no problem of left-overs. We can always pulp everything back and fry them afresh in a new shape.'

Jagan said philosophically, 'After all, everything consists of flour, sugar and flavours . . .' trying to come to a decision which he had been resisting all along; but, after all, one had to take a practical view, with the price of foodstuff going up.

When his staff was gone he put away his scripture book and pulled the drawer of his table half out; it was padded with a folded towel in order to muffle the sound of coin being emptied from the bronze jug. His fingers quickly sorted out the denominations, the fives, tens, and quarters, with the flourish of a virtuoso running his fingers over a keyboard; his eyes swept the collection at a glance and arrived at the final count within fifteen minutes. He made an entry in a small notebook, and then more elaborate entries in a ledger which could be inspected by anyone. In his small notebook he entered only the cash that came in after six o'clock, out of the smaller jug. This cash was in an independent category; he viewed it as free cash, whatever that might mean, a sort of immaculate conception, self-generated, arising out of itself and entitled to survive without reference to any tax. It was converted into crisp currency at the earliest moment, tied into a bundle and put away to keep company with the portrait of Mr Noble in the loft at home.

Jagan gave a final look at the cash in the drawer, locked it carefully, tugged the handle four times, and pushed his chair back with a lot of noise. He put a huge brass lock on the door, turned the key and put it in his pocket, and said, 'Captain! See if the lock is all right.' The captain seized the lock in a martial grip, as if it were a hand-grenade, and gave it a final jerk. 'This is a very strong lock, sir, can't get it nowadays. I know about locks; this must have been made in a village foundry.' He expatiated on the world of locks and locksmiths. Jagan cut him short with, 'Well, be watchful.' The captain gave him a military salute, and that was the end of the day.

Chapter Two

A lull had fallen on Market Road when he walked back home at a little past seven-thirty. An enormous shaft of blue light fell on the road from the Krishna Dispensary. He noticed Dr Krishna at his table peering at the throat of a patient. A street dog lay snoring on a heap of stone on the roadside, kept there since the first municipal body was elected in Free India in 1947 and meant for paving the road. A light was still seen under the door of Truth Printing although it was shut in deference to the Shopping Hours Act. Jagan knew that if he knocked, Nataraj would open the door, and he could always have the excuse of asking if the book was ready. The book had been in the press for years out of count, his *magnum opus* on Nature Cure and Natural Diet. Jagan knew that Nataraj would say again that he was waiting for types, but he could always sit down in one of his chairs and discuss politics. He overcame the temptation and passed on. 'Must be home, the boy will be lonely. Not today.' He fell into a brooding and introspective state as he walked on the edge of the road and was alone with himself. *Jutkas* drove past him with the drivers urging their horses with shrill cries, and then a few cycles, a scooter and a couple of cars loudly honking their horns. The traffic thinned and disappeared and he knew that he had come past Kabir Lane, as no more light fell in the street from the shops. At the junction of Market Road and Lawley Extension there was a short parapet over a culvert. As usual the vagrant was sitting on it, staring at passers-by and spitting into the gutter, and the donkey stood beside the wall as if it were offering itself for target practice. Jagan knew what the vagrant was waiting for: for the dining leaves to be cast out of the homes in Kabir Street: he would collect them, scour them with his hands and fill his belly with any vegetables and rice that might be left on them. 'The remedy would be for our nation to change its habits, for people to eat off plates and not use leaves for the purpose: the plates could be washed and kept, unlike the leaves which are thrown out after dinner for vagrants to pick,' Jagan reflected. He was for a moment racked with the problem of national improvement in various directions. 'If every-one discarded dining leaves, those engaged in the leaf-trade would be thrown out of their profession and an alternative engagement would have to be found for them. But first statistics should be taken of the percentage of the population eating off leaves (and those eating off plates: what kind of plate? Silver, aluminium or what metal?). How many were engaged in gathering the dry leaves from the forests of Mempi and stitching them with little splinters, and how many in cultivating special banana leaves used for dining?' Till all this was done on a national scale this vagrant would continue to remain here. Late in the night he emerged from this culvert and went down the streets crying at every door, 'O good mother, give a handful of rice for this hungry one . . .' He had a deep voice which penetrated the door and reached the kitchen beyond; his tone also quietened troublesome children as he was described to be a man with three eyes. 'He is a disgrace to the nation,' Jagan commented within himself and by the time he reached the statue of Lawley, a furlong off, his head throbbed with several national and human problems and their ramifica-tions. Sir Frederick Lawley faced the city; his back was supposed to be the back of beyond at one time, the limit of the city's expansion, but this prophecy was confounded when Lawley Extension, South Extension, and the New Extension all stretched out beyond the statue, and Jagan's ancestral home which had been the last house outskirting the city became the first one for all the newer colonies.

As Jagan approached the statue, he felt a thrill, not at the spectacle of the enormous gentleman standing in a Napoleonic attitude, benignly surveying the history and fortunes of Malgudi in a grand sweep (Jagan had ceased to notice the statue for over forty years now), but because he anticipated a glimpse of his son Mali on the other side of the statue. The pedestal had broad steps all around, and served as a parkbench for the young and the old of the neighbourhood. Pensioners, idlers, tired workmen, sickly citizens advised by their doctors to inhale fresh air, sat facing east, west, north and south on the steps. Students leaning on their cycles formed a group on the southern steps, all dressed in tight trousers and colourful shirts, hotly discussing film stars and cricket and fashions in dress and deportment. Jagan passed the statue on its north side so that he might not embarrass his son, but he liked to make sure that he was there; with a swift glance at the group, he spotted Mali by the deep yellow of his shirt, and the brief glimpse filled him with joy. He tiptoed away looking elsewhere, muttering to himself irrelevantly, 'Poor boy, poor boy, let him be.' He was very proud of his son's height, weight and growth. 'There are others, but he stands out among them. I wonder what God has in store for him,' he reflected, 'must give him more time.' He reached home, his thoughts still hovering about his son.

He let himself into his house, switched on the light in the front room, took off his upper cloth and hung it on a nail in the wall, took off his *jibba* and thrust it into a basket for tomorrow's wash. He passed through the ancient house, through its triple series of open courtyards and corridors, and reached the back door, lifted the cross-bar, and let it down gently. He stood for a moment gazing at the stars, enthralled at the spectacle of the firmament. 'One still wonders,' he told himself, 'but the problem remains. Who lives in those? We are probably glimpsing the real Heaven and don't know it. Probably all our ancient sages are looking down at us. What are those constellations?' He couldn't be clear about them. His astronomy was limited to the location of the Pole Star from Orion's Belt or Sword or some such point, for which knowledge he had been awarded a second-class badge many years ago when he was a scout. His astronomy did not progress beyond that. For all the million stellar bodies sparkling, as far as Jagan was concerned they might not be more than the two he had been taught to identify. In addition to Orion and the Pole Star he often noticed an extraordinary lively firework in the sky, which sometimes stood poised over the earth in the westerly direction. He called it sometimes Venus, sometimes Jupiter, never being sure, but admiring it unreservedly and feeling proud that he was also a part of the same creation. All this was a habitual second of contemplation whenever he passed into the bathroom in the backyard.

The bathroom was a shack, roofed with corrugated sheets; beaten-out tin was fixed anyhow to a wooden frame to serve as a door on rusty hinges; the wooden frame was warped and the door never shut flush, but always left a gap through which one obtained a partial glimpse of anyone bathing. But it had been a house practice, for generations, for its members not to look through.

13

This bathroom remained very much what it had been in the days of his father, who had resisted all suggestions for improvement, declaring, 'After all, no one is expected to live in a bathroom; one had better come out of it soon so that the rest may have a chance of tidying themselves.' A very tall coconut tree loomed over the bath, shedding enormous withered fronds and other horticultural odds and ends on the corrugated roof with a resounding thud. Everything in this home had the sanctity of usage, which was the reason why no improvement was possible. Jagan's father, as everyone knew, had lived at first in a thatched hut at the very back of this ground. Jagan remembered playing in a sand-heap outside the hut; the floor of the hut was paved with cool clay and one could put one's cheek to it on a warm day and feel heavenly. His father had also trained up a beanstalk on to the thatch and watched its development with anxiety. When he found some money, he put up the walls of the bathroom, laying the bricks with his own hands, and that became practically the starting point of the house. They fetched water from a well across the road and stored it in old kerosene tins and drums. His father expanded the house from the backyard to the front (although stubbornly refusing to improve the bath). As a child, Jagan had no notion how his father's fortune improved, although he heard vague words such as 'appeal', 'lawyers', 'lower court' and 'upper court'. By the time he became an adult, capable of understanding these affairs, they were over and he never could explain what the litigations were about and against whom. There came a time when the hut was finally pulled down, its thatches were used for heating a cauldron of water for the bath, and the cool mud floor was torn up and dug into pits for planting coconut seedlings. His father spent a whole week in these operations. Jagan and his brothers carried off baskets of shovelled earth, screaming with delight, 'Let us build a mountain.' Father had his theories of coconut-rearing and filled the pits with great quantities of salt. 'Salt is the only thing that can make a coconut tree grow,' he remarked every day. 'Show me the man who can grow a coconut tree properly and I will show you one with a practical head on his shoulders.'

Regularly at five in the morning Jagan got up from bed, broke a twig from a margosa tree in the backyard, chewed its tip, and brushed his teeth. He was opposed to the use of a toothbrush.

'The bristles are made of the hair from the pig's tail,' he declared. 'It's unthinkable that anyone should bite a pig's tail first thing in the morning.' It was impossible to disentangle the sources of his theories and say what he owed to Mahatmaji and how much he had imbibed from his father, who had also spent a lifetime perfecting his theories of sound living and trying them on himself, his coconut trees, children and wife. Even after the advent of nylon bristles Jagan never changed his views, maintaining that nylon had an adverse effect on the enamel. 'You disbelieve me. Remember my father who died at ninety without a single tooth loose in his jaw.' Jagan had immense faith in the properties of margosa, and in spite of its bitterness he called it 'Amrita' – the ambrosia which kept the gods alive; and sometimes he called it 'Sanjeevini', the rare herb, mentioned in the epics, which held at the nostrils could bring the dead to life. He never ceased to feel grateful to his father for planting a seedling in his time and providing him with a perennial source of twigs – enough for his generation and the next considering the dimensions of the tree. He chewed its bitter leaves once a month, as it destroyed all bacteria in the system, and he felt elated when the breeze blew – the air passing through the margosa boughs became an anti-typhoid agent, and during the summer rains the place became fragrant as the little yellow flowers drifted down like floss. He collected them, fried them in ghee, and consumed the ambrosia for all his worth once a week. His wife refused to associate herself with any of his health-giving activities. She hated his theories and lived her own life. Their first clash occurred when he forbade her to swallow aspirin and suggested that she should fry a little margosa flower in ghee and swallow it for relief from headache. Seated beside the ancient pillar in their courtyard, she had knotted a towel around her temples and swayed madly back and forth, desperately begging for aspirin. Jagan was very sympathetic, no doubt, but was convinced that aspirin would do her no good. She had just looked up at him and said, 'Oh, this headache is not half as unbearable as your talk. You would sooner see me dead, I suppose.'

'Your headache has made you crazy,' he said, his temper rising. He hated her appearance with that silly towel knotted around her head and her dishevelled hair. She looked ghoulish and no wonder she suffered inexplicable headaches! He suddenly realized the trend of his thinking and suppressed it with a deliberate effort. 'You may do what you like. Only don't suffer.'

'Leave me alone,' she said in reply.

Jagan wanted to ask, 'Why are you disgusted with me?', but passed on into Mali's room. Mali had insisted upon having a room of his own, and in that vast house it was not difficult to find him one. Mali got a long hall without a ventilator or window, known as the 'cool room' in those days, which had a stone-topped round table at the centre and a stool, and seemed delighted to be assigned this room as it was near the kitchen and the main hall and he could enjoy privacy without losing sight of all the goings-on of the house – such as the arguments between his father and mother or their conversation with visitors. He had a few books heaped on the round table and some house-building blocks.

Jagan had asked him, 'Boy, do you know where your mother keeps her headache pill?'

'I know, but she will not let me touch it.'

'Why?'

'Because I may eat it. That's all. It looks so nice.'

Jagan was scared. 'Boy, don't you go near it; it is poison.'

'What's poison?' asked the boy innocently, looking up from a paper kite he was fiddling with.

'Oh,' Jagan said rather desperately. He tried to avoid uttering inauspicious words, but there seemed to be no other way. He said, 'People die when they eat poison.'

Mali listened with interest and asked, 'And then what?' as if listening to a story.

Matters seemed to be proceeding in an unexpected direction. 'Where is the pill?' Jagan asked.

The boy indicated the cupboard in the hall and cried, 'On the very top, so high that you all think I cannot reach it.'

Jagan found his son's attraction to aspirin ominous. He merely replied, 'I'll get you better things to eat than this pill. Forget it, you understand?'

Then he had gone to the cupboard and found the pill for his wife. But that was some years ago, and Mali had grown.

Chapter Three

Mali said one morning, 'I have an idea.'

Jagan felt slightly nervous and asked, 'What may it be?'

The boy paused while swallowing his breakfast. 'I can't study any more.'

The father was aghast. 'Has anyone been rude to you in the college?'

'Let them try!' said the boy.

'Tell me what's happened.'

'Nothing,' said the boy, 'I do not find it interesting, that's all,' and he went on munching his food with his eyes down.

Jagan had never seen him so serious. The boy seemed to have suddenly grown up. He had never spoken before in this tone to his father. Jagan merely repeated, 'If it's something I can do, tell me.'

'I don't want to study, that's all,' repeated the boy.

The morning sun came through a glass tile and touched with radiance the little heap of *uppumav* on his plate – a piece of green chilli and some globules of oil made the stuff sparkle, catching Jagan's eye insistently for a moment, making him wonder if he had made some strange edible gem-set for his son rather than merely frying semolina and spicing it. Shaking himself out of this fantasy, he said, 'All right, I'll come to your college and speak to those people.' The boy looked up angrily. In his anxiety to communicate a new idea to his father, he had become brusque and aggressive. His face was flushed. 'So early in the morning, and the boy showing such a temper!' Jagan reflected as if temper had an approved time-table. 'All right, get on with your eating. We'll talk of these things later,' he mumbled when he should have said, 'Swallow your food and run off to your class.' He was a cowardly father and felt afraid to mention class or college. The boy might scream at their mention or kick away his breakfast. Jagan had an almost maternal obsession about the boy feeding properly. At home he spent all his time cooking for his son; it had started when his wife had her first attack of brain-fever and was taken to the hospital. When he was old enough to notice things, Mali had asked 'Father, why don't you engage a cook?'

'I don't believe in engaging a cook.'

'Why not?'

'Do we engage a servant to do the breathing for us? Food is similar.'

'Oh, Father, Father,' the boy cried, 'don't you engage cooks in your sweetmeat shop?'

'Oh, that's different. It's like a factory and they are specialists and technicians,' said Jagan, giving full rein to his imagination.

The boy failed to grasp the distinction and cried desperately, 'I do not want you to cook for me. We have our college canteen. I can look after myself.' He had stuck to it, relaxing his resolution only to the extent of accepting the breakfast made by Jagan. The practice had continued. Particularly after his wife's death, Jagan became obsessed with his son's diet, and brooded over the question night and day. At night before retiring, he held a long conference with his son on not only what he had eaten during the day but what he would prefer to eat next day. The son, cornered at this hour, answered in his usual manner of half-syllables and clipped sentences, and the day would conclude with Jagan's exposition of his usual theories of nutrition, half-way through which Mali would turn away and bolt the door of his room, leaving Jagan with his unfinished sentence. He would spend a few moments staring at the door, then rise and unroll his mat in the open verandah in the second block and fall asleep before the gong at the Taluk office sounded nine.

Now he felt desperate to know what his son would do if he left the college or rather the college canteen. He asked idiotically, 'Where will you eat?'

His son smiled grimly and replied, 'Why do you bother when you keep saying one need not eat?' He put on his yellow shirt, picked up his bicycle and was off.

Jagan had to bottle up his confusions until the arrival of his cousin in the evening. 'Come here,' he cried the moment he sighted him, much to the bewilderment of the cousin who wanted first of all to go through and try the sweets as they came out of the frying pan. He flourished his arms as if to say, 'Your banalities can wait,' and passed on. Jagan saw him disappear into the kitchen with resignation. 'He is bound to come out sooner or later. No one can stay long in all that heat and smoke. Moreover, he will reach satiety soon with those sweets...' Market Road suddenly became alive with the shouts of school-children just let off. A few of them, satchels slung on their shoulders, as usual stood in front of the Sweet Mart gaping at the display beyond the glass. Jagan watched them from his seat without emotion. 'It's up to their parents to provide them with the money for sweets. I can't be handing out charity-packets.' He felt apologetic sitting there and collecting the cash – a vestige of conscience from his days of public service. If the public could have joined and subscribed, he'd have given away a portion of his profits in order to provide sweets for every child that gazed at his counter. 'But this is a poor country, sir. Per capita income is three annas.' He still stuck to the figure that he had got out of a book called *Poverty and un-British Rule in India* in his college days, but this figure restrained him from demanding of every parent in town that he spend eight annas a day at his shop. 'Poor country! Most people cannot afford even rice for two meals a day. When I cease to be a merchant, I'll . . . But sugar costs one and thirty per kilogramme and flour and butter, real or fake, cost thrice as much, and what about the seasoning? Nutmegs seventy paise each – mark it, each! They used to be got in handfuls for the smallest coin and what *halva* would be worth its name if you did not crush a little nutmeg into it?'

When the cousin emerged from the kitchen wiping his mouth with the towel, Jagan said, as a continuation of his thoughts on social problems which for the moment swamped his private sorrows, 'Do you realize how few ever really understand how fortunate they are in their circumstances?'

The cousin nodded a general approval, secretly puzzled as to what this profound thinker might be driving at. 'They all forget or get used to things; that's the way of the world,' he said, smacking his lips and stating a philosophy that could fit any circumstance.

'Especially young men,' said Jagan; 'they are a problem everywhere. I was reading a little while ago somewhere,' and he tried to quote from some sort of a report on the youth of today, although he could not remember where he had read it or what it said.

'It takes one nowhere,' said the cousin sympathetically, his mind gloating over the memory of the sweets he had eaten.

The conversation was proceeding smoothly thus, when Jagan said abruptly, 'Mali is displaying strange notions.'

The cousin opened his eyes widely to register the appropriate reaction, not being certain how critical he could sound of Mali. Jagan explained. The cousin suddenly assumed a definite stand and said, 'It'd be best to know what the boy is thinking, our educational methods being what they are today.' You could always hit education if you had no other target.

'I was always hoping that he'd be a graduate and that's the basic qualification one should have, don't you think so?' Jagan added with a sigh, 'If I had passed the B.A., I could have done so many other things.'

'But it was not to be, and yet what's lacking in your present state?'

'I had to leave the college when Gandhi ordered us to non-co-operate. I spent the best of my student years in prison,' said Jagan, feeling heroic, his reminiscential mood slurring over the fact that he had failed several times in the B.A., ceased to attend the college and had begun to take his examinations as a private candidate long before the call of Gandhi. 'But what excuse can these boys have for refusing to study?' he asked.

The cousin, ever a man of caution, repeated, 'It's worth finding out from the boy himself. Why didn't you have a talk with him?'

'Why don't you?' asked Jagan in a tone of pointless challenge and added sentimentally, 'He has called you Uncle ever since he could lisp the syllables.'

'The only person to whom I'm not a cousin,' said the gentleman, and both of them laughed. The serious burden of life returning to Jagan presently, he said, 'You must do something about it and tell me tonight.'

At ten that night the cousin came up and knocked on the door softly. Jagan, for once, was awake after nine. The boy had retired and shut himself in his room without giving his father a chance to refer to the day's events. Jagan had noticed the light burning in his room, and resisted an impulse to peep through the keyhole. 'I wish you had peeped in – you'd have seen what he was doing,' said the cousin, when they had stolen on tiptoe from Jagan's house, strolled down the road to the foot of the Lawley statue and settled comfortably on the granite platform there. The cool night air was blowing on their faces. Sir Frederick loomed over them aggressively with his head amidst the stars.

'What do you mean?' said Jagan, leaning back in the shadow of Sir Frederick's spurs. All kinds of morbid and terrifying speculations arose in Jagan's mind. Was the boy counterfeiting money or murdering someone? A hundred evil possibilities occurred to him. He gripped the other's wrist and commanded, 'Tell me everything without concealing anything.'

The cousin shook off the hold contemptuously. 'He is writing, that's all. Wants to be a writer.'

'Writer' meant in Jagan's dictionary only one thing, a 'clerk' – an Anglo-Indian, colonial term from the days when Macaulay had devised a system of education to provide a constant supply of clerical staff for the East India Company. Jagan felt aghast. Here was he trying to shape the boy into an aristocrat with a bicycle, college-life, striped shirts and everything, and he wanted to be a 'writer'! Strange!

'Why does he want to be a writer?' he asked.

'I don't know. You will have to ask him.'

'Where does he want to work? It's degrading,' he cried, 'after all the trouble I have taken to build up a reputation and a status!' He beat his brow in despair.

It never occurred to the cousin that Jagan had misunderstood the word 'writer'. He said, 'I lost no time after you told me this evening to go out in search of the boy. I waited at the college gate . . .'

'Oh, did he go to his college after all?' cried Jagan ecstatically, concluding that he must have eaten in the canteen.

'Yes,' replied the cousin. 'It was only a farewell visit. I saw him come out with a gang of friends, who patted his back and shook his hand and did all sorts of things. A couple of teachers came out, looked at him, and said something. I heard him say, "My father has other plans – probably he is sending me to America." '

'Ah!' Jagan exclaimed. 'What'll he do in America? America indeed!'

'Don't be hasty,' said the cousin slowly. 'He had to tell them something before leaving. Until he demands to be sent to America, don't take any notice of it.'

'All sorts of ideas! All sorts of ideas!' Jagan cried helplessly, tapping his fingers on the granite.

'Well, he may become a second Bharati or Tagore or Shakespeare some day. How can you judge now?' the cousin said.

The truth finally dawned on Jagan. 'Oh, how stupid am I? Yes, of course, writer, I know. I've become illiterate, I think,' he cried happily. It was a great relief that the son was not attempting to be the other sort.

'What else did you think?' the cousin asked and added, 'I have heard that writers earn a lot of money nowadays. They become famous.'

'What does he want to write?'

'I don't know. Poetry, perhaps, easiest to start with, or stories. What else do people write?' said the cousin, not wanting to flounder in unknown seas. 'Actually, it was difficult to get even that out of him. I met him at his school . . .'

'College,' corrected Jagan, feeling somewhat piqued.

'Yes, yes, I meant college. I always think of Mali as a little fellow and it's very difficult to remember that he is no longer a mere schoolboy. At his college gate, when the teachers left him, he saw me and stopped to ask what had brought me there. I didn't want to seem officious and so said something and then asked if he would come for a cup of coffee somewhere.

' "Not just coffee," he said, "I want a lot to eat as well." '

'Poor boy, he must have been starving,' cried Jagan, feeling anguished.

'Not necessarily,' said the cousin. 'Young men eat and still wish to eat a lot more, you know.'

'Certainly,' cried Jagan. 'What is there to prevent his eating as much as he likes and at all hours of the day?'

'Do you leave enough cash with him?'

'Of course I do,' said Jagan. 'Did he say anything about it?'

'Oh, no, oh, no,' cried the cousin. 'He is not that sort of young man. Even if you starved him and denied him everything he'd never complain.'

Jagan felt proud at these encomiums heaped on his son. He remained thoughtful, while the stars in the sky paused in their courses. A couple of dogs trotted in a chase. The vagrant stirred in his sleep, muttering to himself on the other side of the statue.

Jagan peeped around and said, 'Disgraceful that our nation cannot attack this problem of vagrants. Must do something about it, when I find the time.'

The cousin ignored this larger social problem and continued, 'I took him to Ananda Bhavan; you know that place, the loudspeaker deafening you all the time.'

Jagan implored, 'I want to hear nothing about the Ananda Bhavan restaurant. Tell me about the boy, please.'

'Yes, yes, be patient. I know you don't like the Ananda Bhavan people. I know they tried to blackmail you with the sales tax.'

'Oh, please stick to the point. I don't care what they do or did. Tell me what the boy said. Was he unhappy?'

'Yes and no. Happy that he was going to be free to be a writer, unhappy that you should expect him to study at . . .'

'The college,' completed Jagan, almost afraid lest the man should blunder into saying 'school' again.

The cousin took the hint and said, 'College, college and of course college. The very word drives him crazy, although you like it so much. He hates his lessons; he hates his syllabus and all his books. The very thought infuriates him. Do you know what he did? He had his class-books in his hand. I had ordered *dosais* for him and we were waiting. He suddenly tore up the pages of his books savagely, beckoned an attendant and said, "Put these in the fire in the kitchen." '

'Could you not stop him? Didn't you tell him that books must be treated respectfully, being a form of the goddess Saraswathi? How could this boy ever pass his B.A.?'

'I don't know,' said the cousin reflectively. 'It didn't occur to me to argue with him, that's all; what use would it be anyway?'

'Are you also mad?' cried Jagan. 'Don't you see . . .'

The cousin said, 'No. When he tore the books it seemed very appropriate, our education being what it is . . .'

'Oh, stop it. I hope you have not been telling him things.'

The cousin ignored this insinuation and said, 'Do you know what he said after sending his books to the fire? He made up a verse on the spot: "Let us show gratitude to the Great Fire that consumes our horrid books –" or something like it. It sounded very smart and sensible. He ate *dosais* and a number of things, the total bill being three rupees.'

'Great boy!' said Jagan, gratified by his son's verse as well as his gluttony. 'I'll re-imburse you. Remind me at the shop tomorrow.'

'No hurry, no hurry. You can take your own time to return it to me,' said the cousin.

It seemed difficult to keep to the point, there being no precise point to keep to, no main subject to return to. They went on rambling thus until the Taluk office gong sounded twelve o'clock. It boomed through the silent town and Jagan said, 'Even burglars will have gone home to sleep, but still I have got nowhere. I don't know why he cannot write and also read his college books.'

'He said that the one interfered with the other,' explained the cousin.

After a brief pause, Jagan suddenly asked, 'Was Shakespeare a B.A.?' – a question that no one could answer in that place.

The cousin said 'Why go so far? I know Kalidasa never went to a college.'

'Because there were no colleges three thousand years ago,' said Jagan.

'How can you know whether there were colleges or not?'

'College or no college, I know Kalidasa was a village idiot and a shepherd until the goddess Saraswathi made a scratch on his tongue and then he burst into that song *Syamaladandakam*, and wrote *Sakuntala* and so on. I know the story. I have heard it often enough,' said Jagan.

'If you know the story, you must believe in it and hope that some day Mali will be another Kalidasa,' said the cousin soothingly.

Jagan, at the earliest opportunity, applied his eye to the keyhole of Mali's door, which remained shut most hours of the day. The boy seemed to be avoiding him. Jagan prepared the breakfast and left it on the hall table, and also tucked a five-rupee note under the plate so that the boy might eat wherever he liked the rest of the day. Mali would go out and return home at some hour of the night and shut himself in. Jagan went about his sweet-making without any outward sign of agitation, but inside he was all torn up. He could not understand where his son spent the day, or what he ate. He had never suspected that his zeal for education was going to ruin their relationship. He wanted to make it up with his son.

Through the keyhole he saw the light burning in Mali's room. He saw Mali sitting on a stool with his elbow on the table, just brooding. He felt disappointed that the boy was not writing. He had imagined the writer burning the midnight oil and littering the table with sheets of paper in a delirium of inspiration: Kalidasa suddenly bursting into inspired song, the walls of the ancient house reverberating with a new song to be on everybody's lips for a thousand years to come. But the picture that presented itself to him was different. The boy seemed to be moping in dejection and boredom. It was time to pull him out of it.

Jagan realized the time had come for him to forget college education and get completely identified with Mali's fantasies, at least until he came out of his gloom. Jagan beat upon the door with both fists, stooping and squinting at the keyhole having proved irksome.

'What's happened? Why are you bringing down the house?' asked the boy, opening the door.

Jagan pushed his way in, announcing, 'Boy, I like your idea. Come on, let us talk about it.' He breezily paced around and sat on a stool. The boy followed him mutely, his misgivings not totally forgotten. Jagan smoothed his own brow and the corners of his face so that there should be not the slightest trace of a frown and managed to give his face an affable grin, exuding an impression of total approval. They stared at each other uncomfortably for a second, and then the son came over and sat on the circular table with a marble top.

Jagan asked soothingly, 'Do you want a good table?'

'What for?' asked the boy, poised between doubt and trust.

The slightest pressure at the wrong place could topple him over to the wrong side. And so Jagan said, 'A writer needs a lot of space for his manuscripts – they are precious, you know.'

The boy was evidently pleased that the new table was not being planned for college books and notes. 'Who has told you about me?'

'These things become known. A writer has to come out!' He was amazed at his own fluency.

'Oh! I don't care either way!'

Jagan looked about. There was no sign of a book in the making. The marble top was clean, all the college books having been swept out of view. He felt a moment's curiosity about their fate, but checked himself. Not his business, anyway.

'Do you want me to buy you white paper? Have you got a good pen? I think I had better get you a new desk with a lot of drawers.' Peace and understanding were returning after all, and they could grope their way through the world of letters now, each thinking that the other might know better. 'What are you writing now?' asked Jagan with the humility of a junior reporter interviewing a celebrity.

'A novel,' the boy said condescendingly.

'Oh, wonderful. Where did you learn to write novels?'

Mali did not answer the question; Jagan repeated it.

'Are you examining me?' Mali asked.

'Oh, no, I'm just interested, that's all. What story are you writing?'

'I can't tell you now. It may turn out to be a poem after all. I don't know.'

'But don't you know what you are going to write when you sit down to write?'

'No,' said the boy haughtily. 'It's not like frying sweets in your shop.'

This was completely mystifying to the junior reporter. He said pathetically, 'Tell me if you want my help in any matter.'

The boy received that in sullen silence.

'Are your friends also writers?'

'How can they be? They are only readers and want to get their degrees. That's all.' Jagan rigorously suppressed his approval of those friends' attitude. The boy added, 'They are all ordinary fellows who are no good for anything else.'

'I thought you were fond of your friends,' Jagan said, seizing every opportunity to acquire a better understanding of his son's mind. He had thought that the friends were dear to the boy, the way they stood beside the statue leaning on their bicycles and talking loudly. It was also a slight matter of relief, for Jagan had had a fear that his friends might be misleading the boy; now it was some satisfaction to know that he was going astray entirely through his own individual effort. 'For twenty years,' Jagan reflected 'he has grown up with me, under the same roof, but how little I have known him! But the boy has been up to something. He will count for something sooner or later.'

'I saw in *Ananda Vikatan* a competition for novels,' Mali explained. 'They will pay twenty-five thousand rupees for the best.'

'On what conditions?'

'It must be sent before September 30th, that's all, and a coupon in the magazine must be filled in.'

Jagan leaned over to study the dates on a calendar in the wall. 'This is just May.'

'I know,' snapped the boy. 'I've five months.'

'Have you begun to write?' Jagan asked timidly.

'I am not the sort to show my story to anyone before I finish it.'

'What's the story?' asked Jagan, persisting.

The boy shrank away from him and repeated, 'Are you examining me?' in an ominous manner.

'Oh, no, it's not that.'

'You don't believe me, I know,' said the boy half despairingly.

Jagan was for a moment confused. He re-affirmed his faith in his son in the loudest terms possible. Secretly his mind was bothered as to why there was always an invisible barrier between them. He had never been harsh to the boy so long as he could remember, he had always got him whatever he wanted these twenty years; during the last ten particularly he had become excessively considerate, after the boy lost his mother. The scene remained for ever fresh in Jagan's memory – that terrible Friday when their doctor, Krishna, had observed her breathing and just said, 'No doctor could do more; a very rare type of brain tumour; if one knew why it came, one would also know how to get rid of it.' It was nearing midnight and the doctor had been in continuous attendance for forty-eight hours with needle, oxygen and ice-bag, sparing no apparatus in order to save a life: he was physically worn out by the effort and driven nearly mad by Jagan's hints that a nature-cure might have benefited her. 'Nature!' he snapped irritably, turning his head from the bed. 'Nature would sooner see us dead. She has no use for a brain affected by malignant growth, that's all . . .' Jagan had shut his mouth, feeling that the moment was inappropriate for his theories. But when the doctor took his final leave and moved off to his car, Jagan, following him out, could not help putting in a word on the subject: 'You'll see for yourself, Doctor, when I publish my book. I've all the material for it.'

The doctor made an impatient gesture, and said, 'Go back, go back to your wife for the few hours left. Your son is watching us. Protect him.' Turning back from the car, Jagan saw Mali at the door with bewilderment in his eyes. It was harrowing to look at his thin, scraggy frame (he developed and grew tall and broad suddenly after his eighteenth birthday). The boy asked, 'What did the doctor say?' He had been attending on his mother for many weeks now. In her rare moments of lucidity she beckoned to him, and accepted the diet, if he fed her. He came running home from school in order to feed her, rarely going out to play with his friends. At the boy's question Jagan had lost his nerve completely, held his son's hands and broken into a loud wail. Mali had shaken himself off and watched his father from a distance with a look of dismay and puzzlement.

Even with the passage of time, Jagan never got over the memory of that moment; the coarse, raw pain he had felt at the sight of Mali on that fateful day remained petrified in some vital centre of his being. From that day, the barrier had come into being. The boy had ceased to speak to him normally.

'Oh, no!' apologized Jagan, 'I'm sure you are going to write something good, my boy. I do not in the least doubt it. I just wanted to know the story, that's all. You know how much I like stories. Do you remember the stories I used to tell you at nights? The one about a black monkey which you used to like so much!' After taking complete charge of his son, he used to divert his mind by telling him stories from the *Panchatantra*. The boy showed no sign that he remembered those days or wanted to be reminded of them. He showed no reaction. Jagan said, 'You know, I'm also a kind of writer. You will know more about it when Truth Printing lets it out of the press.' And he laughed in a hollow manner.

The boy said simply, 'Father, you do not understand. I want to write something different.'

'Of course, of course . . . Tell me if you need my help.'

It seemed a very simple way of earning twenty-five thousand rupees without frying or baking anything. They sat talking until one in the morning, while Jagan was subjected to a revelation every other minute. He learnt that the boy had cut the coupon from the magazine of his college library, risking punishment and humiliation if caught. 'I did it with a blade, under the very nose of the librarian,' the boy said with a hint of laughter.

'Would that be the right thing to do?' Jagan asked, puzzled.

'Of course, how else could I get the coupon?' the boy asked, producing it from within the pages of a small pocket diary.

Jagan said, looking at it, 'If this is from *Vikatan* you could have bought a copy for four annas, or as many copies as you needed.'

'That anyone could do,' the boy said, and added mysteriously, 'I have always wanted to teach that librarian a lesson; he always thought he was too clever.'

Jagan derived a peculiar thrill in speaking of his son as a writer. Next day, on the way to his Sweet Mart, he stopped at least three acquaintances on the road and spoke to them of his son. The fourth person to be told was the head cook. As soon as he arrived, Jagan summoned him to his throne and said, 'My son is writing a book.' The head cook, between thoughts of the frying for the day, said it was a grand piece of news and evinced interest in the literary progress of Mali.

'He is going to earn twenty-five thousand rupees out of it, and he says he is going to finish it before September, wonderful boy! I never knew that my son was such a genius. Actually, you know, he need not do all this to get twenty-five thousand, that's always there. But I don't want to give it to him to handle. It's not like my generation; we came under the spell of Gandhi and could do no wrong.'

'For all your wealth, you are such a simple man, eating nothing.'

'Eating to live, that's all,' corrected Jagan. 'You will know when my book is printed. I'm also a sort of writer, you understand?'

'No wonder your son takes to it so happily,' said the cook.

The cousin came at the usual hour and heard the story. Jagan repeated himself and concluded, 'I hope he will also emulate my philosophy of living. Simple living and high thinking, as Gandhi has taught us.'

'True, true. But what I don't understand is why you should run a trade, make money and accumulate it.'

'I do not accumulate, it just grows naturally,' said Jagan. 'What can I do? Moreover, I work, because it's one's duty to work.' He pulled the drawer, took out his *Bhagavad Gita*, and read: ' "It's my duty to go on doing something." Moreover' – he raised his voice – 'that man, and the other one, and the one here, it supports

29

them. What would our head cook do if it weren't for this establishment?'

'He'd probably be frying stuff in some other kitchen. He is a master fryer, who'll get a job anywhere.'

'It's not that, my dear fellow. Mine is the biggest sweet-shop in the country. Have you any doubt about it?'

'None whatever; and your fry-master makes unadulterated good stuff.'

Jagan felt soothed by this flattery. All the same he said, 'No wonder Mali wants to try a new line. There are bound to be changes of outlook from generation to generation. Otherwise there will be no progress,' he added in a sudden outburst of theorizing, once again a vestige of his *Satyagraha* days. It was all as agreeable as the fragrance of the ghee, nutmeg and saffron which emanated from the kitchen. He suddenly said, without any provocation, 'I have always resisted the use of essences for flavouring or colouring. You can get any flavour from Germany; it is easy to deceive even the most fastidious nowadays.'

'How false and illusory!' commented the cousin, in a philosophical strain.

'But I'll never use them as long as I am a master of this establishment,' asserted Jagan. The cousin, as a sampler flourishing on absolute purity every afternoon, expressed unqualified approval of this statement.

Chapter Four

Peace reigned at home, with speech reduced to a minimum between father and son. Mali seemed to have brightened up at the fact that he wouldn't be expected to study. Jagan continued to feel gratified that his son was pursuing a fresh course, all his own. 'Instead of reading other people's books, he is providing reading for others,' he often reflected with a lot of pride. 'He is doing a service in his own way.' When he remembered the word 'service', any activity became touched with significance. 'Service' intoxicated him, sent a thrill through his whole being and explained everything. The first time he had heard the word was in 1937 when Mahatma Gandhi visited Malgudi and had addressed a vast gathering on the sands of the river. He spoke of 'service', explaining how every human action acquired a meaning when it was performed as a service. Inspired by this definition, Jagan joined the movement for freeing India from foreign rule, gave up his studies, home and normal life and violated the British laws of the time. Neither the beatings from the police nor the successive periods of prison life ever touched him when he remembered that he was performing a 'service'. 'Everyone should be free to serve humanity in his own way,' he told himself and, 'Mali is really helping mankind with his writing.' What does he really write? he often wondered. Stories? What sort of stories? Poems? Or did he write philosophy? He had a passing misgiving about his son's experience of life, his equipment to be a writer. He had uneasy thoughts sometimes when he sat on his throne in the shop looking at the pages of the *Bhagavad Gita*. However profound the lines before him, his own thoughts seemed to be stronger and capable of pushing aside all philosophy, while revolving round the subject of Mali's manuscript. He wanted to know which language his son's Muses accepted, whether Tamil or English. If he wrote in Tamil he would be recognized at home; if in English, he would be known in other countries too. But did he know enough English, Tamil or any language? He felt worried, his mind was racked with questions. The simplest solution of questioning Mali directly seemed impracticable. What could they discuss? Mali seemed to have become detached, more detached than ever. The only link between them was the five-rupee currency note that he left on the hall table every morning and checked later to find out if it had been accepted. Perhaps the boy lunched and dined at Ananda Bhavan; it was galling to think that his money should find its way into that cash-desk. It could not be helped; it was supposed to be the best restaurant in the town; but Jagan knew that they did not use pure ghee but hydrogenated vegetable oil in unlabelled tins – they were naïve enough to think that if the tins were unlabelled the public would take them to be real butter!

It was long past the thirtieth of September and Jagan would have given anything to know if the manuscript had gone off. But there had been no sign of it anywhere. The boy's movements were so finely adjusted out of his own orbit that, though they lived under one roof, they might be in two different worlds. When he saw the light through the chink in the door, Jagan knew that the boy was in his room. He dared not knock on it. Rarely did they ever reach home at the same time so that there was no chance of their meeting in the hall. Jagan felt harrowed by the lack of information. When the cousin arrived at his appointed time, he found Jagan looking so restless that he felt constrained to remark as he emerged from the kitchen, 'You are blessed with every gift of life: with what ninety out of a hundred people crave for – money, and with what a hundred out of a hundred do not attain – contentment. Yet you have not mastered one thing, that's the art of looking happy. You are always looking care-worn.'

'If one looks worn out by cares, God knows one must have sufficient cause. Do you see Mali at all?'

'Not much. No. No. Long ago, I saw him on a cycle one afternoon in Vinayak Street. Don't ask me what I was doing there. I generally go even farther than that when I have some work – always in the service of someone else, you may be sure. I do nothing for myself.'

'Did he speak to you?'

'Of course not. He was riding a bicycle, I told you.'

'What was he doing so far away?'

'Why not ask him?' asked the cousin.

'He won't answer, that's all,' said Jagan.

'Have you tried?'

'No.'

'Then try.'

'He may resent the question and think I'm interfering.'

'If I meet him, I'll find out, if you like.'

'Please don't. He'll think I have sent you to him.'

'Of course, I'll tell him that I'm talking for you.'

Jagan looked scared on hearing this. Sweat broke out on his brow. The cousin could not help remarking, 'You puzzle me. Why are you frightened?'

'I hate to upset him, that's all. I have never upset him in all my life.'

'That means you have carried things to a point where you cannot speak to him at all.'

'It's not that,' said Jagan, not willing to accept this view.

'Can you tell me when you had your last conversation with him?'

There was a pause while Jagan threw his mind back. The cousin watched him ruthlessly, gently sucking the sweet on his tongue. Jagan remembered that their last speech had been three and a half months ago. He had been reading the paper in the hall, and his son had come out of his room.

'Ready to go out?'

'Hm.'

That had terrified Jagan and at once he had covered up any hint of inquisitiveness. 'Did you see today's paper?'

'No.'

'Don't you want to?'

'Nothing in it for me.' The boy had walked across the hall. Jagan could hear the cycle being taken off its spring stand, and the front door slamming. He sat still with his eyes glued to the newspaper. 'God be thanked that there is no direct exit from his room to the street as my father once foolishly planned; otherwise I'd have lost the memory of my son's identity long ago.'

Reporting this meeting to the cousin was out of the question, so he said, 'The trouble is our hours are so different. By the time I open my eyes from prayer, he's gone; it's been a time-honoured custom in our house not to disturb me when I am praying. But that's all beside the point. We are straying away from the subject. I want you to help me. Please find out, as if you were doing it on your own, where he goes every day and what happened to the story. Did he finish it? Try to meet him and give me some information, please. I'll be grateful for your help.'

'No, no; it's my duty to be of service to you. Don't thank me. I'll see what I can do in my humble way.' He swelled with the importance and the weight of the undertaking. Jagan felt relieved.

The cousin came back four days later, took his seat beside the throne and said, 'New things are coming your way; your son wants to go to America. Didn't I hint to you long ago that it was coming?'

The first shock of the impact blanked out Jagan's mind for a time, and he caught his breath as he had a momentary panic at the thought of his son removing himself geographically so far. He inanely repeated, 'America! Why America? What has happened to his book? Has he written it? Hasn't he written it?'

'He thinks he will have to learn the art in America.'

Jagan was furious at this notion; it was outrageous and hurt his national pride.

'Going there to learn story-telling! He should rather go to a village granny,' he said, all his patriotic sentiments surging.

'Exactly what I told him,' echoed the cousin.

'Did Valmiki go to America or Germany in order to learn to write his *Ramayana*?' asked Jagan with pugnacity. 'Strange notions these boys get nowadays!' he said, avoiding gently any specific reference to his son. The head cook interrupted at this point, bringing in the flavour of kitchen-smoke, in order to announce, 'Saffron stock out. Will last only another day.' Jagan looked at him bemusedly, not able to grasp the subject clearly. The cousin answered for him and promised to arrange for a fresh supply. When the cook retreated into the kitchen, Jagan asked, 'Have you found out where he spends his day?'

'At the Town Public Library.'

'Where is it?' asked Jagan, never having dreamt that his town possessed a library. The cousin himself was not sure and flourished his arms vaguely in the direction of the river. 'Must be one of those things for which a foundation stone is laid, whenever a minister visits this town.'

'I'd have known about it if it had been a thing of any importance. Anyway, do they let him live there?'

'He seems to like it, and does some amount of work there.'

'What sort of work?' asked Jagan, appalled at the notion that Mali should have become a library assistant of all things! 'What has happened to his book?' he asked desperately.

'He will write it in America,' said the cousin.

Jagan felt completely crushed; adverse forces seemed to hem him on all sides. 'What has America to do with writing his book?'

'He has read in one of the magazines at the library about a college where they teach novel-writing.'

Jagan once again felt like bursting out about Valmiki or a village granny, but restrained himself. 'What happened to the prize?'

'Perhaps it's gone. He hasn't written the book yet,' said the cousin. 'Anyway, a book cannot be rushed.'

'True, true,' said Jagan, suddenly remembering his son's words the other night; but added as his own contribution to the theory of writing, 'Still, I suppose, a book has to be written.'

They spent a little time brooding over the mechanics of book-production. 'Why America?' asked Jagan, ignoring the instalment of cash that was brought in, while the cousin made no effort to leave.

'Because, perhaps, it's the only country where they teach such things.'

'They eat only beef and pork in that country. I used to know a man from America and he told me . . .'

'They also drink a lot of intoxicating drinks, never water or milk,' said the cousin, contributing his own bit of information. 'And the women are free,' he added. 'I have seen some of their magazines about films; their women mix freely with men and snap off marriages without ado, and bask in the sun without clothes.'

'Where did you see all this?' asked Jagan, and did not note the answer from the cousin, who flourished his arms vaguely. Jagan went on, 'It may not all be true,' not wishing to think a country to which Mali was going was one to corrupt his body with wine, women and meat, and his soul with other things. He said with a sudden determination, 'But it's unthinkable. Mali shall stay here.'

The cousin smiled cynically. Jagan had a momentary stab of suspicion that this man was at the back of it all, but the doubt passed.

The cousin said, 'He has made all kinds of preparations.'

'Without my permission or help!' cried Jagan.

'They have a typewriter at the library and he has been using it.'

Partly filled with admiration, and partly enraged at the library, Jagan shouted suddenly without thinking of what he was saying, 'If they are going to make use of the library for such nefarious activities . . .!'

The cousin said, 'Did you know that he had gone to Madras for a few days?'

'No? Without my permission or help, without telling me anything? I thought he was in his room.' He remembered that the five-rupee notes left by him had not been picked up on certain days. Thinking that the boy had been saving, he had withheld the allowance, hoping to be asked.

'He has fixed his passport and other such things.'

'How is he going to find the fare?'

'He says he has got it; he said he always knew where to find the money in the house.'

Jagan felt shocked for a moment, but he also felt a sneaking admiration. 'The boy is very practical,' he said with feeling. He sat brooding for some time and then said, trying to put on a happy look, 'See, how self-reliant he has grown! I have always believed in leaving the entity to develop by itself, without relying on extraneous support. As they say in the *Gita*, "Every soul is God . . ." '

'And God can always look after himself,' added the cousin.

'That's the whole point,' said Jagan. 'That's why I never wished to interfere when he suddenly decided to end his education. I said to myself, "Perhaps he wants to educate himself in the school of life," and left him free,' – echoing various tit-bits of banality he had picked up in the course of his life and haphazard reading.

The cousin said, 'Exactly my principle in life. I know much about people and their problems and the world. Did I go to a college to learn the art of living?'

'But I am surprised that he still thinks he can learn the art of writing from an American college!' Jagan sniggered gently at the thought. 'As my good cousin, please try and stop him. I don't know how I can live in that house without him. The very thought depresses me.'

'Yes, I will,' said the cousin mechanically, without conviction. 'But do you know that he has worked out the details minutely? He is getting his American clothes made in Madras.'

'I have always told him to buy a lot of clothes; especially in foreign countries one must always wear tie and shoes and such things, morning till night. Does he want any sort of help from me?' Jagan asked pathetically, almost appealing to the cousin to intercede and do something about it.

'What can you do?' asked the cousin brutally.

'I have a friend in Madras, a deputy minister, who was my prison-mate in those days in Bellary jail.'

'No harm in trying your friend, but Mali needs no help from us. The librarian has a brother in the Aeroplane Company and he has done everything for Mali.'

'Is he going to fly?' asked Jagan, panic-stricken.

'Who does not nowadays?'

Jagan almost wept as he said, 'Please tell him to go by steamer. It's safer. Let him be safe. I don't like aeroplanes.'

'He has almost paid for the air-ticket,' said the cousin, enjoying Jagan's predicament.

'It must be very costly,' said Jagan like a prattling baby.

'But he has doubtless found the cash for it,' said the cousin.

'Naturally. What is the cash worth to me? It's all for him. He can have everything he wants,' said Jagan, making a note mentally to count at the earliest moment his cash hoarded in the loft. He also considered transferring it all, in due course, to a casket behind the family gods in the puja room.

At dead of night, he put up the ladder and climbed to the loft. About ten thousand rupees had been extracted from the bundled currency. He made a rough and ready calculation. 'About four or five thousand rupees for passage; and the balance for clothes and other things. He should ask for more if he wants it, and, of course, a monthly remittance later. Why should he not?' He heard the front door opening, put out the torch and sat still until he felt sure that Mali had safely locked himself in, feeling like a burglar himself, instead of one whose cash had been extracted.

Chapter Five

He had never thought that he could feel so superior about it. Now it seemed to him worth all the money and the pangs of separation. 'My son is in America,' he said to a dozen persons every day, puffing with pride on each occasion. It delayed his daily routine. On his way to the shop he had only to detect the slightest acquaintance on the road, and he would block his path, and instead of discussing weather or politics, as was his custom, would lead the talk on gently to the topic of America and of his son's presence there. After days and days of hopeless waiting, when a colourful airletter had arrived by post, he had almost felt the same joy as if Mali had come back. He hardly had the patience to read the printed instruction 'To open, cut here', but thrust his finger in desperately and gashed the airletter until it split longitudinally, forcing him to piece it together like a jigsaw puzzle for deciphering. The message simply said, 'Arrived. New York is big. The buildings are very tall, not like ours. Thousands of motor cars in the street. Food is difficult. I am in a hostel. Next week I go to school.' Jagan read it with pleasure, although he was somewhat disturbed at the boy's mention of 'school' rather than 'college'. It had arrived by the first post, and he sat on the hall bench and pored over it for nearly an hour, scanning every word and visualizing Mali in that enormous background. He could not keep the good news to himself. The first entrance open to him was the Truth Printing works. Nataraj was at his desk, ever affable and welcoming visitors. The door was only half open, and when the light was blocked Nataraj looked up from his proofs and smiled, and immediately Jagan made the announcement: 'Mali has reached . . .'

'Have you received a telegram?'

'Oh, no, he's prudent. Won't waste ten rupees when ten cents – any idea how much a cent is worth in our money?'

Nataraj made a rapid calculation. A dollar was equivalent to five rupees, seven rupees on the black market as one of his customers had told him, four rupees odd according to the government, a hundred cents to a dollar . . . He gave up the attempt at multiplication and division and thought it best to change the subject. 'You will be getting your proofs very soon.'

'Oh, yes, I know once you take it up, you will get on with it. As you know, it's a contribution and a service, and not written for profit.' After this statement, he switched over to America. 'It's a place of enormous buildings and lots of motor cars. I hope the boy will have a room on the ground floor and not too high up.'

'Our boys are very clever,' said Nataraj, 'and can take care of themselves anywhere in the world.'

Accepting this agreeable statement, Jagan withdrew from the doorway and proceeded towards his shop. On the way he caught a glimpse of the adjournment lawyer at the turning of Kabir Lane. He clapped his hands and stopped him. He could take that liberty with him as they had been classmates at the Albert Mission more than a generation ago and had been together in the National Movement (although the lawyer elegantly avoided going to prison). The lawyer, a one-toothed man with a sprinkling of silver dust on his unshaven cheeks, smiled, exposing his bare gums. 'I've got to go home; some parties are waiting for me.'

'I won't take more than a minute,' said Jagan. 'I felt you'd be happy to know that Mali has written.'

'Have you received a telegram?'

What was the matter with everybody? Jagan felt annoyance at the tendency of people to get obsessed with telegrams.

'After all, why spend ten rupees when ten cents bring over a letter in four days?'

'Four days!' said the lawyer. 'No, no you must be mistaken. It takes longer than that. It takes at least fifteen days.'

That was the limit. How presumptuous of the man to talk of America, while he was there to provide first-hand information! People's notions were fixed. Stupid fellows! Frogs in the well!

Ahead of him, he saw the chemist at his door, looking down at the street. He greeted Jagan warmly. 'Rather late today?' he said with a lot of friendliness.

'Yes, I know, I know,' Jagan said, approaching him eagerly.

'The postman was rather late today. Well, when one has a son living so far away . . .'

'Has he reached America safely?'

'Yes, I was somewhat anxious for two or three days! Other boys would have wasted money on a telegram, but a letter at a tenth of the cost takes only a couple of days more. He's prudent, you know.'

'What's the postage? I want to send for a free catalogue from Sears Roebuck. You know, it is an interesting book. It'll give us wonderful ideas on all sorts of things.' Jagan almost groaned when the other asked, 'What's the equivalent of fifty cents, which is the postage for the catalogue?'

He passed on. None so good as the cousin, who deserved all the sweets he ate for his listening capacity: all the others in the town were obsessed with their own notions, were ignorant and resisted enlightenment on the subject of America. When he was sitting in his seat, the head cook came to ask for the day's programme. Jagan repeated the formula and then added a postscript as a favour to the cook: 'Mali has safely reached the other end, and that's a big relief to me. It's a huge country with a lot of motor cars. Everyone has a car there.' The cook listened respectfully and turned away without comment. Jagan felt relieved that the fellow had not stopped to ask about telegrams or the equivalent of a cent.

He had to hold his soul in peace until four-thirty when the cousin arrived, passed straight in to savour, and came out of the kitchen. Jagan said with a quiet firmness, 'The boy has reached the other end safely.' He flourished a fragment of the airletter, as a special favour affording the cousin a glimpse of the letter while he had only mentioned it to others.

'Excellent news! I knew he'd be all right,' he said, smacking his lips.

'He didn't send a telegram.'

'Yes, yes, why should he? Letters arrive so quickly nowadays. You must offer a couple of coconuts to Ganesha at the corner temple.'

'Surely, it goes without saying,' said Jagan as if there were a specific contract between himself and the god in the matter of his son's safety. 'It shall be done this very evening.'

'I'll buy the coconut on my way,' said the cousin, and immediately Jagan snatched up a coin from his drawer and handed it to the other.

'I feel a great burden off my head today. When someone goes

on such a long pilgrimage, especially if he is flying, it's always a worry, although one doesn't talk about it.'

'I know, I know,' said the cousin. 'What does he say about himself?'

'He likes the new experience, of course. Lots of tall buildings and cars everywhere. I hope he will walk carefully in the streets . . . He says the food is good. I'm relieved. You know it's a country of millionaires. Everyone is so rich.'

Mali proved unusually communicative from across the seas, and although at times he sounded brusque, disconnected or impersonal, he generalized a good deal about the civilization in which he found himself. The blue airmail letters grew into a file. If only Mali had taken the precaution of leaving a proper margin to his epistles, Jagan would have bound them into a neat little volume at Truth Printing; surely Nataraj would have realized its importance and obliged him with speedy execution. Jagan stuffed his *jibba* pocket with the letters, and pulled them out for choice reading of passages to all and sundry, mostly to his cousin who, as ever, remained an uncomplaining listener. Gradually his reading of the *Bhagavad Gita* was replaced by the blue airmail letters. From their study he formed a picture of America and was able to speak with authority on the subject of American landscape, culture and civilization. He hardly noticed to whom he spoke; anyone on the road seemed good enough. His acquaintances feared that he was afflicted with the Talking Disease.

From the minute he stepped out of his house, he scanned the landscape for a familiar face, pounced hawklike on the unwary victim and held him in thrall; he even stopped the vagrant on the culvert one day in order to describe the Grand Canyon. 'Actually, there is nothing like it anywhere in the world,' he concluded and gave him five paise for listening. It was a matter of luck for another, whether he could slip away in time or got entangled in American lore. Jagan found everyone restless when he spoke, but he rushed through his narration breathlessly. He had the feeling of having to bottle up his ideas until the blessed hour that brought his cousin in, who displayed such an enthusiasm for American information that Jagan could hardly tell him enough.

The cousin often wanted to see the letters himself, but Jagan resisted the idea: he held them in sacred trust and would not allow a third person to touch them.

Day after day, the cousin collected information on American life and manners and passed them on to his own circle of listeners. Very soon most people in Malgudi knew that fifty thousand human lives were lost in road accidents, every year, in America; and how people broke down on hearing of the death of Kennedy at street corners and crowded round anyone with a transistor radio. Jagan felt quite competent to describe, as if he had watched it himself, the route of Kennedy's motorcade on that fateful day, and he felt choked when he recounted how on that very morning, in Dallas, Kennedy had mingled in enormous crowds which grabbed and tore at his clothes and hair in sheer affection; nor did he spare his listener any detail of Oswald's death later.

The only letter Jagan rigorously suppressed was the one in which Mali had written after three years' experience of America, 'I've taken to eating beef, and I don't think I'm any the worse for it. Steak is something quite tasty and juicy. Now I want to suggest why don't you people start eating beef? It'll solve the problem of useless cattle in our country and we won't have to beg food from America. I sometimes feel ashamed when India asks for American aid. Instead of that, why not slaughter useless cows which wander in the streets and block the traffic?' Jagan felt outraged. The *shastras* defined the five deadly sins and the killing of a cow headed the list.

While he was cogitating on how to make his feelings felt on the subject and collecting quotations from the *shastras* and Gandhi's writings on the cow, to be incorporated in his letter to Mali, there came a cable one morning: 'Arriving home: another person with me.' Jagan was puzzled. What sort of a person? He had terrible misgivings and the added trouble of not being able to talk about it to the cousin, as he might spread the news of 'another person' all over the town. His worst misgivings were confirmed on an afternoon when the train dumped Mali, 'another person' and an enormous quantity of baggage onto the railway platform and puffed away. The very sight of the streamlined trunks, suitcases and corded cartons filled Jagan with uneasiness and a feeling of inferiority. The old porter at the railway station could hardly handle this quantity of baggage, although normally he would seize and carry scores of boxes and baskets without a thought. Now he had to call in the boy at the cigarette shop for assistance. Mali kept muttering without moving his head or lips much, 'Be careful, awful lot of things that might break. Have spent a fortune in airfreight.' Jagan slipped into the background, pushing his cousin to the fore to do all the talking and receiving. He was overwhelmed by the spectacle of his son, who seemed to have grown taller, broader and fairer and carried himself in long strides. He wore a dark suit, with an overcoat, an airbag, a camera, an umbrella and what not on his person.

Jagan felt that he was following a stranger. When Mali approached him, extending his hand, he tried to shrink away and shield himself behind the cousin. When he had to speak to his son, with great difficulty he restrained himself from calling him 'sir' and employing the honorific plural.

Matters became worse when Mali indicated the girl at his side and said, 'This is Grace. We are married. Grace, my dad.' Complete confusion. Married? When were you married? You didn't tell me. Don't you have to tell your father? Who is she? Anyway she looks like a Chinese. Don't you know that one can't marry a Chinese nowadays? They have invaded our borders . . . Or perhaps she is a Japanese. How was one to find out? Any indiscreet question might upset the gentleman with the camera. Jagan threw a panicky look at his cousin and fled on the pretext of supervising the loading of the baggage into Gaffur's taxi outside. A small gaping crowd followed them to the car murmuring, 'He's come from America.' Mali took notice of Gaffur by saying, 'Jalopy going strong?' Gaffur did not understand the word (which sounded to everyone like the *jilebi* prepared in Jagan's shop). Jagan and the cousin sat with Gaffur in the front seat, leaving the back for Grace and Mali. Gaffur said without turning his head, 'Why didn't you bring a car for me?' Jagan feared that Gaffur's familiarity might upset Mali, but the young man, fresh from democratic surroundings, said, 'I wish you had told me; oh, I sold my Pontiac before coming.' Gaffur, driving the car, entered into a description of the state of the nation with reference to automobiles, how you had to wait for five years to get a Fiat, three for an Ambassador, and so forth, how no importation was allowed and how a brand-new Plymouth was seized and destroyed at the customs, all of which upset the young man, freshly come home. Mali occasionally peeped out to say, 'Nothing has changed.'

Grace gazed with fascination at the streets and bazaars and cooed, 'Oh, charming! Charming! Charming!'

'Honey, live in it and see what it is like,' said Mali, on hearing which Jagan wondered whether he should address her as Honey or Grace. Time enough to settle that question. When they approached the statue, she asked, 'Who is that?' No one answered her. Jagan became tense at the approach of the house beyond the statue. When they stopped, he jumped out of the car and panted up the steps in order to open the main door. He had spent the fortnight in rigging up his house to suit his son's requirements. Under the guidance of the doctor's wife known to the cousin, he had spent a fortune in building a modern toilet and bathroom adjoining Mali's bedroom and had scrubbed and colour-washed the walls and put up new tables and chairs. Mali went straight to his room to wash and change. Gaffur and the cousin left after piling the boxes in the passage. Grace was left alone, standing uncertainly in the hall. 'Sit in that chair,' Jagan said, unable to find anything else to say. He added, 'Tell me what you want. I will get it. I do not know exactly what you will like to have.'

'Oh, how kind you are!' she said, genuinely pleased with his attention. She drew a chair for him and said, 'Please be seated yourself, you must be tired.'

'Oh, no,' Jagan said. 'I am a very active man. The whole secret of human energy . . .' he began and cut short his sentence when he noticed the bewilderment in the girl's face. 'I must really be off, you know, must go back to my shop, otherwise . . .'

'Oh, please do go and attend to your work.'

'Make yourself comfortable,' he cried and hurried out while Mali was still in the bathroom.

He began to avoid people. His anxiety was lest the lawyer or the printer or anyone else should stop him in the street to inquire about his daughter-in-law. He walked hurriedly to his shop with downcast eyes. Even his cousin found great stretches of silence when they met. Jagan had grown unwilling to talk about his son. Everything about him had become an inconvenient question. The cousin wanted to know what Mali had qualified himself for, what he proposed to do, and, above all, who was that casteless girl at home. He was dying to know what dietary arrangements were made at home and if they cooked meat. He inquired indirectly, 'Does Mali still like our coffee or does he ask for tea as some of these foreign-returned people do?'

Jagan understood the purpose of this question and said in order to put an end once and for all to inquisitiveness, 'What another person eats or drinks never interests me; why should I pry into it? The kitchen is there and they should know what to do with themselves.'

'It'd be all right for Mali. But it's the girl I'm thinking of . . .'

'Oh, she is all right. She was cooking for him and feeding him before, and she is able to do it now, I suppose.' Feeling suddenly that after all the cousin did deserve some enlightenment, he added, 'I can only provide what I'm used to. If they don't like it, they can go and eat where they please.'

'The Palace Hotel in the New Extension, I hear, provides European food.'

'Whatever it is, one can only do one's duty up to a point. Even in the *Gita* you find it mentioned. The limit of one's duty is well defined.'

The cousin changed the subject: he'd agreed with so much of the *Gita* day after day that he felt weary of it. As long as Mali's blue airmail letters had been the theme, the *Gita* had receded into the background. Now it was coming back, which showed that Jagan was becoming mentally disturbed again.

Occasionally one of Mali's old friends came to meet him. He seated the friend in the hall and conversed in low tones, as became a gentleman, and Jagan had no means of knowing what they talked about. Perhaps Mali was describing the Grand Canyon and Niagara and the Statue of Liberty and the traffic jams in New York; he knew all about such things and could have joined in if they'd let him, but he felt it might seem presumptuous unless he was invited. In that hope he sometimes let his feet lag crossing the hall while Mali was playing a gramophone or a tape-recorder or displaying to his friend a polaroid camera or one or other of the hundred things he'd brought with him, which had included a wrapped package for Jagan. Grace had pressed it into his hands with: 'Father, this is for you.' It was a pale yellow casket with compartments containing spoons, forks and knives. He had examined it, turned it round in his hand and said, 'Beautiful! But what is it?'

45

Grace replied, 'It's a picnic hamper. Mali thought you would appreciate it.'

'Of course, it's welcome,' Jagan had said, wondering how one used it, and locked it up in his almirah.

Mali never wore a *dhoti* at home, but a pair of dark trousers over a white shirt and always had his feet in slippers. He hardly ever left his room or visited any part of the house. He seldom went out: if he did, he waited for darkness to descend on the town and then, dressed elaborately in socks, shoes, jacket and tie, stepped out in the company of Grace and strolled up a deserted part of New Extension Road, but never in the direction of the statue or Market Road. He carried himself like a celebrity avoiding the attention of the rabble.

One morning, Grace parted the mustard-coloured curtain which divided the house into two sections, came into Jagan's quarters, and tidied them up. He was not used to being helped and felt uneasy while his roll of mat was shaken and put away, and his pillow of hard cotton patted. She washed the vessels in his kitchen and arranged them neatly on a shelf. His protests went unheeded. She clutched the broom and raked every corner of the floor, saying, 'Father, you think I mind it? I don't. I must not forget that I'm an Indian daughter-in-law.'

Jagan did not know what to say in reply and mumbled, 'That's true indeed.' She was stooping and scrubbing the ancient granite sink in the kitchen at floor level, tucking up her sari (which she had learnt to wear), exposing her ivory hued kneecap. Jagan could not take his eyes off that ivory patch as he protested, 'Oh, Grace, Grace, you must not. I'm not used to it. Don't you bother yourself. I believe in doing all my work myself.'

'And I believe in not letting you do it, that's all,' she said. 'I like to work. What else should I be doing all day?'

Jagan, who had been in the puja room before the gods, was now following Grace about, turning the rosary between his fingers. He said, 'What will people think if they see a modern girl, brought up in New York, doing all this drudgery? Mali may not like it.'

'It's not his business anyway,' she said. 'He is writing letters, and I'm doing the house, that's all. This is the loveliest house I have ever seen in my life.'

'Don't you find it musty and old?'

'No, it's lovely. I've always dreamt of living in a house like this.'

Nowadays he left home late, as he had got into the habit of waiting for Grace. He was getting used to the extreme air of orderliness that the feminine touch imparted to one's surroundings.

One day Grace said, 'I wish you would let me cook for you.'

'Oh, that is impossible. I'm under a vow about that.'

He explained how he ate to live only on what he could cook with his own hands.

Grace cried, 'Oh, you sound thrilling!' This was the first time someone had had a good word to say about his habits. Encouraged by her enthusiasm, he expatiated on his own creations of salt-free and sugar-free food, and concluded by saying that she should really look forward to reading his book when Truth Printing let it out of the press. She said ecstatically, 'I'm sure it's going to be a best-seller.'

At the earliest chance he inquired, feeling very awkward, 'What did Mali . . . ? I mean, what I want to ask is, has he finished his studies and acquired a degree in America?'

Grace looked up from a vessel she was scrubbing, and asked, 'Why, didn't you know?'

Jagan, feeling that he must cover up his relationship with his son and not betray the actual state of affairs, said, 'I've had no time actually to talk to Mali about all these matters, and so . . .'

'Yes, yes, I understand,' Grace said. 'Still, he ought to have told you.'

'Oh, no,' cried Jagan. 'Don't take it that way. I am not complaining . . .'

'Of course not,' she agreed. 'I still say that Mali should have told you. Suppose I tell him to speak to you about it; it is pretty important, you know. Unless he talks to you, what can he plan, really?'

'Yes, I was also thinking that. I'd like to know his plans.'

'You will, you will . . .' she said.

Jagan said, 'I thought he would mention something in his letters, but, you know, I only learnt a great deal about your country from them.'

At this she rose to her feet with a peal of laughter, and said,

'Oh, oh, Father, Father, get me one of the letters and I will tell you . . .'

'What?' Jagan asked, rather puzzled. 'What do you mean?'

'Have you any of those letters? I will explain . . .'

He went to his favourite cupboard and took out a cardboard box in which all the blue letters had been neatly treasured, and riffled through the lot. 'Here they are; I do not know which one you want to see.' He was still hesitant, being averse to letting anyone touch these valuable documents, but he could not say so to Grace.

'Wow! What a lot!' she exclaimed, and pulled out a letter at random. 'Ah, here it is!' She pointed to the signature at the end. 'Can you read this?'

Jagan fumbled for his glasses, put them on, and read aloud. ' "G M", is it?'

'Surely, didn't you notice it before? I thought you knew, "G M" is Grace and Mali, that's me and him, after we . . . we . . .' She tailed off. 'I composed all those letters, though both of us signed them.'

'You wrote them?' Jagan said, gulping down the saliva in his awkwardness. 'How should I know? I never even knew that you were there.'

'Didn't Mali ever write to you himself?'

Jagan remained silent. This was not going to do anyone any good; he silently prayed to Gandhi's spirit to forgive the lie he was about to utter. 'Yes, yes, but I did not know these letters were yours.'

'What did Mali have to say about me? Were you shocked?'

'He didn't describe you. How can one write about a person fully? Words after all convey so little; that's why I thought he was taking up a very difficult line when he said he wanted to be a writer . . .' He was rambling on thus when Grace put away her mop and brooms, came up, and sat down by his side, dangling her legs down the steps of the courtyard. 'I didn't gather much about you from him,' He let his clumsy imagination soar. 'He only wrote that he was going to marry. I didn't know much about you; even now I don't know much about you except that you are a good girl.'

'That is all one should bother about, don't you think? Why should we ask or know more?'

Jagan did not like to let this opportunity slip and said, 'It is a custom in this country to inquire where one was born and bred and who is who generally, and then we go on to other things.'

'Only the passport and income-tax people ask for such details in other countries. However, since I am an Indian now, I might as well get used to things and tell you something. My mother was a Korean and my father was an American soldier serving in the Far East after the Second World War. I was born in New Jersey when my father went on home leave and took my mother along; he was recalled while my mother was still confined, and . . .' She remained silent for a moment and said, 'He never came home again. My mother decided to stay in America and I studied at Margaret's. Have you heard of it?'

'No,' Jagan said. 'What is it?'

'A girls' school. How I adore the memory of it!'

'Must be a good place,' Jagan said. It was his habit to pick up tit-bits of American information and build on them.

'I studied Domestic Science at Michigan and met Mo when he came there for his Creative Writing course. We sat side by side at a football game. Oh, you must see the football matches in Michigan; have you such things here?'

'Yes, yes, we have football too. All the schoolboys play it.'

'I thought he must have written to you all about it.'

'Yes, yes, but you know sometimes letters get lost. The other day I heard a friend complaining to the postmaster that his letters never reach him properly . . .'

'You are happy, aren't you?' she asked suddenly. Jagan nodded.

She said, 'I had heard so much about the caste system in this country, I was afraid to come here, and when I first saw you all at the railway station I shook with fear. I thought I might not be accepted. Mo has really been wonderful, you know. It was very courageous of him to bring me here.'

'Well, we don't believe in caste these days, you know,' Jagan said generously. 'Gandhi fought for its abolition.'

'Is it gone now?' she asked innocently.

'It's going,' Jagan said, sounding like a politician. 'We don't think of it nowadays,' hoping that the girl would not cross-examine him further.

*

Mali suddenly dashed into Jagan's presence one day to ask, 'Can't you get a telephone for the house?'

Jagan said, 'I've not thought of it.'

'Yes, that's it. This is awkward and backward. How can we do any business without a telephone?'

Jagan wanted to say, 'After all, Malgudi is a small town; everyone is within shouting distance.'

'Even in your business,' Mali went on, 'if you had a telephone, more business would flow in. People might order by telephone.'

Jagan merely said, 'I've not thought of it,' while he wanted to reply, 'My daily sale is such and such even without a telephone, which shows that when one wants to eat sweets one doesn't wait for a telephone.'

The boy said, 'I felt embarrassed because I could not give my associates a telephone number.'

'Who are your associates? What's the association?'

'Grace!' Mali called. 'Will you join us? We are discussing business now.'

Jagan was seized with a cold dread at the prospect of a business discussion with Mali, although pleased that after all Mali was going to talk to him. He was in one of his rare moods of communication. Jagan could see by the deliberate manner in which Grace kept herself in the background that she must have been responsible for this meeting. Mali suggested, 'Father, let us adjourn to the hall. We have chairs there.' Jagan was getting ready to leave for his shop, but thought it worthwhile to postpone his routine. Nowadays, with one thing and another, his time-table was getting slightly upset.

Jagan obediently trooped behind his son and took his seat in the hall, where he had not stepped for many weeks now. He noticed that Grace had transformed the place with curtains, mats, tablecloth. A couple of modern paintings hung on the walls: Jagan found them bewildering, but said 'Yes' when Grace asked, 'Aren't they marvellous?' The bamboo chairs were piled with coloured cushions. A little vase on a table held a sprig of margosa leaves. Jagan's heart throbbed at the sight. He said, 'Margosa is the ambrosia mentioned in our *vedas*, did you know that, Grace?'

She almost hugged the flower-vase and cried, 'How grand! How did they know? They know all about everything in the *vedas*, don't they?'

50

'Of course they do, all the *vedas* have emanated from God's feet.'

'Ah, what a conception!' Grace cried. She found everything thrilling. Everything stirred in her some poetic feeling, deep within.

Mali cautioned her, 'Don't start swallowing margosa leaves, my dear.'

Jagan said, 'No harm in it. It is a natural antiseptic, purifies the blood, supplies iron . . .' His eyes lit up when he spoke of margosa leaves. 'I've explained it in detail in my book. When you read it, you will understand better . . .' Grace was now readjusting the flowers in the vase with a deliberate interest, as if she were privileged to handle ambrosia as a result of marrying an Indian.

It was a long time since Jagan had observed his son's face at close quarters. Now he noticed that the freshness and the glow of foreignness that he had possessed when he arrived was gone; he looked even a shade below par. He had not re-acquired the taste for South Indian food, but seemed to be eating his meals out of hermetically sealed tins. Jagan repressed his remarks on this subject, although he sadly noted that Mali's eyes were dark-ringed. What was he worrying about? Jagan patiently waited for the other to speak. He noticed that Mali wore socks under his sandals, and wanted to cry out, 'Socks should never be worn, because they are certain to heat the blood through interference with the natural radiation which occurs through one's soles, and also because you insulate yourself against beneficial magnetic charges of the earth's surface. I have argued in my book that this is one of the reasons, a possible reason, for heart attacks in European countries . . .' While he was busy with these thoughts, he was also dimly aware that Mali had been talking. He had been aware of the sound, but he had missed the substance of the words. He had anticipated this meeting for a long time and he realized now with a shudder that he had probably missed the opportunity of a lifetime. He woke up with a start and became extra-attentive, bending to the task all his powers of concentration, as Mali was concluding his passage with, 'You get it?' Jagan was at a loss whether to say 'yes' or 'no', but sat staring ahead and making noncommittal sounds in his throat.

'Well, think over it; you have all the data,' said Mali. Then he glanced at his watch and rose muttering, 'I must check at the rail station about my unaccompanied baggage, expected today; if only we had a telephone . . .' He went to the door, turned to Grace and said, 'Don't wait for lunch.' They heard his scooter palpitating away.

Jagan sat still, quietly enjoying the thought that his son had spoken to him at such length. When he rose to go, Grace held the door open for him and asked, 'Did you have any questions for Mali? Was everything clear?'

Jagan replied, 'I can always go back to the subject, can't I?' with a significant smile, and Grace said, 'Of course.'

————

Chapter Six

The cousin nowadays found Jagan rather hesitant about speaking of his son, but on the theory that conversation must go on he said, 'Did you hear that there was a fight at the market? The jaggery merchant as usual was cornering the stock; and . . .'

Jagan, seated on his throne, with the flavour of frying ghee filling the hall, said, 'Our merchants are becoming heartless.'

'You just wait and see what's going to happen to the rice dealers; they are playing with fire.'

'Even when one wants to make profits, one should retain some sense of service. I have not raised the price here, in spite of the sugar crisis.'

'Oh, everybody is not you,' the cousin flattered, giving a soft back-stroke to his tuft. Flattery was his accredited business in life; even when he joked and disparaged it was all a part of his flattery. He said, 'You are not one who knows how to make money. If you were unscrupulous, you could have built many mansions, who knows?'

'And what would one do with many mansions?' asked Jagan and quoted a Tamil verse which said that even if eighty million ideas float across your mind, you cannot wear more than four cubits of cloth or eat more than a little measure of rice at a time.

'Ah!' jeered the cousin genially, stuffing a piece of tobacco into his mouth, 'that's why I say that you do not know the art of living and flourishing, and yet the Goddess of Wealth chooses you for her favours!'

Jagan laughed happily, and, feeling that now the other deserved a little dose of information about Mali, said, 'I came late this morning because Mali wanted to discuss his plans.' He was very proud of being able to mention something so concrete about his son. The cousin became alert and sat up attentively in order not to miss a word. Jagan paused after the announcement and the cousin filled the momentary gap with, 'I had a glimpse of him this morning on a scooter. Has he bought one?'

'It's a friend's, I hear. He must have a conveyance.'

'Who could that friend be?' the cousin speculated. 'Scooter-riding boys – one is that kerosene agent's son; another is the man who has come from the Punjab to establish a button factory. Another scooter belongs to the District Judge's nephew – you know, that young man in the Public Works Department in charge of the new roads in the hills.'

'Boys must have their own vehicles nowadays; they don't like to walk,' generalized Jagan. 'I always like to move on my feet, but these are days of speed; people must go from place to place quickly. They have more to do than we had, don't you think so? Mali has never fancied walking. He has always cycled. I bought him his first cycle when he was seven years old, and he could go wherever he pleased. I sometimes found that he would cycle up to Ellaman Street, not in the least minding the crowd on Market Road.'

'Even adults shy away from Market Road in the evenings.'

'But that boy grew up fearlessly, full of self-reliance at an age when other boys were being mollycoddled.'

'But poor boy, his mother was so ailing.'

'That's another reason why I tried to keep his mind diverted.'

The dialogue was rambling off into a series of side issues. The cousin tried to pull it back to the main theme. 'You were starting to tell me about Mali's plans. You must be feeling relieved now.'

'Yes, yes, but I always knew that everything must be going well, with nothing to bother about.'

'Now, have you any idea of his plans?'

'Yes. He was in a hurry to go to the railway station this morning, and he could give me only a general idea. Of course, he'll tell us the details later.' This was the utmost Jagan could essay without betraying his ignorance.

The cousin asked abruptly, 'Are you in favour of his scheme?'

'Which scheme?' Jagan asked, looking surprised. He hadn't suspected any scheme. The cousin paused for a second, while the noise of school breaking up next door enlivened the air. A group of children as usual hung about the front stall gazing at the sweets arranged on trays. 'Captain, don't allow crowds to stand there; they obstruct the traffic.' Traffic was not Jagan's real concern – there were many obstructions on Market Road: a couple of cows belonging to a milk-seller always stood in the centre of the road in their off-hours, not to speak of a rogue bull, belonging to no one in particular, which sometimes chased the cows amorously, scattering the pedestrians, *jutkas* and cycles alike on to the steps of the shops; there were groups from villages, bringing in grain and fruit to the market, who sat on the edge of Market Road in a circle, overflowing onto the middle; cycles and bullock-carts and automobiles threaded their way through without damage to themselves or to others. No one protested or bothered, but Jagan always mentioned the word 'obstruction' because the sight of the children at the counter made him uneasy, even guilty at times. He preferred them to go away without looking at the sweets so hungrily. It was his habit to call out the captain and issue an order whenever he felt any sort of mental strain.

The cousin now realized that the word 'scheme' had set up an agitation in Jagan's mind; he watched Jagan's face with satisfaction. Jagan's studied avoidance of the subject of his son had not been to the cousin's liking. It made him feel that he had been suddenly converted into an outsider; he didn't like the status, and so here he found an opportunity to bring himself back into the fold. 'I didn't want to speak to you unnecessarily about it, but I'm so happy that the boy still calls me "Uncle" whenever he meets me; although he has travelled to the other end of the earth, he has not forgotten his uncle. You see, I didn't like to thrust myself on him after his return home. People change, you know, especially when they go abroad. I know of a foreign-returned I.C.S. officer who disowned his parents when they came to meet him at the railway station.'

'Horrible fellow, he must have been mad! Mali could not be in the least like him.'

'I know, I know; that's what I am telling you. I went to the Registrar's house last week, and Mali was talking to his son. You know their house in the New Extension? I'd gone there because I'd promised to find a suitable cook for them; the lady is not in good health. I have to do various things for various persons.'

'The Registrar's son and Mali are friends, I suppose?'

'Oh, yes, they were conversing on the front verandah. As I passed in, Mali himself addressed me. "Give me a few minutes before you go." "Yes, Mali," I said. "I'm at your service." After finishing my business inside, I came out and Mali said, "I'll walk with you." '

'Did he want to walk? I thought he never cared to walk.'

'Only up to the gate, because he did not like to let his friends overhear what he wanted to say.'

'What did he say?' Jagan asked, now completely at the mercy of the cousin.

'He wants to manufacture story-writing machines,' said the cousin.

Jagan felt so baffled by this statement that he couldn't phrase his surprise properly. He blurted out a couple of questions incoherently and lapsed into silence.

The cousin watched his face, relishing the bewilderment he saw in it, and said with an innocent look, 'Haven't you heard of story-writing machines?' as if they were an article of daily use. This was a minor victory for him in the matter of American knowledge. Jagan felt it best to acknowledge defeat and give up all pretence. The cousin rubbed it in by saying, 'I thought he would have told you everything. What else was he telling you this morning?'

Jagan said loftily, 'We had other things to talk about. He was telling me of other matters.'

'But this proposition is uppermost in his mind; he is thinking of it night and day.'

'Yes, yes,' said Jagan, 'I knew of course that he was speaking about a machine, but something else came up before I could ask him to explain.'

'This is not just an ordinary machine,' said the cousin.

At this moment Jagan let out his periodic shout: 'Captain! Why is there a crowd?' but the cousin continued in a tone of authority, 'Now listen carefully. This story-writing machine, as you might have guessed, is a story-writing machine.'

'How does it do that?' asked Jagan, genuinely surprised.

'Don't ask me,' said the cousin, 'I am not an engineer. Mali constantly used the word "electronic" or "electric" or something like that, and explained it at length. It sounds very interesting; why don't you ask him? I am sure he will be able to explain it to you satisfactorily.'

Jagan bided his time and the next morning when Grace came in to clean his kitchen, applied for an interview. 'I want to talk to Mali; is he free?'

'Of course,' she said, 'if he isn't, he will free himself for your sake.' She paused and then heard the clatter of a typewriter from Mali's room. 'He is busy, I think,' she added. 'I will tell him.' She went up and came out a few minutes later with an air of importance. 'He will see you in fifteen minutes.'

For a moment Jagan felt as if he were a petitioner in his own house, and there flashed across his mind those far-off days when Mali used to stand at his door, cringing for some concession or for cash, and for a brief second he was aghast at the transformations that had come with time. 'I have to be off myself,' he said to redress the balance of importance, but Grace went back to her work in the kitchen without a reply. Unable to make up his mind, he idly opened a cupboard and stood gazing at the old bottles and packing paper that he had preserved on the theory of keeping a thing for seven years.

Grace said from the kitchen, 'Another day I will clean up that cupboard for you. We need to do some spring-cleaning in this house.'

Jagan, aghast at the implications, said with some intensity, 'Don't do anything yet.' Meanwhile the typewriter ceased and a bell sounded, and Grace said, 'He is ready for you. You want to go in?' She seemed to have built up Mali into a celebrity. She led him forward. 'He is very methodical, you know.'

Jagan was pleased and baffled at the same time. He gritted himself for the interview. He glanced at the clock on the wall and muttered, 'Must be going in fifteen minutes.'

Jagan took the visitor's chair, looked for a moment at his son and plunged into the subject straight away. 'How exactly does the story-machine operate?'

'I explained it to you yesterday,' said Mali.

'There were some points which I did not quite grasp, but I was in a hurry.'

The son looked pityingly at him, rose, opened a packing case, pushed aside a lot of brown paper and thread and lifted out a small object which looked like a radio cabinet and placed it on the table. 'I was only waiting for this to arrive; yesterday I had to clear it from the railway office. What a lot of time is wasted here! I have never seen a more wasteful country than this.' Jagan refrained from retorting, 'We find it quite adequate for our purpose.' Now Mali stood beside the cabinet in the attitude of a lecturer; he patted it fondly and said, 'With this machine anyone can write a story. Come nearer, and you will see it working.' Jagan obediently pushed his chair back, rose and stood beside his son, who seemed to tower above him. He felt proud of him. 'God knows what he eats out of those tins; he looks tired, no doubt, but how well grown he is!' he reflected as Mali explained, 'You see these four knobs? One is for characters, one for plot situations, one for climax, and the fourth is built on the basis that a story is made up of character, situations, emotion and climax, and by the right combination . . .' He interrupted his oration for a moment to pull a drawer out and glance at a cyclostyled sheet of paper; he shut the drawer and came back to say, 'You can work on it like a typewriter. You make up your mind about the number of characters. It works on a transistor and ordinary valves. Absolutely fool-proof. Ultimately we are going to add a little fixture, by which any existing story could be split up into components and analysed; the next model will incorporate it.'

Jagan asked, 'Do you want to use this for writing stories?'

'Yes, I am also going to manufacture and sell it in this country. An American company is offering to collaborate. In course of time, every home in the country will possess one and we will produce more stories than any other nation in the world. Now we are a little backward. Except for *Ramayana* and *Mahabharata*, those old stories, there is no modern writing, whereas in America alone every publishing season ten thousand books are published.' He rushed back to his desk-drawer and gazed on the cyclostyled sheet again before repeating, 'Yes, ten thousand titles. It is a "must" for every home; all a writer will have to do is to own one and press the keys, and he will get the formula in a moment, on a roll of paper, from which he can build up the rest . . .'

Jagan left his seat and went over to examine the machine as if it were something from another planet. He approached it so cautiously that Mali said, 'Touch it and see for yourself.' Jagan peered at the apparatus closely and read the headings: 'Characters: good, bad neutral. Emotions: love, hate, revenge, devotion, pity. Complexities, characters, incidents, accidents. Climax: placement and disposal and conclusion.' It looked pretty, its mahogany veneer was grained; its keys were green, red and yellow to indicate the different categories. 'How can one write a story with it?' Jagan asked.

'Exactly as one does with a typewriter,' Mali answered, and Jagan admired him for the fund of information he had gathered on the subject.

Just at this moment, Grace came in, stood beside them and said, 'Isn't he clever?' in a jocular manner. Jagan could not answer her immediately, his mind was too full of confusion and questions. He felt hemmed in: the room had lost its original appearance and looked like an office in a foreign country. What was Mali trying to do? What was his own part in all this activity? What was going to be the nature of his involvement? He said with some trepidation, 'Grace, do you know that our ancestors never even wrote the epics? They composed the epics and recited them, and the great books lived thus from generation to generation by the breath of people . . .'

Before he could proceed further, Mali said with a gesture of disgust, 'Oh, these are not the days of your ancestors. Today we have to compete with advanced countries not only in economics and industry, but also in culture.' While on the one hand Jagan felt delighted at the way his son seemed to be blossoming after years of sullen silence, he was at the same time saddened by the kind of development he noticed in him now. The boy went on, 'If you have the time, I'd like to explain to you one or two other points.' Jagan helplessly glanced at a travelling clock on Mali's table, and jingled the keys of his shop in the depths of his *jibba* pocket. 'Ultimately, you may have to give up your sweet-making and work in our business. I'll give you a nice air-conditioned room with a couple of secretaries.'

Jagan had never known his son talk so fluently; he wished secretly that he would speak differently. He felt the time had come for him to ask his questions. 'Do they write all their stories with this machine in America?' he asked as if he wished to fill a lacuna in his knowledge of that land and its civilization.

'Mostly, mostly,' said Mali.

'Most magazines,' added Grace, 'are nowadays switching over to the machine in their fiction departments, and out of the best-sellers last year at least three were a product. The proposition is that we get American collaboration worth two hundred thousand dollars, provided we find fifty-one thousand to start the business.'

'Fifty-one thousand dollars would be the equivalent of . . .' began Jagan, starting the age-old calculation.

'Work it out yourself,' said Mali with a touch of irritation in his voice. 'Let me first finish my sentence. They will be responsible for the know-how and technical personnel, help us set up the plant, run it for six months and then quit; they will also provide us with promotional material.' What a lot of new expressions the boy had learnt, Jagan reflected with admiration, while Mali added, 'We shall have to collect forty-nine thousand dollars by public subscription, and then the controlling stock will be in our hands.'

Jagan had thought till then that his son was a moron. He looked for a brief second at Grace and asked, 'What was your subject in the college?'

She answered, 'I've told you I post-graduated in Domestic Economy at Michigan.'

'Why go into all that now?' asked Mali.

Jagan said, rising, 'I was wondering if Grace had also studied business subjects.' And now it was Mali's turn to wonder why his father said that.

Jagan left without further comment. At four-thirty when the cousin arrived, he told him, 'Have you any idea what fifty-thousand dollars is in rupees?'

The cousin said, 'A little over two lakhs of rupees.'

'How do you know?'

'By a simple calculation and I also verified it yesterday when I met Dodhaji, our banker, after I left Mali.'

'Two lakhs!' mused Jagan. 'Where does one find it?'

'In your bank-book,' said the cousin promptly in a jocular way.

'Are people under the impression that I have amassed wealth?'

'Yes, of course, although everyone admires your simple living and high-thinking habits.'

'How can wealth accumulate with the price of foodstuff standing where it is? I just keep up the business so that these poor fellows may not be thrown out of employment, that's all.'

'That everybody knows,' said the cousin. 'Are you interested in buying raisins? I saw a fresh stock arrive at the *sait*'s shop, handpicked quality.'

'Have you asked the cook?'

'He told me that he needed them because I found the *sohan papdi* rather tame without raisins today.'

Jagan cried furiously, 'Is that so? Why didn't he tell me?'

The cousin said, 'You didn't come in time, that's all, and he couldn't wait for the stuff. Why do you get upset?'

'It's because I do not like the idea of cheating my customers.

Do you realize that the price for the customer remains the same with or without raisins?'

'And your own margin of profit is improved,' said the cousin. Jagan glared at him. The cousin added, 'You are a rare being, but that would be the line of thought of some of your compatriots in this city.'

Mollified, Jagan said, with a touch of pride, 'I was held up by Mali, poor boy. I have to give him the time he needs now and then; otherwise there is bound to be a lot of misunderstanding. His ideas turn on big figures nowadays. He seems to have learnt many things in America.'

'He wants me to use my influence to sell the shares of the company.'

This was a relief to Jagan. 'I'm sure many people will be interested in the proposal.'

'Including your good self.'

'No harm in finding five or ten along with the rest.'

'Mali's idea is different. He has reserved five or ten for people outside, and counts on you for the fifty-one thousand dollars for a start.'

'And you have found its rupee equivalent?'

'About two and a half lakhs.'

'Where does one find it?'

'I've already indicated.'

'Does Mali think so?'

'Of course, and he also says he knows where you keep cash not sent to the bank.'

'He says so, does he?' said Jagan, laughing within himself at the fact that he had changed the venue of the immaculate cash. 'Money is an evil,' he added with great feeling.

The cousin said, 'Shall I ask the front-stall boy to throw away that bronze jug?'

They both laughed at the joke, but the relaxation was short-lived for Jagan. He became very serious suddenly and said, 'I hope you will find an occasion to tell my son that I have not got all that money.'

'Now you are both on speaking terms, why don't you tell him yourself?'

Jagan sighed and said, 'I do not wish to spoil his mood.'

*

The tempo of Mali's demand increased. Though at one time Jagan had sighed for a word from his son, he now wished that the thaw had not occurred.

He was being hunted. When he passed in and out of the house he felt his steps were being watched, his face being secretly studied for a yes or no. Grace gazed at his face meaningfully. Mali, if he was at home, kept on coming into his quarters on some excuse or other. After the first day's demonstration Jagan had studiously avoided all literary topics. 'Here is a scheme to make me a bankrupt,' he said to himself whenever he heard footfalls approaching his room. 'Fifty-one thousand dollars! I am not growing over-fond of money, but I'm not prepared to squander it. Why should we want stories or machines for writing them?'

One morning Mali stood at the doorway of the puja room after breakfast, in blue pants, with his hands resting on the top of the threshold as Jagan sat before his gods. 'They do everything with machines nowadays. Washing machines, have you seen one?'

'No,' said Jagan, trying to cut all mechanical references to a minimum.

'Grinding, powdering or calculating – nowadays one uses electricity for everything.' Behind him stood Grace, adding, 'Even for mending pencils we have machines.'

'We should have brought one with us,' Mali said, turning to her. Mali, who never used to seek him before, was now intruding even into the privacy of his puja room, interrupting his prayers. Jagan met this disturbance passively by shutting his eyes and muttering some incantations until Grace said, 'We should not disturb his prayers.' Prayer was a sound way of isolating oneself – but sooner or later it ended: one could not go on praying eternally, though one ought to.

He had become rather sneaky nowadays. Soon after his prayers, he tiptoed to the kitchen to prepare his salt-free food, bolt it down, put on his *khadi jibba* and slip away with the least noise, but he always found Grace at the passage ready to open the door for him with some remark about the weather or politics, gazing on his face with an unmistakable inquiry about his views on the machine. He was amazed at the intensity of her interest in Mali's fortunes. As ever, he had two opposite feelings: appreciation of her interest in Mali and resentment at her effort to involve him in their business. Mali never thrust himself forward more than a minimum; he seemed to have left the task to Grace; even his visitation at the threshold of the puja room in the morning seemed to have been dictated by Grace. An occasional misgiving tainted Jagan's thoughts – might not Grace's interest, friendliness and attentiveness be a calculated effort to win his dollars? Walking to his shop with head lowered in thought, as the vagrant at the statue corner greeted him and begged for money, Jagan paused to ask, for the hundredth time in a year, 'You are sturdy; why don't you seek work?'

'When have I the time, master? By the time I have gone round begging and returned here the day is over . . .'

Jagan tossed a five-paise coin at him as he remembered an ancient injunction: 'Perform thy charity without question.'

In appreciation the beggar said, 'Master does not tell me much about America nowadays. Why?'

'Because I have told you all you should know.'

'What's the little master doing?' asked the beggar.

'Well, he'll be starting a factory soon,' replied Jagan, without conviction.

'What'll he make?'

'Some machinery,' Jagan said, not wishing to elaborate and wishing the beggar would leave him alone. Fortunately he slipped off to pester some other person coming in the opposite direction, and Jagan quickened his pace. Passing Truth Printing, he spied Nataraj alone at his desk and on an impulse stopped to ask, 'I hope you have not forgotten my work?'

'How could I?' said Nataraj. 'As soon as the pressure of the seasonal printing lessens, yours will be the first. I'm your family printer, you know. Your son has given me an urgent work which he wants in three days, the prospectus for his new enterprise.'

'Ah!' cried Jagan. The 'scheme' seemed to dog his steps.

'Your name is in it!' said Nataraj.

'Ah! ah!' exclaimed Jagan.

Nataraj pushed up his roll-top and produced a proof sheet and Jagan saw his name in print as one of the principal promoters of Mali Enterprises. The others in the list were Grace and a few of Mali's scooter-riding friends. Nataraj studied his face and said, 'Why, aren't you pleased?'

Jagan replied in a hollow tone, 'Yes, yes, no doubt.'

'Seems to be an interesting new kind of enterprise . . .'

'Yes, yes, no doubt.'

He hurriedly left for his shop. As the cook stood before him taking instructions for the day, he feared he too might begin to speak of the story-writing machine, but luckily this man's universe of kitchen smoke and frying oil had not lost its insularity yet. Occupying his throne, with the scent of incense and frying, Jagan recovered a little bit of his sense of security. He opened the drawer and let his eyes rest on the copy of the *Bhagavad Gita* for a while, opened a page at random and tried to get absorbed in its eternal message, but part of his mind was deeply injured by the sight of his own name in print on the prospectus. How could Mali perpetrate such a deed, take so much for granted? But the poor boy probably had complete confidence in his father's support, and there was nothing heinous in that. It was natural. Still, he should at least have had the courtesy to mention it to him. Neither Grace nor Mali . . . But perhaps they had only been hanging about his puja room to inform him of that rather than ask for capital; and he blamed himself for not giving them a chance.

Whoever was the American associate, he had done his coaching perfectly; and Nataraj proved extraordinarily prompt. The city was soon flooded with the prospectus of Mali's company. The first one came by post to Jagan himself at his shop. It went into the cultural shortcomings of the country, and the need for it to take its place in the comity of nations, and how this machine was going to cut time and distance, and lift the country out of its rut, and then followed many facts and figures. One thing Jagan noted was that the jungles on Mempi Hills would provide the soft wood required for some part of the machine, and so it could be had for a song. Then they went into details of production and marketing and location. Jagan now realized that the son of the kerosene agent was actually the economic brain behind the whole show – a young fellow in jeans and striped shirt, who rode a scooter and carried Mali on the pillion.

Very soon they abandoned the scooter and were seen moving about in an old automobile. Grace explained to Jagan one morning, 'The company have now made a start with an automobile. Although it's an old one, it is useful. One has to move about so much on business, nowadays.'

'What car is it? It looks green,' said Jagan, out of the polite need to say something, and not wishing to ask, 'What is its price? Who has paid for it?'

Grace replied, 'It's pretty, isn't it?' and Jagan lapsed into meditation before the gods, and remained in meditation until she moved away from the threshold and he could hear her talking to Mali in the front portion of the house.

'Gandhi has taught me peaceful methods, and that's how I'm going to meet their demand. These two are bent upon involving me in all sorts of things,' he reflected. He was bewildered by his son's scheme and distrusted it totally. He was aware that pressure was being subtly exercised on him to make him part with his cash. He was going to meet the situation by ignoring the whole business; a sort of non-violent non-co-operation.

But he found his domestic life irksome. He had lost the quiet joy of anticipation he used to experience whenever he turned the Statue Corner. He felt nervous as he approached the ancient house. The expectant stare of Grace when she opened the door and the significant side-glances of Mali got on his nerves. He was aware of a silent tension growing. He felt happy if nobody came when he turned the key in the door, at the times when both were away, Grace shopping and Mali with his local associates in his green car. 'Thank God,' Jagan thought, 'for the green car.' When he was in, if he heard them open the front door, he retreated far into the backyard of the house or sometimes even locked himself in the bathing shack.

But the state of non-co-operation could not last for ever. Grace asked him one morning point-blank, 'Have you thought over the proposition?'

Jagan felt cornered – if he had just picked up his upper cloth a minute earlier, he could have reached the street by now. Grace had studied his movements and timed her interception perfectly. He had dodged this encounter for two weeks by sheer manoeuvring of arrival and departure. Now he felt trapped. He wanted to say, 'Leave these questions for menfolk to settle; keep away, charmer from Outer Mongolia or somewhere.' She had stuck a flower with a pin in her bobbed hair and he longed to tell her, 'Take off that flower, it's ridiculous.' He merely remarked, 'I see you have jasmine in your hair this morning.'

'As it's a Friday, I have remembered my duties as a Hindu wife. I have also washed the doorsteps and decorated the threshold with white flour. I went to a shop yesterday to get it. See what I have done!' She was so importunate that he had to look cheerful and follow her out. She pointed at a floral design on the ground and cried, 'Don't you believe now that I could have been a Hindu in my last life? I am able to bend down and draw the design on the floor as I see a lot of others do.'

Jagan wanted to say, 'An orthodox Hindu woman would never clip her hair as you have done,' but actually remarked, 'It's a long time since anyone attended to these things in this house. How did you know that Friday is auspicious?'

'I have friends who tell me what is proper,' she said.

Just as Jagan was thinking of slipping away, a window opened, and Mali peeped out and commanded, 'Father, come in for a moment. I must talk to you.' Jagan felt that Grace had only been holding him in a trap and scowled at her accusingly, but she merely said as though she were the usherette at a Presidential interview, 'Certainly, go in,' suggesting that he should feel honoured at the summons.

Muttering, 'I have to go and open the shop,' Jagan went in.

Mali was at his desk and flourished a finger towards the visitors' chair. Jagan lowered himself into it gingerly, still muttering, 'I must go and open the shop.'

Mali ignored his plea and asked, 'Have you thought it over?'

'What?' asked Jagan, trying to look absent-minded, but he knew he was not bringing it off successfully, for Mali, with Grace sneaking up behind, as if to complete the trapping operation, held him in a pincer movement. Mali tossed a prospectus at him. 'I mailed you one, didn't you get it?'

Jagan said neither yes nor no; there was danger in either statement. His mind wandered off in another direction: how could Nataraj have managed to issue this piece of work so quickly from his press, while his own book had remained untouched for so many years? What charm did Mali exercise? As he sat brooding on it, Mali suddenly said, 'You don't even care to look at it.'

Jagan feared that the season of sweet temper was coming to a close, and replied mildly, 'I have looked at it, and I have also noticed that you have put my name in without even telling me.'

'What is happening to you? On the very first day I spoke to you, I spent over thirty minutes in explanations; I asked if I might print your name and didn't you say "Go ahead"?'

Jagan cast his mind back. 'What day was that?'

Mali's temper had now risen. Grace saw the symptoms and stepped in to say, 'On the very first day when he told you about his scheme.'

'Oh, yes, yes,' said Jagan, realizing that he might have said anything at any time. He added mildly, 'Yes, but I naturally thought you would tell me again before actually going to the press, you know.'

'I really do not know what you mean. You expect everything to be said ten times; no wonder nothing gets done in this country.'

'Why do you blame the country for everything? It has been good enough for four hundred millions,' Jagan said, remembering the heritage of *Ramayana* and *Bhagavad Gita* and all the trials and sufferings he had undergone to win independence. He muttered, 'You were not born in those days.'

Mali made a gesture of despair. 'I do not know what you are talking about. I want to get on with the business. We had two long sessions, and I told you everything, and now . . .'

Grace interposed to say, 'Father, if you have any questions, I am sure Mali will answer them.'

Jagan felt, like a man in a witness-box, that anything he uttered might be used as evidence against him and so he said, 'I must be going now, I have to open the shop.'

Mali said, 'We have to make a beginning, our associates are waiting on us. We will lose everything unless we act at once. I have explained to you the basis of our participation.'

Fifty thousand dollars! Whatever its equivalent might be, it was a staggering sum. 'I am a poor man,' Jagan wailed, and immediately noticed the shock on Mali's face and the embarrassment he had created in the presence of Grace. It was as if he had uttered a bad word. Seeing this, Jagan said, 'Gandhi always advocated poverty and not riches.'

'And yet you earn your thousand rupees a day,' said Mali with a vicious smile.

'If you feel you can take up the business and run it, do so; it is yours if you want it.'

'You expect me to do that? I have better plans than to be a vendor of sweetmeats.'

Jagan did not wait to hear more. He pushed the chair back very slowly and gently, pausing for a second to study the faces of

67

the other two. For once he saw Grace's eyes unlit with a smile. It was impassive. 'Is she a good girl or a bad one?' Jagan asked within himself. 'I wish I could decide.' Mali was biting his thumbnail and kicking the foot-rest below the table. Jagan did not have the courage to stay and face him. Without another word he took his upper cloth off the hook and was out of the room in a moment. When he passed the culvert at the confluence, the vagrant said, 'My master does not even look at me nowadays.'

'I gave you five paise only . . .' He couldn't remember when, but he concluded, 'I am a poor man like you. Do you think I have inexhaustible cash?'

'Master should not say such a thing.'

At least this fellow spoke better than Mali in similar circumstances, who didn't want him if he did not claim to be a wealthy father!

He remained morose throughout the day. At four-thirty the cousin entered, went into the kitchen and came out. He knew that Jagan was waiting to spring some terrible information on him. Wiping his lips with the towel, he sat down on his stool, remarking, 'Chandra Kala (Digit of the Moon) tastes absolutely divine today, and if the reputation of this shop is going to shoot sky-high in this town, it will be on account of it.' As always, flattery helped; a few webs spread around Jagan's eyes and he said, 'It is purity that is important. Yesterday I came early to see that pure cow's butter was melted for frying. I won't touch buffalo butter, though it may be cheaper: Gandhi was opposed to buffalo products. I had sent one of the cooks to collect cow's butter from Koppal, he came back at five in the morning, and I came straight in before eight in order to melt it right. A fortune had been spent on it, and I didn't want to risk over-boiling it.'

'You pay attention to every detail. I have often wanted to ask you, why did you choose this business? Rather a specialized job, isn't it?'

'When I was in jail, I was given kitchen duties, and after coming out this seemed to me as good a business as any other.' He was slipping into a reminiscential mood, much to the relief of the cousin. 'But the reputation of the shop is all due to Sivaraman; but for him I don't know where I would be. I wanted to serve the public in my own way by making available pure sweets, particularly for poor children.'

'An excellent ideal,' said the cousin, deliberately refraining from the reminder that poor children were just the ones who could not afford to buy sweets. He said it another way: 'If the stuff is to be pure a price has to be paid for it.'

'That's true,' said Jagan. He sat brooding for a while and then announced, 'From tomorrow the price of everything will be reduced. I have made up my mind about it.'

'Why?' asked the cousin in consternation.

Jagan spurned an explanation. He just said, 'We buy provisions for, let us say, a hundred rupees a day, and the salaries of our staff and the rent amount to, let us say, a hundred,' he lowered his voice, 'and the stuff produced need not earn more than, let us say, two hundred in all. Now, the truth is . . .' he began but slurred over the details at the last minute, not wishing to reveal the actual figures. 'More people will benefit by a reduction.'

'But you are opposed to the eating of sugar, aren't you?'

Jagan took time to digest this contradiction before saying, 'I see no connection. If others want to eat sweets, they must have the purest ones, that is all. I am thinking particularly of children and poor people.'

'What about your share?' the other asked testingly.

'I have had enough,' Jagan said.

The cousin sought further explanation, like someone scrutinizing and assaying a tricky diplomatic statement. 'Enough of what?' he asked.

'Of everything,' Jagan said.

The cousin looked appropriately serious and gloomy. 'If you are thinking of retiring from the business I am sure someone will be willing to take it over and run it.'

'Oh, it is not so easy,' Jagan said. 'I told Mali so this morning and he said . . .' He remained silent. The recollection of the scene, he felt, would overwhelm him; he might break down and it would be silly to be seen in tears while he was occupying the throne. He had a mental picture of himself standing like a ragged petitioner in the presence of Mali and the Chinese girl, being sneered at for his business of a lifetime, a business that had provided the money for Mali to fly to America and do all sorts of things there. 'Vendor of sweetmeats', indeed! Jagan became aware of the cousin waiting for his reply and said quickly, 'He was not interested in vending sweets.'

The cousin felt that this was the time to sound sympathetic and said, 'What better income could one have? But, you see, his ideas are different, as you know.'

'Money is an evil,' Jagan said, uttering an oft-repeated sentiment. 'We should all be happier without it. It is enough if an activity goes on self-supported; no need to earn money, no need to earn money. Captain!' he shouted. 'Who are those boys? What do they want?'

'I will send them away, sir.'

'No, no, tell that boy at the counter to give them each a packet and then send them away.'

'They may not have the money.'

'Who cares? I can afford to give away. Boy,' he shouted from his throne, 'treat those children.' The children got their sweets and went away greatly surprised.

'If those boys go out and tell others, you will be mobbed and unable to leave the place.'

'We will manage, don't worry,' said Jagan. 'In a day or two some changes are coming.'

The cousin looked scared and said, 'Don't be hasty; go on a pilgrimage to the temples and bathe in the sacred rivers. I will mind the shop, if you like, while you are away.'

'I will tell you when I am ready.'

The boy from the front stall now brought in the bronze jug. The cousin, who usully timed his departure at this point, got up but did not leave, curious to know whether Jagan would accept the cash or just throw it out. Jagan pulled out the drawer, spread the folded towel to deaden the noise of the coins cascading down, looked up at the cousin and said, 'Tonight and tomorrow I will have to do a lot of reckoning with concentration. I have left things to drift too long.'

The cousin, worrying where these hints were leading, said, like the peace-maker he was, 'I will speak to Mali; I know I can talk to him. Even to that girl Grace; she is so trusting!'

'By all means, speak to him on any matter you like,' Jagan said and added with firmness, 'But not on my behalf.'

Chapter Seven

Two days later, coming at the usual time, the cousin found the shop entrance crowded. A placard hung from the counter: 'Any packet 25 paise.' There was such a clamour for the packets that the boy at the counter looked harried and exhausted. Old men, young men, children, beggars and labourers, everyone fell over each other with outstretched arms, and the trays were emptied as fast as they were filled from the kitchen. By five o'clock the entire stock of sweets for the day was exhausted. Sivaraman and the other cooks came out of the kitchen, stood before Jagan and asked, 'What do we do now?'

'Go home,' said Jagan. 'If the sweets have been sold, our work for the day is over.'

'I do not understand,' said Sivaraman, turning the golden bead at his throat. 'What has happened? What is all this for?'

'Let more people eat sweets, that is all. Aren't they happy?'

'Do you plan to close down?' asked Sivaraman, and his assistant said, 'At this rate, we will be swamped.'

'It will make no difference to you,' said Jagan. 'We shall reduce nothing, either in quantity or quality.'

'How? How can we?' asked Sivaraman.

Jagan could not easily explain what he was doing or why. The cousin, sitting on the stool, came to his rescue: 'We are only trying some new measures to meet the competition. I will explain it all to you tomorrow.' The cooks went away, and the shop emptied itself at six o'clock, the boy bringing in the bronze jug earlier than usual, saying, 'Still a crowd outside waiting, sir. They are angry that they are not getting anything today.'

'Tell them to come tomorrow.' They could hear the shouts of the crowd outside and the captain swearing at them.

'Our people must learn to be disciplined,' Jagan observed.

He felt light at heart after this arrangement, but it took time for his staff to get adjusted to the idea, as they were afraid that stagnant business might limit prospects and promotions. Jagan had not thought of that, but he pretended to have taken into consideration all aspects of the question and just brushed off comments. They returned to the subject again and again. They had more time to stand around the throne and discuss things now that the frying operations lasted only three hours from mid-day and the sales only an hour; but for the crowd at the counter vainly clamouring for more, the place became free from all activity. This was a cause of great concern for Sivaraman, who felt that the crowd might turn unruly. Jagan replied, 'Be patient and watch; our people have to learn discipline and will certainly learn soon. Don't worry.' To everyone else in that little hall it sounded irrelevant, but they were too polite to say so. 'Maybe we shall have to prepare more,' said Sivaraman, chewing a piece of tobacco in a most leisurely manner.

'No harm in trying it, but what for?' asked Jagan.

They merely mumbled, 'So that no one is turned back.'

'What for?' asked Jagan again.

Sivaraman and his four assistants were pure technicians in the matter of confectionery; they floundered over questions of economics, marketing and politics. Sivaraman had a sudden inspiration and answered, 'Because more people are asking for our sweets now that the price has been so much reduced.'

'Oh, that is a brilliant explanation,' Jagan felt, but he did not think it politic to say so, he merely remarked, 'Well, that is a point of view; we will consider it after we see how it all goes for at least fifteen days.' He knew that his staff viewed him as an astute businessman; although his decision was baffling, doubtless, they thought he must have some sound reason for taking this step; they credited him with some canny purpose, and he could not bring himself to disillusion them. He felt curiously flattered and gratified, and, although a lover of truth generally, in this instance he enjoyed shining in a false light.

Sivaraman finally said, 'Is it possible that you have found a way to draw all the business in the town to your door?'

He had just enough tact and vanity to permit himself a meaningful smile and they felt pleased and smiled meaningfully too. He then held before them greater treasures than mere profit. He said, 'You have leisure now and do not know how to use it. Let me help you. Sit down and learn how best to utilize the precious hours that come to us, not by lounging in the market-place or discussing money matters. Sit down, all of you. I will read to you from the *Bhagavad Gita* every day for an hour. You will benefit by it. Call in the captain also, if he likes to join us.' He commanded them to be seated again, looked on them with benign pity from his throne, took out his *Bhagavad Gita*, opened it on the first page and began: 'On the field of Kurukshetra two armies arrayed and ready for battle faced each other. Do you know why they were there?'

Sivaraman, now completely relaxed, sitting cross-legged and bolt upright on the floor, said, 'Of course, we all know why they were there. I am sure all these boys know too.' They murmured an assent; the captain, standing respectfully apart with arms folded and his short stick under his right arm, nodded appreciatively.

Not minding what the head cook said, Jagan began again from the first line in a singsong, and felt a thrill at the sound of Sanskrit. 'At this moment the great warrior Arjuna had a misgiving as to how he could fight his own uncles and cousins; his knees shook at the thought. Then God himself, who had chosen to be his charioteer, explained to him the need to fight for a cause even if you had to face your brothers, cousins, uncles or even sons. No good has been achieved without a fight at the proper time. Do you understand?' All their heads nodded an assent although their minds were wandering a little: they were anxious lest he should inflict on them a repetition of the same stanza. After further explanation Jagan said, 'There is no such thing as reading this book finally; it is something to be read all one's life. Mahatma Gandhi read it to us every day; was it because he did not know it or thought we did not?'

'True, true,' all of them chorused.

'Mahatmaji placed his fight against Britain in the same category.' The place was beginning to take on the look of a schoolroom, and that the pupils were not quite enjoying it became evident by the number of times Sivaraman got up to spit out tobacco and the others went out to blow noses or take snuff. Even the captain, the very picture of good manners, at one point pretended to notice some intruders at the door and slipped away. It was doubtful how long this could have gone on, for these men, after all, flourished in kitchen smoke and preferred frying to enlightenment, but to everyone's relief three visitors burst in. The captain strutted up, saluted and ushered the visitors before the throne, as was his duty, and withdrew. The cooks lounging on the floor presented an odd spectacle at this hour when business should be at its peak and the kitchen belching fire. Jagan became incoherent and effusive when he recognized his visitors; one was the *sait* from Ananda Bhavan, the man who had built an enormous business on eating within a span of fifteen years although he hailed from a province a thousand miles away; the second ran a canteen at the law-courts, and the third man, who had a white beard, was a stranger. 'Perhaps someone's brother,' Jagan reflected. 'Ah, what an hour,' he kept repeating, and almost embraced them. His audience for the *Bhagavad Gita* melted away unobtrusively. There were not enough seats for all the visitors, but luckily the cousin's stool was available today and Jagan fussily offered it to the bulky *sait*. The captain brought in an iron chair from the soda-shop next door which Jagan allotted to the law-court canteen man, leaving 'someone's brother' to fend for himself, and resumed his seat on the throne; it was impossible for him to occupy any other position within this hall. 'Someone's brother' stood about uncertainly while they talked of politics, the weather and general market conditions for half an hour, before coming to the point. Then the *sait* asked, 'What is it that you have been trying to do during the last . . .'

'Four days,' said the 'brother'.

The *sait* added, 'He is our friend.'

Jagan threw a smile at him and, encouraged, the bearded man edged nearer and sat on the platform at Jagan's feet.

The *sait* said, 'You are making a drastic reduction in the price of your sweets?'

'Yes.'

'May we know why?'

'So that more people may enjoy the eating of sweets,' replied Jagan with a beatific smile.

The others looked shocked at this heresy. 'What prevents more people from eating at the right price?'

'The price of the stuff itself,' said Jagan, hitting upon a lucid explanation.

'It is bad business,' said the canteen-owner.

In answer Jagan said, 'I am unhappy, my distinguished guests, that I have nothing to offer you, all our trays having become empty an hour ago.'

'Then that is good business,' said the *sait* with a twinkle in his eyes. Jagan accepted the compliment with a knowing nod, looking gratified at his own cuteness. 'But why should you upset all our business?' asked the *sait*.

'I will ask the customers who clamour here to go to your shop, provided you promise them pure quality.'

'Do you mean to say that we don't use pure stuff?'

'I don't know. I use the purest butter for frying and the best flour and spices.'

'And yet you say you are able to sell a packet for twenty-five paise?' They all laughed at the joke. The *sait* went on, 'In 1956 I used to do that myself, but now where can we get pure stuff at the right price?'

'I can help you to get the supplies if you like. As Lord Krishna says in the *Gita*, it is all in one's hand. Make up your mind and you will find the object of your search.'

The bearded man sitting on the platform butted in to remark, 'Ah, the *Gita* is a treasure, truly a treasure-house of wisdom.'

'I never spend a moment without reading it.'

'One can go on reading it all one's life,' agreed the *sait* himself, and the canteen man said, 'We all know it. The *Gita* also says every man must perform his duty in the right spirit and the right measure. Do you think you are doing that?' he assailed Jagan directly.

Jagan's composure was lost. He merely said, 'Oh!' and covered his confusion with a simper.

Now the *sait* leaned forward to say with all the grimness he could muster, 'If one person does it, all the others will do it also, are you aware of that?'

Jagan's mind did not take in the implications of his statement but he felt he ought to match its sharpness and answered, 'What if they do?'

'Is that the line you wish to take?' asked the canteen man.

Jagan, wondering what there was so sinister in taking the line, mumbled some irrelevancy and suddenly shouted, 'Captain! Get four drinks for these gentlemen from the soda-shop . . .'

There were murmurs of refusal from the assembly, but they softened towards Jagan and the *sait* said 'Oh no, don't take all the trouble, sir. We have come to talk serious business. Let us get through it first. Business first is my motto always.'

'Otherwise how can we get on? That must be the beacon-light of conduct for all businessmen, the only philosophy,' said the canteen man, and the bearded man quoted a passage from the *Upanishads* which proved nothing.

'What are we all talking about?' asked the *sait* suddenly. Jagan and the rest said nothing. The *sait*, who was evidently the leader of the delegation, continued, 'My time is precious; at this hour I am hardly able to leave my counter, and yet I have come; does it not show the seriousness of the business that has brought us here?'

The canteen man said, 'It is nearly a year since I visited this part of the city. Where can one find the time?'

'Each man is busy in his own way,' said the bearded man.

'I am very glad to see you all here. We must all meet once in a way like this and discuss our problems,' said Jagan, feeling that he had been left out too long.

'I am very happy that you should think so,' said the *sait*, looking genuinely relieved. 'We must all learn to live together and voice our feelings nowadays; otherwise we will be left behind in the race.'

'Union is strength,' said the bearded man; he attempted to illustrate his thesis with a story from the *Panchatantra*. 'There was once upon a time . . .' he began.

This was too much for the delegation and the *sait* cut him short with, 'Of course, Panditji, we all know the story and its moral. As I was saying,' he went on, feeling that he had the first right to speak in this assembly, 'as I was saying, we have many problems. Today we are all bewildered and we ask ourselves why we should continue in business.'

'Exactly what I have felt, but I keep it up more for the sake of my staff,' said Jagan, understanding the words in the simplest terms possible.

The *sait* felt inspired to continue, having fallen into the groove of talking shop, 'There is really no answer to our problems; people mind their own business and think that we can somehow exist and continue to exist. How they expect us to continue is more than I can understand.'

'If we close our business even for a single day, then they will know,' said the canteen man.

'It would actually be more economical to close down our business, but we cannot do it; people would suffer; innocent office-workers, labourers and students who depend upon us for their nourishment would be the real ones to suffer,' said the *sait*, feeling as if he were a benevolent angel conferring boons on humanity. 'Our problems are numerous.'

He was excessively fond of the word 'problem'. He had mentioned the word so often that Jagan felt constrained to ask, 'What problems?'

Both the *sait* and the canteen man turned an astonished glance at him as if they could hardly conceive of anyone in his senses asking such a question. Both of them started to talk at once, and the voices clashed and became indistinguishable as they said, 'The sales-tax inspectors who will not accept the accounts we render, the income-tax people who assess arbitrarily, the health inspectors, the food control which has practically driven everything underground – how are we to get the provisions for our recipes? And above all, the frying medium: we can't always use pure ghee, and the government forces us to announce what we use; how can we do that when our customers like to be told, whatever they may actually consume, that they are being served pure butter-melted ghee?'

'The ideas about pure butter-melted ghee are antiquated,' said the canteen man. 'In fact, scientists have proved that pure butter and ghee bring on heart disease; the artificial substitutes have more vitamins.'

'They are not much cheaper, either.'

'Their prices are going up nearly to the level of pure ghee.'

'So why not pure ghee?' asked Jagan, which really irritated his visitors. As they were mustering their wits for a repartee, the captain brought in four bottles of soda, opened the first one with an enormous pop and held the bottle dripping, overflowing, whizzing and hissing to the *sait* as the courtesy due to the leader of the delegation.

The *sait* said with some annoyance, 'I told you, I want nothing.'

Jagan said, 'It is only soda, a lot of gas in it; take it.'

Meanwhile, like a machine, the captain was popping open the other bottles and the bearded man was snatching each from his hand and passing it on; the floor became wet with the effervescence. When a bottle was offered to Jagan, he took it, but turned it ceremoniously over to the captain.

The *sait* said, 'You wanted us to drink the soda.'

'Because I know it is good,' said Jagan.

'But why don't you drink it yourself?'

'I don't drink more than four ounces of water a day,' said Jagan, 'and that must be boiled at night and cooled in a mud jug open to the sky. I drink no other water. Even when I was in prison in those days . . .' he began, but the rest cut short his reminiscence with the question, 'Have we spent this afternoon usefully?' Jagan was not sure whose responsibility it was to find an answer, but remembering that he was the host, said, 'Of course, it has been an honour to receive you.'

'We are happy that we have understood each other now,' said the *sait*. 'I hope we can count on your co-operation.'

Without thinking what they meant Jagan said effusively, 'Certainly, surely, I believe in co-operation fully.'

The canteen man remarked, 'If it is just some temporary policy of yours, it is not for us to question you.'

'But if it's anything else,' interrupted the *sait*, 'we must all strive to maintain the tone of business; that is our common aim.'

Jagan made some indistinct sounds in his throat and they all left. He heard them drive off, and prepared to wind up for the day. The captain came in to take the iron chair back to the soda-shop, and placed on Jagan's table a bill for the drinks. Jagan had emptied the cash collection into his drawer hours ago, and now proceeded to open it and was sorting out the various denominations, when the bearded man who had gone out with the *sait* came back. Jagan said, 'Forgotten anything?'

'No,' said the man, approaching and taking his seat on the stool, 'I sent them away in their car. I actually live in the next street; they gave me a lift, and I thought I might come in with them and meet you. They were so busy talking to you, I did not like to disturb your meeting.'

'I don't think I have seen you before,' said Jagan.

'I live in Kabir Street but seldom pass this way,' he said, settling down on the stool for a conversational evening.

Jagan said, 'I thought you were going with them.'

'Why should I when my house is so near?'

'I didn't know that,' said Jagan. 'I don't know your name yet.'

'People who knew me used to call me Chinna Dorai as distinct from my master, who was known as Peria Dorai. The small master and the big master – ah, in no way to be compared.'

'Who was your master?'

'How many temples have you visited in your life?' the bearded man asked.

Today everyone seemed to be firing questions at him, but Jagan answered, 'A hundred temples of all sorts, maybe more.'

'The god or gods in every one of the temples were carved by my master.'

'Oh, how wonderful to know that!' said Jagan.

'The figures of Shiva, the Destroyer, Vishnu, the Protector, Devi, who vanquished the demon Mahisha with the dreadful weapons she bore in her eighteen arms, the Dwarapalakas, gate-keepers at the shrine, and the designs on the doorways and the friezes on the walls, were alike all done by my master, all over the South.' His eyes blazed and his beard fluttered while he spoke.

Jagan was impressed by his elocution although he did not quite understand what he was driving at; it was at least a relief from the talk of butter and frying. His description of the gods made Jagan regret that he had not gone near the temple for months, being wrapped up in this monotonous job of frying and cash-counting. He declared fervently, 'Of course, I have visited every temple in this part of the universe, times out of count, and I know all the one hundred and eight gods and saints enshrined along both the banks of the Kaveri. I know the songs that Sambhandar composed in honour of those gods.' And he assumed a falsetto voice and sang a couple of pieces for sample.

The bearded man shut his eyes, listened and showered praise on Jagan's musical ability and memory; which ballast of flattery he needed today because he was beginning to have misgivings about his practical wisdom. Jagan in turn expressed approval of the other's taste in music. In all this demonstration of mutual esteem the purpose of the conversation, was, as usual, lost. The bearded man sang a couple of songs himself, not in a falsetto, but a full-throated voice without inhibition, and the captain at the door peeked in to make sure that things were normal within, at this business hour, with its noise of traffic and crowds on Market Road. After the songs the bearded man returned to his main theme. 'All those gods you have seen in the temples were done by my master or his disciples.'

'What was his name, did you say?'

'Don't mind what I said. We called him "Master" and that's sufficient. There has been no other who could assume that title.'

'Was he your master?'

'Yes. In his last years he didn't like to admit anyone near him except me.'

'Where did he live?'

'Not far from here. Any day you can spare a little time, I'll take you there. It's just on the other bank of the river. You can see the trees of his garden. Do you ever go across the river?'

Jagan sighed at this reminder. For years his fixed orbit had been between the statue and the shop, his mental operations confined to Mali, the cousin and frying. He recollected with a sigh the blaze of colours at sunset, the chatter of birds in Nallappa's Grove; how he had often wandered along the river, lounged on the sands or sat on the river-step with his class-fellows; how Mahatma Gandhi used to address huge assemblies on the sands of the river and how he himself, a minute speck in such a crowd, had felt his whole life change when he heard that voice. Where now were those friends, whose faces and names he could not recollect – dead, flattened out by life or existing in the same place under new masks like that toothless lawyer, or that man who was so bent that he hardly looked at anyone, or a dozen other familiar faces, at one time bench companions at school and playmates around the statue every afternoon – passing each other daily but hardly uttering four syllables in twenty years? 'You have become contemplative,' said the bearded man accusingly.

'Gandhi was my master,' Jagan said. The bearded man showed no interest in the statement, perhaps because he was jealous of the term 'master' being applied to any other claimant but his own. Eager to go back to the business on hand, he asked, 'When will you find the time to go out with me?'

'Tomorrow,' said Jagan promptly, and then asked, 'Where? Come here at one o'clock in the afternoon. Are you going to show me your master's sculptures?'

'No, they are all in various temples, I told you. He was regularly besieged by temple-builders. He was not the sort to keep his handiwork in his own house.'

There was such intensity in his speech that Jagan apologized. 'Oh, I didn't mean that. Where do you want to take me?'

'To show you the place where he lived and worked, that's all.'

'Do you work there now?'

'No, I told you, I live behind this road.'

'Do you make your images there?'

At this, the man burst into a big laugh and said, 'Did I not tell you what I do now? I make hair-dyes. I can make the whitest hair look black. That *sait* is my best customer in the town. Once in four weeks I go and personally colour his hair, which otherwise would look milk-white. On those days he fetches me in his car; that's how I came to be with him today. A lucky day, because I have come to know your good self.'

'I'm also happy. I have never seen an image-maker before.'

'You are not seeing one now, either. I'm only a blackener of white hair. I have come, too, to ask if you need my services. My responsibility is to make people look young. The *sait* appreciates my services. Ask him if you have doubts.'

Jagan hesitated for a moment, and said apologetically, 'I do not know if I could do it,' trying to imagine the remarks of Mali and Grace. Probably Mali would not even notice; he hardly ever looked at him. Why not try at least to amuse him? He suddenly remembered that he himself was a specialist in this and allied subjects. 'Diet has a lot to do with the colour of one's hair. My book on this subject will be out one day and then you will see for yourself; if your diet is controlled according to Nature's specifications, you will never see a grey hair anywhere.'

'That may be the reason why the bear never has a grey hair,' said the bearded man and laughed at the joke.

For Jagan, though, this was a serious line of inquiry. He said solemnly, 'I must consider that point when my book is finally prepared.'

Chapter Eight

The pond was covered with blue lotus, the steps were mantled with moss and crumbling. On the bank stood a small shrine supported on stone pillars, with a low roof of granite slabs blackened by weather, time and the oven smoke of wayfarers. Over this little building loomed banyan, peepul and mango trees and beyond them stretched away a grove of casuarina, the wind blowing through their leaves creating a continuous murmur as of sea waves. The surroundings were covered with vegetation of every type; brambles, thorn-bushes, lantana and oleander intertwined and choked each other. The sun glittered on the pond's surface. The bearded man who had led Jagan to this spot remained brooding, watching some birds dive into the water.

'So quiet everywhere!' Jagan remarked, deciding to puncture the oppressive silence.

The other shook his head. 'Not as it used to be. Too many buses on the highway, ever since that project in the hills . . .' His voice trailed away. 'In those days,' he said, 'when I lived here with my master, you could not meet a soul unless you walked all the way to Nallappa's Grove and crossed into the town. In those days people did not go up the mountain as much as they do now; robbers hid themselves in the jungles, and tigers and elephants roamed the foot-hills.' He seemed depressed at the thought of their giving place to highway buses.

'Why did you choose to live here?' Jagan asked.

'Where else could one live? We needed all those stones.' He pointed through the thickets. 'You see the nose of Mempi? For softer panel-work that stone is excellent; for images of the inner sanctum one has to cut the stone at the belly of the hill further up, though it is difficult to hew and there are more breakages than in other portions.' His head seemed to throb with stony problems.

Jagan watched him in silent wonder and asked, 'What would one do for food, and with one's wife and children, in a place like this?'

The bearded man made a flourish as if to ward off such a petty question. 'My master never bothered about such things. He never married. I came to him when I was five years old. I don't know who my parents were. People used to say I was picked up by my master on the river-step.'

Jagan wanted to ask, but suppressed the question, whether he might not have been born to a passing concubine of his so-called master who never married. While the bearded man remained thinking of his past, Jagan reflected, 'He has the whitest beard and sells the blackest hair-dye. Why does he not apply it to his own beard?' He asked aloud, 'How is your business?' – a question that he must have asked every few minutes, whenever there was a pause.

The bearded man said, 'Nothing to worry about, and the sales-tax people have still not come my way yet.'

'That is a real blessing,' said Jagan, remembering the visitations he had to endure, the inspectors and their minions rummaging his desk for day-books, ledgers and vouchers. In the end they accepted his accounts, unaware of the cash that grew from out-of-hour sales at the counter and filled the smaller jug, but he could no more help it than he could the weeds flourishing in his backyard. He had a habitual, instinctive and inexplicable uneasiness concerning any tax. If Gandhi had said somewhere, 'Pay your sales tax uncomplainingly,' he would have followed his advice, but Gandhi had made no reference to the sales tax anywhere to Jagan's knowledge.

The bearded man said, 'But they are bound to wake up sooner or later, when they notice fewer grey hairs around,' and chuckled.

Jagan seized this opportunity to say, 'Anyway, you are an exception to your own rule.'

'I like my white beard and so keep it. There is no compulsion for anyone to blacken his hair. I would not have dreamt of blackening people's heads if I had had a chance to work on stone. But you know how these things happen. My master supported me for years.' ('How could he not, as you were his only son by a passing concubine?' Jagan retorted inwardly.) The bearded man pointed to a corner in the pillared hall. 'He worked on those details of ornament and I had to move the block here. He lived his whole life here. All that he possessed could be contained within the palm of one's hand. I cooked a little rice for him in that corner, where you see the walls blackened. All day he sat here working on the image or we went to the quarry to hew slabs. He never saw anyone except when some temple men came to order an image. People were afraid to come here because of the snakes, but my master loved them and never approved of clearing the wild growth around. This tree was full of monkeys; you can see them now. "I'll share the fruits of those trees with them," he used to say. He enjoyed the company of snakes and monkeys and everything; once there was even a cheetah in the undergrowth. "We must not monopolize this earth. They won't harm us," he used to say, and, true to his word, nothing ever did. When he died one night I sat at vigil by a small oil lamp, and cremated his body beyond that pond, heaping on the dead wood and withered leaves. Next day I walked off to the city and lived on charity here and there, until I got the idea for my business. That is all. I have nothing in my life to complain of now, but I was well off in those days . . .' Still brooding, he walked around the small hall, peered into an alcove, 'There used to be a god in the sanctum which had been stolen years before we came here. One night my master woke me up and said, "Let me make a new god for this temple. Then it will flourish again." He had dreamt of a five-faced Gayatri, to be seen nowhere else, the deity of Radiance. He had even hewn the slab for it and knocked the first dents. It used to be in that yard somewhere. Let me look for it . . .' He became suddenly active, peeped into every corner of the hall, went round to the backyard, where oleanders and hibiscus flourished and bloomed wildly. He discovered a bamboo staff amidst a clump – 'Ah, this is still here!' – seized it and strode about, looking like a statue of many thousand years' antiquity.

Watching him in this setting, it was difficult for Jagan, as he mutely followed him, to believe that he was in the twentieth century. Sweetmeat vending, money and his son's problems seemed remote and unrelated to him. The edge of reality itself was beginning to blur; this man from the previous millennium seemed to be the only object worth notice; he looked like one possessed. He pointed to a grassy spot under a palmyra tree and said, 'This is where my master's body was burnt, that day. I can remember that terrible night.' He stood under the palmyra with his eyes shut for a moment, muttering some holy verse. 'We should not let the body deceive us as to the true nature of our being. One is not really bone and meat. My master proved it,' he declared, and as if seized with a sudden frenzy beat down every bush with his bamboo stick, startling a variety of creatures – lizards, chameleons, birds and frogs, which had lived undisturbed for years in the green shelter. He seemed to enjoy their discomfiture and inhaled noisily, with relish, the smell of crushed greenery. He said, 'I'm sure the cobras that live here must have quietly slipped away when we came; they are uncanny in their habits. Very alert, very alert and watchful . . .' Chipped-off blocks of stone and odds and ends of sculptural pieces came to view beneath the weeds. He pointed his staff at them, explaining, 'This was the pedestal of Vishnu, meant for some temple; those are the arms of Saraswathi, the goddess of learning – they could not be used because of a slight crack in the stone. My master got so upset when he noticed the defect that he flung it out through the door, and remained speechless for three days. At such moments, I used to stay away from him, shielding myself behind the trunk of that tamarind tree. When the mood passed he would call me. But where is that other block? Where is it? The two-foot-square one? It could not have grown limbs and walked off – although, let me tell you, if an image is perfect, it cannot be held down on its pedestal. I always remember the story of the dancing figure of Nataraj, which was so perfect that it began a cosmic dance and the town itself shook as if an earthquake had rocked it, until a small finger on the figure was chipped off. We always do it; no one ever notices it, but we always create a small flaw in every image; it's for safety.'

He went on talking and Jagan listened agape as if a new world had flashed into view. He suddenly realized how narrow his whole existence had been – between the Lawley Statue and the frying shop; Mali's antics seemed to matter naught. 'Am I on the verge of a new *janma*?' he wondered. Nothing seemed really to matter. 'Such things are common in ordinary existence and always passing,' he said aloud.

The bearded man, suppressing his surprise at this sudden remark, said, 'True, true, you must not lose sight of your real being, which is not mere bone or meat.' He reached up to a branch of a guava tree, plucked a fruit and bit into it with the glee of a ten-year-old urchin. 'This tree always gave the best fruit. Monkeys thrive on it, and during certain seasons the tree-top would be as full of monkeys as leaves, you know.' He pulled down the branch again, plucked off another fruit and held it out to Jagan. Jagan took it from courtesy, but did not eat it. 'I keep off sweets and salt.'

'Why?' asked the other.

'Well . . .' how to express his whole philosophy of life in a limited jargon? He concluded, 'You will find it all explained in my book.' At the mention of 'book' the other began to lose interest. He was used to inscriptions on stone and on palmyra leaf, and he was not enticed by the mention of the printed book. Jagan, unaffected by his attitude, added, 'The printer, Nataraj, do you know him at all?' The bearded man had lost interest in the subject totally by this time. Ignoring Jagan and talking on, he failed to observe that Jagan had overcome the temptation to take a bite and had let the fruit slip to the ground, unable to decide whether it would be good or bad from the point of view of dietetics. What a shame if it was good to eat and he had surrendered it, for it was attractive, with green turning yellow on top and yellow turning red in the middle, and soft to the touch. Before he had developed his theories of sane living, he used to eat a dozen of them each day and it might well be said that between seven and twelve years of age the aroma of guava had permanently clung to him! A huge tree had grown in their backyard, right over the tin shed, and one day his father took an axe and cut it down, remarking, 'These little devils will eat nothing else as long as this cursed tree stands. See how one by one they are going down with colic . . .' As he followed the other about, vaguely aware of his speech, his mind was obsessed with the fruit he had abandoned, until the bearded man asked, 'Are you listening to me?'

'Yes, yes, of course,' Jagan said.

'We have gone round and round, but not found the slab. It must be somewhere,' said the bearded man. He hugged the stick, resting his chin on it, and was lost in thought.

Jagan could not help asking, 'Why are you bothered about it?'

'Very important, very important, I tell you. When I have found it, you will know.' He unwrapped himself from the stick abruptly and said, 'Now I remember; come with me.' He moved briskly towards the pond. 'Come down with me. Mind the steps – they are slippery.' He went down the steps and up to his knees in water. Jagan lagged behind, unable to comprehend the other's action. 'Perhaps he is going to knock me into the pond and go

back to the town and report, "The maker of sweets has vanished." '
The other's face was flushed with excitement as he looked up and
cried, 'Won't you come down? What if your *dhoti* gets wet? You
can dry it later.' His tone was peremptory.

Jagan descended the moss-covered steps, which gave him a
creepy feeling under foot. His *dhoti* did get wet and he shivered
slightly as he watched with fascination bees swarming on the blue
lotus. He felt a sense of elevation – it would be such a wonderful
moment to die, leaving the perennial problems of life to solve
themselves. While he was busy with his thoughts the other, who
had stopped on all fours, looked up and said, 'Come here,' with
his eyes blazing and his beard fluttering in the wind. 'There is no
retreat for me,' thought Jagan. 'He is preparing to hold my head
down in the water. Should I turn back and rush away? No, not a
chance of retreat,' and he took a further step down. He was now
wet up to his waist. 'Cold water may be good for rheumatism, but
I am not a rheumatic,' he told himself. 'If I do not perish in this
water, I shall perish of pneumonia. In my next life I'd like to be
born . . .' His mind ran through various choices. Pet dog?
Predatory cat? Street-corner donkey? Maharajah on an elephant?
Anything but a money-making sweet-maker with a spoilt son.

The bearded man, still on all fours, now commanded, 'Plunge
your hand in here and feel . . .'

Jagan obeyed, precariously poising himself on the slippery
surface.

'What do you feel there?' the other asked imperiously.

Jagan noted that ever since they had stepped into this garden,
the man had become more and more authoritarian. He was no
longer the tame hair-blackener of Kabir Street, but a sort of leader
of the forces, a petty chieftain used to having his orders carried
out without question. Nothing like implicit obedience. Jagan
plunged his arms into the water, and shuddered when something
clamped its jaws on his hand. 'Oh!' he screamed. It was only the
other's hand-grip. Now a smile appeared on the bearded face as
he propelled Jagan's hand through the water over a stone surface.
'This is the stone I meant. Let us take it out. Hold it at your end
properly. Can't you lift it? I am not surprised. If you ate normally
like other human beings, or at least consumed some of the sweets
that you sell, you would be in better shape. I remember my master
put this stone into the water because it needed the treatment to

87

bring out its surface grains. Do you feel the notches, the first ones he made? He had started to work on it but suddenly decided that it needed water-seasoning; he always said that the longer a stone stayed in water . . .' He looked about in despair. 'If you could only make up your mind to lift it; it is only will-power you lack. This is not after all a big statue but a small one, hardly a couple of feet; when it is fully worked, it will hardly be eighteen inches. Can't you lift a stone that is going to be just eighteen inches high? I am surprised. I only want you to give me a hand, not lift it yourself. Help me.'

He was so cajoling and bullying by turns that finally Jagan began to feel that he ought to exert himself. He gritted himself for the task by tying his upper cloth around his head and tucking up his *dhoti* in a businesslike manner. He held his breath, gripped his end of the block, pausing for a moment to consider whether at his age he was well advised to carry a slab of stone up wet steps. But this was no time to consult one's own inclinations or welfare. When they reached the top of the steps, he just let go the stone, threw his entire length flat on the grass, and shut his eyes.

When Jagan revived, he found the other rolling the stone over and explaining, 'This would be the top; come closer and you will see the lines marked by my master with the bodkin, the outline of the goddess.' He scraped the moss off the stone, which was drying in patches, and stood lost in contemplation. To Jagan's eyes it was no different from any other block of stone; even the scratches originally made by the master were hardly convincing; but the bearded man seemed to feel intoxicated at the sight of it. 'This is where the goddess's hands come; she is ten-armed, and except for the one which indicates protection and the one offering a blessing, all the other arms hold a variety of divine articles.' For some time he was lost in visions of the goddess and then began to narrate a story.

'I know the story of the goddess,' said Jagan.

'Who doesn't?' replied the hair-blackener. 'But still it's always good to hear it over and over again; you will always have the protection of Dvi, and everything you attempt will turn out successful.' And he broke into a loud Sanskrit song. The birds in the trees fluttered at the sudden outbreak of noise. Frogs at the edge of the pond sprang back into the water, and Jagan's gaze was held by the delicate tracks on the surface left by the newts and other aquatic creatures invisibly coursing.

'If I can devote my life to the completion of this task I will die in peace,' said the other.

'How old are you?' asked Jagan.

'Do you want to know? Then guess.'

Such speculation always embarrassed Jagan. He could never be sure whether people asking that question liked to look younger or older than their years. In either case, he felt he could not be drawn into a debate, and so said, 'I can't say . . .' observing the man's head, which was bald. ('No place for his dye there,' he thought.)

'I am sixty-nine,' said the other abruptly in a matter-of-fact manner. 'I'm prepared to die peacefully on my seventieth birthday, if I can finish that image and instal it on its pedestal.'

'Will you be able to complete it in a year?' Jagan asked.

'I may or may not,' said the other. 'How can I say? It's in God's hands. With all that water-seasoning, the slab may suddenly split in the middle, and then what does one do?' Several possibilities occurred to Jagan. While he was fumbling for an answer, the other declared, 'Bury the broken image and start anew with a fresh quarrying and fresh seasoning in water, that's all.'

'If that breaks?'

'That'd be an inauspicious thought and question,' said the other grimly and added, 'The second stone does not generally crack.' They sat in silence, which the other broke, 'Ten hands! Oh, the very picture thrills me.' He burst into a song in Sanskrit, 'Mukta-vidruma-hema...' When he had completed the stanza he asked, 'Do you understand the meaning of that?'

'Yes, in a way,' replied Jagan cautiously.

'It only means the goddess whose countenance has the radiance of *mukta*, that is pearl, and *hema*, that is gold, and then the blue of the sapphire or the sky, and then the redness of the coral . . .' He took a deep breath, paused and continued, 'Since She is the light that illumines the Sun himself, She combines in her all colours and every kind of radiance, symbolized by five heads of different colours. She possesses ten hands, each holding a conch, which is the origin of sound, a discus, which gives the universe its motion, a goad to suppress evil forces, a rope that causes bonds, lotus flowers for beauty and symmetry, and a *kapalam*, a begging bowl made of a bleached human skull. She combines in Her divinity everything we perceive and feel from the bare, dry bone to all beauty in creation.'

Jagan was filled with awe and reverence at the picture. The bearded man sat brooding for a while, then said, 'My master always meditated on this form and wanted to create the image for others to contemplate. That was his aim, and if I can carry it out, I'll abandon all other work in life.' He came down to business. 'It's only a man like you that can help in this task.'

Jagan gave a start on hearing this. He had not thought that the task would concern him. 'How? How?' he asked anxiously, and before the other could collect his thoughts, added, 'Don't think too much of me. No, no. After all I'm a humble merchant.'

The other said, 'Why don't you buy this garden and instal the goddess?'

'I – I – do not know,' replied Jagan, thickening his armour of self-defence, and tried to laugh the question off, but the other became deadly earnest, half rose and, waving a finger close to Jagan's eyes, said, 'Very well, I understand. I only thought it would do you good to have a retreat like this.'

'Yes, yes, God knows I need a retreat. You know, my friend, at some stage in one's life one must uproot oneself from the accustomed surroundings and disappear so that others may continue in peace.'

'It would be the most accredited procedure according to our scriptures – husband and wife must vanish into the forest at some stage in their lives, leaving the affairs of the world to younger people.'

Jagan felt so heartily in agreement that he wanted to explain why he needed an escape – his wife's death, his son's growth and strange development, how his ancient home behind the Lawley statue was beginning to resemble hell on earth – but he held his tongue. He felt shy and reserved about talking of his son – like one not wishing to exhibit his sores.

Chapter Nine

Jagan now had a separate key with which he let himself into his house softly, crossed the passage and shut the door between his part of the house and his son's. Then he hooked his upper cloth on a nail in the wall, stripped off his *jibba*, passed on to the backyard, poured a lot of cold water over himself and came out of the bathroom. Feeling hungry today he set a bowl of water on the kitchen oven, and cut up a few vegetables, and threw them in, along with a small measure of coarsely ground wheat. The day had been hot and he preferred to remain without a vest. While his dinner was cooking, he stood before the gods for a second with eyes shut, then lit an oil wick and took out his small *charka* (wooden spinning-wheel) from behind a large bureau, inserted a hank of cotton, turned the wheel and drew a fine thread out, watching its growth with a sensuous pleasure: the slight whirring noise of the wheel and the thread growing out of it between one's thumb and forefinger was very comforting, stilling the nerves and thoughts. Gandhi had prescribed spinning not only for the economic ills of the country, but also for any deep agitation of the mind. Jagan's mind was in a turmoil; at the same time he had a feeling that his identity was undergoing a change. If that was so, why should he bother or resist the idea? Committed to various things until yesterday, to the shop and the family, he was a different man at this moment. An internal transformation had taken place; although he still cared for the shop and house, this latest contact had affected him profoundly. The gods must have taken pity on his isolated, floundering condition and sent this white-bearded saviour. As he turned the spinning-wheel, sitting there in the courtyard, with the sky-reaching coconut trees of the neighbourhood waving amidst the stars, his mind analysed everything with the utmost clarity. He wondered if the bearded man might not be a visitation from another planet – otherwise what had brought him into his shop exactly when he needed him? Who really needed help and from whom? The man had said he needed help installing the image of the goddess, while he himself thought that he was being helped. He could not solve the puzzle easily, and so left it alone. Anyway it was a reposeful memory: the man had really communicated a thrilling vision when he described the goddess with five heads. Should he help him or not to complete his task? He knew nothing about him. How could he trust him? On what basis? After he finished the image, what then? Live in his company in that wilderness and encourage him to carve more images? What would happen to the hair-dye? Perhaps he'd be expected to take charge of the business and run it in addition to his sweets. Run after white hair on a large scale, earn more money and ruin Mali further? He suspended his reflections and his spinning for a moment in order to attend to the vegetables on the stove, then he came back to his wheel, thinking of the fixed law of Nature by which wheat was cooked in exactly thirty minutes; if it was cooked for forty minutes, it became gruel and was no good nutritionally; in food, food-making and food-eating, what was important was precision. It was a science – that's what he was trying to establish in his book, which would have been in the hands of the public but for Nataraj. Why was Nataraj so indifferent to this task, while he had printed the prospectus for Mali with alacrity? Perhaps he didn't like his ideas; but printers did not have to like an idea in order to print it. He should rather be like Sivaraman, who had to fry something even if he didn't care for it himself. The cotton got thinner and longer as if it were the soft dough from which Sivaraman sometimes drew fine vermicelli strands; the wheel groaned and purred and cleared its throat. Through the open roof he could see the crescent moon passing behind the coconut trees, a couple of wispy white clouds racing across its face. 'Perhaps the monsoon will be breaking earlier this year?' he reflected. 'One enters a new life at the appointed time and it's foolish to resist.' He was no longer the father of Mali, the maker of sweets and gatherer of money each day; he was gradually becoming something else, perhaps a supporter of the bearded sculptor – or was he really his ward?

There was a knock on the door, which was lost in the purring of the spinning-wheel. The middle door opened and Mali came in, looking like an arrival from another planet in that dim light (Jagan had fitted ten-watt bulbs in the light sockets in order to benefit the human retina). Excited at the sight of his son, Jagan snatched a towel and hid his chest under it; if he had known that he was coming, he'd have had his *jibba* on. He left his spinning and leaped up to fetch a stool to seat Mali. Mali took it from his hand, muttering, 'What a fuss you make!', planted it in the open court and sat on it, while Jagan stood about uncertainly. 'Sit down, Father,' Mali commanded, 'but don't turn that wheel; it's noisy and I want to talk to you.'

At this Jagan felt a sinking in his stomach and smacked his drying lips. He moved away from his spinning-wheel, folded his arms across his chest, and asked, 'Now, tell me, what do you want?'

'Everyone talks about you in the town,' said Mali in a tone of accusation.

Jagan slightly stiffened but said nothing. The sinking in the pit of his stomach was gradually leaving him as he remembered that one ought not to resist when circumstances pushed one across the threshold of a new personality. 'What do they talk about?' he asked. He was beginning to shed the awe in which he had held his son. 'Who are "they"?'

'The Ananda Bhavan *sait* and a number of others were discussing you yesterday.'

Jagan did not wish to pursue the subject and so mumbled, 'Let them.' He felt unhappy having to speak in a new tone of voice to Mali, from whom he used to pine for a word; 'I am a new personality and have to speak a new tongue.' He could not judge the expression on his son's face because the crescent moon was now completely gone and his bulb enveloped everything in a pale yellow light, making all faces and all moods look alike.

Mali took a paper from his pocket, tried to read it and said petulantly, 'Why can't you have brighter light?'

Jagan replied, 'Light rays should soothe the optic nerves and not stimulate them.'

The boy smiled cynically and said, 'This cable came in the afternoon from my associates.'

When he heard the word 'associates', Jagan did not need to hear anything more. He was not scared, as he would have been forty-eight hours ago. 'In a few hours, I have undergone a lot of changes, but the boy doesn't know it,' he reflected. 'Let me be kind to him. No harm in showing him kindness. After all . . .' He felt a stab of habitual tenderness, and regret at sounding so officious to Mali. 'What does the cable say?'

Mali spread it out again to catch the light, failed and repeated from memory, 'Please cable . . . status of our project.'

Jagan looked bewildered. This was not the English he knew. Except for the word 'cable', the rest did not mean anything. He said, 'Why should they ask you to cable? An ordinary letter will do.'

The boy said, 'We have to move pretty fast in business matters. Why can't you leave that to me? I know what to do. What shall I say in reply?'

'What is "status"? Whose status are they talking about?'

Mali clenched his fists and said, 'Are we going through with our manufacturing business or are we not?'

'Do you propose to talk about it now?' asked Jagan.

'I must know about it.'

Jagan felt a sudden pity for the boy sitting there forlorn and puzzled, and he cursed the barrier which seemed to raise itself whenever they came together. He pleaded, 'Son, I'll leave you in charge of the shop, it's yours. Take it.'

The boy made a wry face at the mention of the shop; fortunately the dim light did not reveal it fully. 'I tell you once and for all, I don't want to be . . .' He merely concluded, 'I have learnt valuable things in the United States at a cost of several thousand dollars. Why can't our country make use of my knowledge? I . . . I can't . . .' Although he avoided the phrase 'vendor of sweets', his repugnance for the occupation came out unmistakably. They remained silent, and Mali added the final touch: 'In any case your business is worth nothing now.'

'Who told you that?'

'Everyone in the trade is talking about you. What are you trying to do anyway?'

Jagan remained silent. Whereupon Mali again described his fiction-writing machine in detail, and repeated the contents of his prospectus. Jagan listened while the stars ran their course. When Mali paused, having reached the end of his prospectus, Jagan just asked, 'Where is Grace?'

'Why?' asked the son.

Jagan had no answer; he was not bound to answer every question. Mali insisted, 'I have to know whether you are coming into our business or not.'

'What'll you do if I say no?'

'Grace will have to go back; we will have to buy her an air-ticket, that's all.'

'What has it to do with her?' asked Jagan; the connections were baffling, like the wiring at the back of the radio panel.

'Why would she stay here?' asked the boy plainly. 'She has nothing to do here.'

'I do not understand what you are talking about. I have never been able to understand you at all. Call her, let me talk to her.' He had got used to the presence of Grace in the house and he felt desolate at the thought of losing her.

'She has gone out,' said Mali briefly.

'Where, at this time of the night?'

'She can go where she pleases. Why should anyone question her?'

'No, it's not that,' said Jagan. Fate seemed to decree that there should be no communication between them. Some invisible force twisted their tongues when they wanted to speak and made them say the wrong things. Jagan stood up desperately, bent close to his son's face and cried, 'Where is she going? Why is she going? Is she unhappy here?'

Mali rose to his feet and said, 'Who are you to stop her from going where she pleases? She is a free person, not like the daughters-in-law in our miserable country.'

Jagan said, 'I just want to know why she is thinking of going, that's all. She is, of course, free. Who says she is not? Has anything made her unhappy?'

'What is there to keep her happy?' cried Mali. 'This is a miserable place with no life in it. She was used to a good life. She came here to work, and she is going back because she has no work to do.'

Jagan swallowed back the words he wanted to blurt out: 'But she is sweeping and cleaning the house. This is a big house and she has enough work to keep her engaged for a whole day. What more does she want?'

Mali announced, 'She came here for the project, to work with me; didn't you see her name in the notice?'

Jagan had learnt the art of ignoring questions. Mali got up, saying, 'If she has nothing to do here, she goes back, that's all. Her air-ticket must be bought immediately.'

'But a wife must be with her husband, whatever happens.'

'That was in your day,' said Mali and left.

Jagan lost his sleep that night. The obscurity of the whole business worried him. Grace was out of sight. He liked her presence in the house; it filled a serious lacuna. Where had Mali hidden her at the moment? He wouldn't even admit that he knew where she had gone. Was this how a man kept track of his wife?

Chapter Ten

He had to wait for his chance to meet Grace. He knew by the sound of the duster in the front part of the house that she was back, but would she come as usual to his rooms and attend to things? No. It was over ten days since she had come near him. She seemed to be avoiding him. He felt depressed at the thought. What had he done that she should avoid him? Had she shown all that consideration only in order that he might invest in their story machine? Now that he had made his position clear, the barrier between him and the other two was growing more impregnable than ever, and there was absolutely no way of his approaching her and asking for an explanation. He wondered if he could go in and talk to her, but what would be the use? With Mali there, how could he ask her for verification? It would be at best a formal greeting. Though he was ready to leave for his shop this morning, he sat on his cot vaguely hoping that either Grace would come his way or that Mali would go out on one of his errands and he could have a word with her. But there was no sign of either happening. Mali went on typing in his room; after a while the sound of sweeping ceased, and he could hear some exchange of words between the two; then even that ceased and he was left alone; a tremendous stillness reigned over the house. There seemed to be no hope. He quietly slipped out of the house and reached his shop, where life went on as usual, only the clamour at the counter destroying the peace of the afternoon. Of late, Jagan had been unable to concentrate on the *Bhagavad Gita* until the crowd had dispersed. They behaved as if they were entitled to their sweets irrespective of whether there was a stock or not, which made Jagan wonder if he had been wise in reducing the price and whether he should not go back to the original rate.

The cousin had been absent for several days. He explained, 'I had to be away in the Tirupathi Hills with the Judge's family; they had taken two of their grandchildren to the temple for their first shave. It was a grand trip; they had engaged three cottages and the whole temple was open to them – an influential man. They would not listen when I told them that I could not afford to keep away so long; they nearly abducted me.'

'You are wanted everywhere,' said Jagan. 'I have wanted you very badly since yesterday.'

'I am at your service.'

'Has the reduction in prices affected the quality of our sweets?'

'Such a thing is unthinkable, I tell you.'

'The Ananda Bhavan *sait* was here . . .'

'I know, I know,' said the cousin. 'They are talking about you all the time!'

'What do they say?' Jagan got suddenly interested in the market reactions.

'It seems you have agreed to resume your prices soon.'

'I don't know . . . I don't think I have said any such thing,' said Jagan.

The cousin said, 'At least that is what they think. It will do them good to stand in the line and see how you do things. I wouldn't be at all surprised if their men are in the crowd and buy the sweets cheap here and sell them at their own price in their shops.' It hadn't occurred to Jagan that this was a possibility. He looked desperate and the cousin had to say, 'I was only joking, don't let it worry you.'

Jagan asked, 'Have you seen Mali recently?'

'He was at the Judge's house last evening. His son is his friend. He called me aside. He is ever so fond of me as his uncle. Nothing changes him . . .'

Jagan sighed. 'Why does he not talk to me properly? He can't speak even two sentences without upsetting me.'

The cousin, pleased at the superior position he was enjoying, said rather patronisingly, 'Don't let it upset you. You are a wise man and you must not think of these things too much.'

'What did he tell you?'

'He called me into the garden while his friend had gone in to wash and told me that Grace was going back to America soon. Did you hear that?'

'Yes, yes, but I did not understand why.'

The cousin said, 'She is going on business. That's what he told me. Something to do with his machine. You see how plucky these girls are! She goes thousands of miles to settle business matters, while we do not even understand what they are doing!'

98

Jagan did not correct him but kept his knowledge of the facts to himself. 'Well, of course, I had heard that, but I wanted to know if there was anything more.'

'His business seems to be promising,' said the cousin.

'The Ananda Bhavan *sait* and a few others have promised to buy shares in his company.'

Jagan asked with genuine wonder, 'How does he talk to them?'

'He is all over the town and very active. I meet him here, there and everywhere.'

'I want your help,' said Jagan. 'Don't laugh at me. I have to speak to Grace and find out a few things for myself.' He explained the situation in a round-about way without letting the cousin know too much.

The cousin knew that a lot of things were being hidden from him, but he did not mind. He said, 'I see Grace sometimes visiting Dr Kuruvilla's house. She has a friend there whom she knew in America. Shall I speak to her and say that you want to see her?'

'Won't Mali be with her?'

'Sometimes she spends her time with the girls in that house, while Mali goes out with his friends.'

Jagan had to hold his soul in peace for the next two days, while the cousin thought out ways of decoying Mali, leaving the line clear for Jagan to speak to Grace. One afternoon he arrived on his usual tasting duty. Wiping his mouth with his towel, he said, 'If you are prepared to leave the shop, you can meet Grace at home. Mali is waiting for me at the Judge's house. I have promised to go with him to look for a plot of ground on Hill Road.'

'What for?'

'For building his factory.'

'What rubbish! He is talking like a big financier! If he has the money for it, why does he ask me?'

'Everyone in the town thinks of him as a big businessman. He talks well!'

'Yes, to everyone except me,' said Jagan resentfully.

The cousin said, 'We'll talk of all that later. Will you go home? This is the right moment. Mali is going out of town and won't be back until evening. I'll stay here until you come back. There will be others to go with Mali.'

Jagan went home, washed himself, went into the puja room,

stood before the gods and prayed, 'Please help me, enlighten me. I don't know what to do' He stood in meditation for a second, then, reinforced in spirit, knocked on the middle door in the hall. It was unusual for him to come home at this hour; the place looked strangely different, with the afternoon sun coming in at odd corners through the open court. 'This looks like somebody else's home,' he reflected, and it confirmed his recent feeling that he was no longer his old self. He recollected the bearded man's advice during their rambles: 'At first don't hurry, but when you decide, be swift and positive.' That was more or less what he had learnt from Gandhi, but the lesson seemed to have worn out. He remembered how as a volunteer over twenty years ago he had rushed into the British Collector's bungalow and climbed the roof in order to bring down the Union Jack and plant the Indian flag in its place. Helmeted police were standing guard in the compound, but the speed of his action completely took them by surprise and they had to clamber after him to the roof, but not before he had seized the Union Jack in a crocodile grip and hugged the flagpost while attempting to plant his own flag. They had to beat him and crack open his skull in order to make him let go his hold. He opened his eyes fifteen days later in the hospital, and lay forgotten in a prison afterwards. 'There are times when a *Satyagrahi* has to act first and think afterwards,' his leaders had advised. Once a *Satyagrahi*, always a *Satyagrahi*. If one was not acting for truth against the British, one was acting for truth in some other matter, in personal affairs, in all sorts of things. His training was always there, but somehow had dimmed inexplicably. With these reflections, he reinforced his ego before venturing to knock on the door of Mali's apartment.

Grace opened the door and exclaimed, 'Father! You here at this hour! How unusual!'

Jagan went straight to the point. 'I have to talk to you. Will you come here or should I go in there?'

'Please come in. Come to the hall. The chairs there are comfortable.'

He followed her and took his seat on the sofa. She sat in her chair, one finger twirling a chain around her neck. She had a book open on a side table. She was wearing a yellow kimono and looked very much like a Japanese. 'She looks different each day!' he thought and, suppressing his impulse to ask, 'Are you sure you are not a Japanese today?' said aloud 'What are you reading?'

'Nothing very important,' and she mentioned some title.

'Go straight to the point,' he told himself. 'You have beaten about the bush and practically lost contact with your son; don't lose your daughter-in-law too.' His first question was: 'I don't see you in my house nowadays. Why?'

She went red in the face. Her lips twitched and she remained silent.

Observing her discomfiture, he said, 'Don't bother to answer my question.' He left her a little time to recover her composure, then asked, 'Do you wish to go back to your country?'

Once again, her lips twitched, her face went red, and she cast her longish eyes down and remained silent. A crow cawed, perched on the tiles of the open courtyard. Its raucous note broke the awful silence. She muttered 'Ah, that crow has come! Excuse me.' She bustled out, went into her kitchen, came out with a piece of bread in her hand, and tossed it onto the roof; the crow picked it up and was off. Presently more crows came and sat on the roof and cawed. 'This is the worst of it. They all clamour, but I don't really have enough for all of them,' she said.

Jagan could not help saying, 'The same thing is happening to me in my shop. The whole town clamours for my sweets, but really the sales are closed before four in the afternoon.'

She received this in silence. Jagan felt nervous. All the resolution he had made vanished without a trace. He was scared of Grace. He felt she might break down if he asked any more questions. He sensed a deep-seated disturbance in her and became anxious to leave her alone, whatever the mystery might be. When a clock struck four, he got up, saying with extraordinary clarity, 'I must be back at the shop.'

She walked to the door with him silently. When he was about to pass out, she said in a matter-of-fact way, 'Father, Mo wants me to go back.'

'Why?' Jagan asked, halting.

She hesitated. Jagan feared she might cry, but she said very calmly, 'It's all over, that's all.'

'What's over?'

She didn't answer.

He asked, 'Is it his idea or yours?'

She repeated, 'He wants me to go back. He says he can't afford to keep me here any more.' These new facets of Mali now revealed were startling and Jagan found himself tongue-tied. She went on, 'I used to work. I had two thousand dollars when I came here. All that's gone.'

'How?'

She merely said, 'Mo has no more use for me.'

'Use or no use, my wife – well, you know, I looked after her all her life.'

Grace said rather shyly, 'The only good part of it is, there is no child.'

He found some portions of her talk obscure but could not ask explicitly for explanations. He said, 'If you read our *puranas*, you will find that the wife's place is beside her husband whatever may happen.'

'But we are not married,' Grace said simply. 'He promised he'd marry me in the Indian way, because I liked it, and brought me here.'

'And the marriage didn't take place, after coming here?'

'Wouldn't you have known it, if it had?' she said.

It was too much to swallow and digest at one sitting. Jagan wailed, 'I don't know what to make of it all.'

'Will you come back for a while and take a seat? I'll explain. I feel awkward standing here,' Grace said.

He stood looking at the girl. She looked so good and virtuous; he had relied on her so much and yet here she was living in sin and talking casually about it all. 'What breed of creatures are these?' he wondered. They had tainted his ancient home. He had borne much from them. He said coldly, 'No, I'm not coming in now. Let me go back to the shop.'

When the cousin came at 4.30 p.m. Jagan shouted, 'Come here, I am waiting for you.' The cousin held up his arm as much as to say, 'Wait till I finish my savouring duties.' While he was in the kitchen, Jagan's ardour cooled. He had mentally rehearsed a speech beginning 'Do you know . . . ?' but actually, when the cousin emerged from the kitchen he asked, 'How well do you know Mali?' The cousin spent a little time gazing at the tailor across the road pedalling his sewing machine, which, as Jagan knew, was a sign that the cousin was in deep thought. He shook him out of it by saying, 'Mali is not married.'

The cousin, suppressing many questions that arose in his mind, wondered if he was expected to attempt some new match-making for Mali and began, 'Of course, if you give the word, people are ready to snatch his horoscope; even the Judge was mentioning that he had a brother's niece-in-law who was anxious for a match with your family . . .'

Jagan felt slightly elevated by this news, but suddenly remembered that he was not fated to live an ordinary peaceful life. 'Captain, those schoolchildren!' The captain, not knowing whether he was expected to shoo them off or give them gifts, cried back, 'What shall I do with them, sir?'

'Send them away. If you show some consideration once, they expect it for ever and ever; our people have no self-respect.'

'I know you want to reduce the price of all stuff further, but cannot,' said the cousin.

'No sense in upsetting the social balance. I don't wish to make enemies of that Ananda Bhavan *sait* or the others. There are all sorts of persons at their back.'

The cousin agreed in order to dispose of the question then and there, and let the other go on with the more interesting subject of Mali. He egged him on. 'Did you meet the girl today?'

'Why do you say "the girl" instead of Mali's wife?' Jagan asked with a certain amount of vicious pleasure.

The cousin, feeling trapped by this question, said generally, 'She seems to be a good girl. When I met her yesterday at . . .'

Before he could finish his sentence Jagan said, 'I am not doubting her goodness, but she is not married to Mali at all.' The cousin received the statement in silence, fearing that anything he said might smack of scandal. Jagan went on, 'She told me so herself; why should I doubt her?'

The cousin said simply, 'Then why not let her go back to her country, as Mali wants?' This sounded such a rational approach to the crisis that Jagan had nothing further to say for a long while. It was very difficult to recollect what he had meant to say or to refresh his memory with the righteous indignation he had felt. The cousin added, 'Our young men live in a different world from ours and we must not let ourselves be upset too much by certain things they do.'

This sounded a sage-like statement, but Jagan could not accept the theory of indifference which the cousin, still not knowing the exact facts, was developing. Jagan said, 'This sort of thing is unheard-of in our family. Even my grandfather's brother, who was known to be immoral, never did this sort of thing. When he was not married he never claimed that he was married, although . . .'

'I have heard my father speak about him. He was certainly married to three wives and had numerous other women. He never shirked a responsibility.' They were deriving a vicarious pleasure from going into the details of lechery practised by their forefathers.

'I can't understand how two young persons can live together like this without being married,' said Jagan and fell silent, letting his mind revel in sensuous imaginings of what had gone on within the walls of his house. 'I feel my home is tainted now. I find it difficult to go back there.'

The cousin said, 'You have heard only one side of the story. Why not speak to Mali and find out the other?'

'He has already told me he wants her to go.'

'It is because his business is not developing,' said the cousin.

'What business?' cried Jagan so emphatically that the cook carrying a tray to the front stall stood arrested and nearly dropped it from his hand, at which Jagan glared at him and said, 'You get on with your job. I am not speaking to you.' He added in a whisper, 'These boys are not what they used to be; they are becoming awfully inquisitive. I am sure he knows all about this affair.'

The cousin now brought the matter down to a practical level, as he always did. 'Why do you let this affect you so much? It is, after all, their business.'

'But I feel it is my home that is being dirtied. Mali is my son. Grace is not my daughter-in-law.'

'Oh, that is a very wrong, selfish view to take,' said the cousin, feeling his way now and getting the measure of Jagan's mental needs. His role was to help Jagan crystallize his attitudes in a crisis. He added, 'What is all your study of the *Gita* worth if you cannot keep your mind untouched by all this? You yourself have explained to me that one should not identify oneself with objects or circumstances.'

Jagan accepted this compliment with great pleasure although, if he had questioned it, he might not have been able to find out exactly what he had said, or why or when. Obliged to admit his devotion to the *Gita* and the wisdom derived from it, he mumbled, 'We are blinded by our attachments. Every attachment creates a delusion and we are carried away by it . . .'

'Too true, too true,' said the cousin. 'Equanimity is more important than anything else in life.'

'That is what I am seeking but never attain!' Jagan wailed and quietened his thoughts for a moment. Suddenly he remembered that he had been fooled by the young people and that the house which had remained unsullied for generations had this new taint to carry. How could he live in the same house with them? He was on the point of saying, 'I have half a mind to tell them to go where they please and do what they like, but not in my house . . .' But he checked himself; it was a statement that his tongue refused to phrase. Certain things acquired an evil complexion if phrased, but remained harmless in the mind. 'How do you expect me to go on living there?'

'If you have the back-door entrance, use it and don't go near their portion. Where else could they go now?'

'That is true, housing conditions being what they are. More-over, people will talk.' He begged, 'Please don't let anyone know.'

The cousin threw up his arms in horror. 'Unthinkable. What you say to me is a sacred trust, believe me.'

Assured by this protestation, Jagan said, 'What shall I do now?'

'About what?'

'About Mali and that girl.'

The cousin gave a clear-headed statement: 'Get through their marriage very quickly in the hill temple. It can be arranged within a few hours.'

'Alas, I don't know what her caste is, so how can I?'

'Oh, she can be converted. I know some persons who will do it.'

A burden was removed from his shoulders. Jagan said, 'You are my saviour. I don't know where I should be without you.'

Chapter Eleven

Jagan barricaded himself in completely. He derived a peculiar excitement in performing all the actions of a purificatory nature. He shut the communicating door between his part of the dwelling and Mali's and locked it on his side. He did everything possible to insulate himself from the evil radiations of an unmarried couple living together. There was a ventilator between the two portions of the house; he dragged up an old stool, and with the help of a long bamboo shut it tight. Now the isolation, more an insulation, was complete. He gave up the use of the front door, as it took him through a common passage trodden by the feet of the tainters. A whole morning he kept himself busy with these arrangements, dragging the stool hither and thither and shifting the ladder. After locking the back door of his house when he left for his shop, he took a side-lane which led to the main street. He noted that this path was over-grown with thorns and weeds. 'I must take out my spade and clear it,' he said to himself. Nearly fifty years had elapsed since he had traversed this lane. In those days, when his father's family had lived in a hut in the backyard and the front portion was growing up little by little, he and his brother used to hunt for grasshoppers amidst the weeds. All the blazing afternoons they would be active in this pursuit while the Malgudi summer scorched everything, and even the grasshoppers were reluctant to leave the paltry shade of the weed-plants. His elder brother carried a small tin; he cupped his palm over the grasshopper and trapped it, and, if it was a large one, transferred it to his tin as befitting an elder brother; if it was a little one, it was passed on to Jagan; but on no account would Jagan be permitted to catch one himself. He could only stand behind his brother and wait for his luck, with his own little tin in hand. This would go on all afternoon, until the grasshoppers learnt to anticipate their footfalls and to hop off to safety.

Sometimes their sister would trace them down here, and follow them doggedly, uttering sinister remarks: 'You are killing the animals here. I'll tell Father; they are found dead every day in the tins. You will both go to hell.' Jagan, afraid of this blackmailer, would plead with her to leave them alone, but his elder brother would say, 'Let her talk. No one wants her here. If she speaks to Father, I'll wring her neck,' and rear himself up menacingly and she would run away screaming in terror. 'They never liked me,' reflected Jagan. The sister had married a wealthy village idiot, became a rustic and brought forth an ugly brood of children, and the brother had cut all contact after the division of their father's estate. Ah, how intrigued they would be if they knew the full story of Mali! Since the advent of Grace, all his relations had ostracized him. The only reminder he had had from his sister was a postcard a year ago on the back of which she had written, 'We are ashamed to refer to you as a brother. Even when you joined Gandhi and lost all sense of caste, dining and rubbing shoulders with untouchables, going to jail, and getting up to all kinds of shameful things, we didn't mind anything. But now is it a fact that you have a beef-eating Christian girl for a daughter-in-law? I can hardly call you a brother in the presence of my in-laws. No one can blame Mali, with a father like you, etc . . .' And she had concluded with the gratifying thought that their parents were fortunately dead and spared the indignity of watching these unsavoury activities. Jagan had heard that his brother, who lived in Vinayak Street, often spoke of him in anger and shame; and he never invited him to join him in performing the anniversary ceremonies for their father. He was an orthodox man who managed the. headquarters of a religious order, established ten centuries ago with a million followers, and he had begun to disapprove of Jagan's outlook long ago.

His remarks were brought to Jagan from time to time by common friends and relatives and occasionally by the cousin, whose standing was secure everywhere. The elder brother had once remarked, 'How can you expect a good type of son when you have a father like Jagan?' What would they say if they knew the latest development? They would doubtless remove themselves even further. Jagan felt grateful for being an outcast, for it absolved him from obligations as a member of the family. Otherwise they would be making constant demands on his time and energy, compelling him to spend his time in family conclaves, sitting on carpets with a lot of kinsmen exchanging banalities while awaiting the call for the feast. Thus he had escaped the marriages of his nieces, the birthdays of his brother's successive children and several funerals.

Jagan was passing the statue when the green car with Mali and Grace drove past him. Mali applied the brake and waited for Jagan to come up. Grace opened the car-door and asked, 'Want a lift anywhere?'

'No,' said Jagan and tried to pass on.

'Were you spring-cleaning your home, Father? I heard the sounds of your activity.'

'Yes, I was trying to clean my surroundings,' Jagan said, putting into the word a new meaning. Mali sat staring ahead saying nothing. Jagan noted the serious care-worn look in his eyes, and felt a tug at heart. If he could have recklessly announced, 'Long live your story-writing machine! Here, take my bank-book, it's yours. I have no use for it,' all problems would be at an end. No, not all problems. Marriage? These two sitting so close with their legs touching and not married! What was their relationship? Now they were saying things against each other and yet they were nestling so close!

Later Jagan confided in the cousin, 'I had half a mind to accost them then and there, but I let them go. I will find another opportunity to clear up this whole business once and for all.'

By his architectural arrangements, Jagan had isolated himself so thoroughly that he didn't notice until a fortnight later that Grace was no longer there, and that there had been hardly any movement in the front part of the house. One morning he was so intrigued by the silence that he stood beside his door and applied an eye to the keyhole, after removing a little paper ball he had plugged into it. He saw no one, but he heard some movement in another room. He put the plug back into the key-hole, straightened himself, went round by the backyard and arrived at the front window and stood peering through the half-curtain. He couldn't see anything, but Mali called from within, 'Who is it?' Jagan tried to tip-toe away. A little later, Mali opened his window, saying, 'You could have knocked.'

'No, no,' said Jagan, 'I didn't want to . . .' He tried to retrace his steps through the side-lane. Mali watched him for a moment then cried, 'Father!' Jagan was thrilled. After many days he was called 'Father' again. He stopped.

The boy asked, 'Why do you prowl around like this?'

Jagan said in confusion, 'Where is Grace?'

'Why do you want her?' Mali asked gruffly.

'Because I have not seen her for a long time,' said Jagan, feeling bold enough to make that statement.

Mali said, 'How can you hope to see anyone when you have sealed yourself off and use the back door? It looks silly.'

Jagan pretended to attend to a jasmine bush as he noticed his neighbour watching them with great interest. 'Ever since he bought that house, this man has done nothing except watch our house. I wish I had bought it when it was offered. I could have given it to Mali. He'd have been near enough and far enough too.' Jagan was lost in these speculations for a moment, and Mali, also noticing the neighbour, suppressed his conversation. Jagan said, 'I want to talk to you both; why don't you come out?'

Mali withdrew his head from the window and came out by the front door. He wore a fancy dressing-gown, and had stuck his feet into slippers. He seemed to cower back and recoil from the bright Indian sunlight. It was as if he was unique and could not come out except with a fanfare and appropriate pageantry. He approached his father and said, 'I don't like that guy over there watching us. Don't talk loudly.'

'All right,' Jagan whispered hoarsely. The effort to suppress his natural tone choked him and puffed up the veins on his neck. He was unused to secrecies.

Mali said, 'Why should we talk in the garden? Can't we go in?'

Jagan was afraid to mention the actual reason, and slurred over it by saying, 'I thought it was pleasant here.'

'Yes,' said Mali cynically, 'with the sun scorching and all the neighbours providing an audience.'

The sting was lost on Jagan, whose only delight was that he had today caught his son in a talking mood. 'Let us move on to the shade in that corner. The man won't see us there.'

'But all the passers-by will watch us,' said Mali.

Jagan asked, 'Why should not people look at us? What's wrong with us?'

'People must respect other people's privacy, that's all. We don't find it in this country. In America no one stares at another.'

'If we avoided each other's looks, how should we understand each other? What is one ashamed of, that one's face must be hidden?' Mali could not carry on this debate. He found his father in an extraordinarily controversial mood today. He gave up his point. Jagan, triumphant, asked, 'Is Grace inside or not? I'd like to talk to you both on a matter of importance.'

'She is not here. She has gone to stay with some friends for a few days.'

'When did she go?' Jagan felt that his son was likely to resent his questioning tone, and so expanded the theme, 'I was wondering if it was not a very long time since I saw her.'

'You have sealed off the middle door and use the back door. What's your idea, Father?' While Jagan was choosing words for a plausible answer, the boy went on, 'Do you think my business is going to be dropped because you have shut the door? Our correspondence goes on and I must know where we stand. Do you imagine you have made me drop the project?'

It's a pity that they should be rushing to the edge of the precipice as usual. Jagan tried to give another turn to their talk. 'You must both be married soon.'

'What are you trying to say?' screamed Mali. Jagan explained. Mali merely said, 'You have been listening to nonsense. I never knew you could listen to such gossip.'

Jagan noted with pleasure that the boy had refrained from calling him 'silly' again. He asked, 'Does Grace gossip about herself? Anyway, I do not want to go into all that again. There is a very small temple, where you can go through a quick marriage. No one need be invited, just the three of us and a priest, and you can be done with the whole business in an hour.'

'Grace has been getting funny notions, that's why I told you to pack her off some weeks ago, but you grudged the expenditure,' said Mali. 'She is not in her right mind; she must go to a psychiatrist.'

'What's that?'

'Don't you know what a psychiatrist is? What a backwood this is, where nothing is known.' With that Mali turned and went in, leaving Jagan transfixed to the spot. He tried to recollect the words that Mali had said and to make out their meaning. There was no meaning. What was a psychiatrist? What would he do? Before he could sort it out in his mind, the neighbour edged along to the fence, commenting, 'So rare to see you! What is your son doing?'

'He is in business with some American businessmen.'

'Oh, that's very good. So he will earn dollars for our country. Very good, very good . . .' On this pleasant note Jagan tore himself away, because he felt that the next question was going to be about the daughter-in-law. Funny situation – not knowing whether she was a daughter-in-law or not! He was totally at a loss to decide who was lying.

Chapter Twelve

He was worried. The entire day passed with his mind completely obsessed. He was functioning with only a part of himself. Sivaraman's enquiries, the coming in of cash and the arrival and departure of his cousin at the appointed hour were all mechanically gone through. His cousin ate, spoke of various things, and waited as usual to talk of Mali, but Jagan was in no mood to encourage him, and the cousin gave up with resignation. 'Sometimes he talks, sometimes he doesn't. Take him as he comes, that's all,' he thought and slipped away at the right moment.

Jagan counted the cash and made the entries, but his mind worked on one theme only: the puzzle created by Mali. At every encounter he displayed a new facet, which might or might not have relevance to the previous one. Jagan was reminded of the concept of *Viswarupa* that he had read about in the *Bhagavad Gita*. When the warrior Arjuna hesitated to perform his duty on the battlefield, God came to him in the guise of his charioteer and revealed Himself in all His immensity. On one side he was thousand-faced. 'I behold You, infinite in forms on all sides, with countless arms, stomachs, mouths and eyes; neither Your end nor middle nor beginning do I see . . .' quoted Jagan inwardly, at the same time remaining rational enough to realize the irreverence of the comparison.

That evening Jagan sat all alone on the pedestal of the statue. All the others who had congregated around it were gone. Sir Frederick thrust his top into the world of sparkling stars. The night was hot; the still air and heat were suffocating. He saw his house beyond the statue; unless he went and switched on a light, there would be no light in it. It stood up, sinister, and silent. There was a time when it had seethed with life, lamps burning in every room, and during the festivals hundreds of mud lamps would be lit and arrayed all along the parapet. Theirs had been the brightest home in those days. That was long before the birth of Mali, years even before his marriage. He suddenly recollected the exact point in time when he had shed his bachelorhood, that day when he had travelled to the village of Kuppam in order to take a look at the bride proposed for him by the elders of his family. He had to go by train to Myel, a tiny red-tiled railway station set amidst emerald-green rice-fields, two stations beyond Trichy. From Myel he had to go on in a cart drawn by a pair of bullocks over a bumpy mud track, and in some places even over cultivated fields. The future bride's younger brother, who had come to meet him as a piece of courtesy, was also in the carriage. Jagan was in a happy mood and laughed uncontrollably at the way they were progressing in the cross-country run. Every time the wheels sank into a sandy patch and the cartman got down and heaved them out with oaths, Jagan felt tickled; but the boy stuck to his seat and remained grim and silent. He had been trained to show respect to a brother-in-law by being reserved; that boy had the grimmest face in the country. Ultimately he grew a long moustache as a commissioned air-force officer, and was lost sight of in the Burma campaign of 1942.

Jagan's father had sent his elder son to accompany him and had commanded Jagan, 'Don't stare at the girl. I have seen her and I know she is good-looking. Don't imagine you are a big judge of persons.' At the end of the bumpy journey, he was received with a lot of fuss and seated on a carpet spread on the *pyol* of an ancient house. His future father-in-law and a number of his relations had assembled to have a look and measure the proposed bridegroom from different angles. They all engaged him in conversation and tried to judge his intelligence and outlook. Jagan had already been warned by his elder brother not to be too communicative, as a certain mysteriousness was invaluable in a son-in-law. Everyone kept asking as if in a chorus, 'How was your journey?' Jagan stroked his tuft with one hand, fumbled with the rim of his cap and threw furtive glances at his brother for a signal. When his brother nodded slightly, he answered, 'Oh, it was good.' 'Did you have comfortable seats in the train?' asked one examiner sitting at the farthest corner of the *pyol* and this time Jagan said on his own, 'Of course.' It was a matter of propriety to say a good word about the journey because the railway ran over their territory. 'What is your subject of study at the college?' asked another one, and Jagan answered, 'History' without waiting for his brother's sanction. (Later, when they were alone his brother nudged him and said, 'You should have said "mathematics"; I know these people would prefer a mathematical son-in-law; all the boys in this part of the country are first-class mathematicians.' To make matters worse Jagan had not only said, 'History' but had also attempted some humorous explanations about his capacity in mathematics.)

While talking Jagan cast furtive glances into the hall in the hope of catching a glimpse of his future bride. He had as yet no idea what she would look like. He had been shown a rather over-touched shiny photograph of her, mounted within a floral board: a sharp-faced young person with tightly braided hair. The photographer had managed to achieve his task without revealing what the girl's eyes looked like, and Jagan when presented with the photograph had been unable to scrutinize it for long, for his father was watching him; but he was racked with a doubt whether the girl might not be squint-eyed, since it was well known that photographers tried to slur over such facts for purposes of marriage. He liked her height as she stood with her elbow resting on a corner stand with a flower vase on it; her fingers looked slender and long. She had been decorated with so many ornaments that it was impossible to guess what she really looked like, and, of course, the photographer had imparted the appropriate complexion.

Now Jagan was going to clear up his doubts; engaged in answering the questions of the assembly, he was simultaneously wondering when the call would come for him to enter the house and examine his bride. They brought a silver tray heaped with golden-hued *jilebi* and *bonda* made of raw banana, and coffee, brown and hot, in two silver tumblers, at the sight of which Jagan became hungrier than ever. Left to himself he would have gobbled up the entire lot (his food theories had not yet begun), but a glance from his brother restrained him. The protocol was inflexible: they were honoured visitors, on whose verdict would depend the future of the girl; it was a highly serious and important role, and they were expected to carry themselves with dignity and not show any emotion even at the sight of *jilebi*; even if one was maddeningly hungry one had to say, 'Oh, why all this? I cannot eat. We have just had coffee and everything in the train . . .' Jagan mumbled this sentence with the utmost reluctance, jointly with his brother, who uttered it with great clarity. All the same, the code demanded that their hosts should press the delicacies upon them. Then one would have to break off the *jilebi* minutely with the tip of one's fingers and transfer it to one's mouth, and generally display reluctance or even aversion until pressed again, and then, just to please others, eat two or three bits in succession and then take an elegant sip of coffee. The essence of behaviour in these circumstances consisted in seeming to do things for the sake of one's hosts. One left half a cup of coffee undrunk and the edibles practically untouched; one peeled a banana indifferently, broke off a couple of inches and ate them without moving a muscle, leaving the rest of the fruit to be thrown away. This was Jagan's first occasion for displaying ceremonial behaviour. At home he was well known for his gluttony, indeed his mother admired him for it. When he came home from school he always rummaged in the kitchen cupboard and stuffed his mouth with cashew nuts, coconut, jaggery, and varied fried edibles which his mother prepared for his benefit. On Saturdays and Sundays, when he stayed at home, he ate non-stop, and this always elicited the utmost appreciation from his father, who would remark, 'This son of ours must have been a rat in his last life, considering his nibbling capacity.' For one with such a reputation it was rather hard to observe the restraints of protocol; his fingers itched, his palate was agitated. However, after tasting a minute portion of the repast, Jagan resolutely pushed away the tray.

Then his future mother-in-law appeared at the doorway, unobtrusively studied the features of her son-in-law, and announced with all gentleness, 'Why not adjourn inside?' addressing no one in particular. Whereupon the master of the house rose to his feet, saying, 'Why don't you all come in?' which was again a kind of code. Although everyone was fully aware of the purpose of the young man's visit, one had to view it casually, neither side displaying too much interest or anxiety. Everyone sitting on the *pyol* got up. Jagan's brother, a born diplomat, was the last but one to respond, and the last was Jagan, though he was burning with impatience. He was worried, too, lest he should perpetrate some silly *faux pas* and become a disgrace to his family, whose previous experience in such matters was none too happy. Jagan had become an eligible bachelor three years before and had inspected four would-be brides so far. On two occasions he had kept staring at the girls in open-mouthed wonder because they happened to be stunningly ugly; on another occasion he undisguisedly watched the legs of the girl as she walked in because she was reputed to be lame. For these lapses he had been severely reprimanded, and his action went into the repertory of family jokes. Whenever his maternal uncles or others from his mother's side arrived and gathered after dinner in the courtyard looking for scapegoats for their gossip, invariably Jagan supplied the text. This time, they had tried to prevent mistakes by sending his elder brother to chaperon him through this delicate mission. The brother was certainly not going to spare the authority vested in him; he was keeping his eye on him, commanding and manipulating him by narrowing his eyelids or opening them wide.

Next they were all led to the central hall of the village home. In honour of this visit many cluttering benches, rolls of bedding and other odds and ends had been moved to a corner and covered with a huge carpet; on the floor was spread an enormous striped carpet; incense sticks were lit so as to overwhelm the smell of the cowshed in the backyard. 'These fellows from the city are fussy and don't know how to live with domestic animals,' her father had said, or so Jagan's wife reported later in life. For Jagan the scene was heavenly; he felt a momentary satisfaction at the thought that all these preparations were for his sake (even if it was the brother who was the controller). They showed him a seat and the rest arranged themselves around. Jagan kept thinking, 'With so many around, my view is going to be obstructed and then no one should blame me if I demand a second appearance.' There could be no such thing as a second appearance, but his imagination was running wild. Some voices approached and Jagan stiffened and resolutely avoided his brother's glance. A harmonium sounded mysteriously somewhere inside, and to the accompaniment of its discordant notes a slightly masculine voice (he was to become familiar with it later in life) sang Thyagaraja's 'Telisi Rama Chintanamu . . .' (The power of the very thought of Rama . . .) 'Ambika is singing with the harmonium; she felt too shy to sing in the presence of so many, so she is singing in the room. She can sing very well. I have got her a teacher from the town.' The father mentioned a place six miles away. Jagan was certainly not in a critical enough mood to say they should have spared themselves the trouble. The music ceased. There were stirrings inside, some arguments and protests, and then a little girl with tightly pleated hair emerged grinning with the comment,

'Ambika refuses to come out, she feels shy,' at which all the elders joked and laughed. The master of the house raised his voice and called, 'Ambika, come on, come on, there's nothing to be afraid of in these days.' And he addressed the women inside in a general way: 'Don't make fun of her, she will be all right . . .' After this preamble a tall girl emerged swishing her lace *sari*, facing the assembly and smiling, and Jagan's heart gave a thump. 'Not at all like the photo, so tall! I can't believe . . .' The master of the house saved further speculation by announcing, 'She is my first daughter,' and the tall girl said, 'Ambika is coming.' The rest Jagan did not hear; he lost interest in the tall girl who was only a sort of advance guard for her younger sister, who came with downcast eyes and bowed head and moved across the arena so fast that Jagan could not take in any detail. 'Not short nor tall, nor fat nor puny . . .' Jagan could not arrange her in any clear outline. The details overlapped, but producing only impressions of an agreeable nature, and not provoking aversion as on the previous occasions.

'How is she to know what I look like if she flits by so fast?' Jagan speculated. 'I don't care what my brother is going to say later; for the present I am going to stare, gaze and study. I don't care what anybody thinks.' He stared unwinkingly at the girl. She had a thick wad of wavy hair, plaited and decorated with flowers, and many pieces of jewellery sparkled on her person. She wore a light green *sari* which suited her complexion. Was she fair or dusky? Who could say? His vision was clouded with a happy haze and he might keep peering at her a whole day with none to disturb his study, yet he could never clear his doubts about her personality. During these muddled moments, she shot one lightning glance at him, which somehow, through the fates, coincided with a look he was himself shooting at her, their eyes met, and Jagan's heart palpitated and raced, and before he could do anything about it, it was all over. The assembly was on its feet, people were leaving and the vision was gone.

All through their journey back, Jagan remained pensive. His brother did not try to disturb his mood. Their train was due to arrive two hours later, but the double bullock cart had put them down at the little railway station before sunset and had returned to the village. Jagan sat on a weighing platform, looking away at a range of mountains beyond the green fields. His brother, who was pacing up and down impatiently, stopped by for a minute to say, 'Why should they have dumped us down here so early?'

Jagan merely said, 'They have their own reasons, I suppose. I heard the young fellow say that the bullocks had some difficulty at night . . .'

'Ah, you are already assuming the role of their spokesman? Does that mean . . .?'

Jagan nodded an assent somewhat shyly and stood up and asked eagerly, 'How will they know? Should we not tell them?'

His brother stood stiff and said, 'I hope you have not been a fool, telling anyone that you like the girl. One doesn't cheapen oneself.'

'No, no,' protested Jagan. 'I was with you all the time and never spoke to anyone except to say goodbye . . .' When he had had to leave at last his feet had tarried and moved at a snail's pace in the hope that the girl would peep out of the doorway, at least to prove that she loved him as conveyed by her lightning look; he wanted somehow to assure her that he would marry her and that he was not in the least prejudiced by her harmonium music; in his excited state of mind it seemed to him a matter of the utmost urgency to convey to her his message, and if she really cared for him she would show some slight sign at parting. He had never expected that such factors as train-times and the poor sight of bullocks would tear him away from his beloved's aura so unceremoniously.

On the train journey, he remained brooding. He was troubled by the feeling that he had missed the chance, somehow, to say farewell to his beloved; the thought of her was extremely comforting, soothing and also in a quiet way thrilling. His brother, now having no policing to do, was asleep in his seat, leaving Jagan free to go back to the village in his thoughts and roam unfettered. Thinking it over, Jagan felt charmed by every bit of the expedition: their house was nice and cosy, their hall smelt beautifully of incense which somehow blended successfully with the cowdung smell from their cattle-shed; the harmonium was out of tune, but it would not be proper to judge her music from it. Her voice was gruff because she had had to adjust it to that horrid instrument; he was sure that she really had a sweet voice to suit her face . . . Then he too fell asleep during the rest of the journey. They had to get off and change into another train at some junction and they arrived at Malgudi station early in the morning. His brother hailed a *jutka*, haggled with the man, and they started out for their ancient home at Lawley Extension. Milkmen were out with their cows, a few cyclists were on the move to reach the single textile mill of the town by the time its doors should open. Except for these the city was still asleep.

When the brothers arrived home, their mother was sprinkling water on the front doorstep and decorating it with flour. While his brother was still arguing with the *jutka* man who was demanding two annas more than the agreed fare, Jagan picked up his little bag and passed into the house. His mother just smiled at him but asked no questions. His father was drawing water from the well in the backyard; he glanced at Jagan and went on with his work. His sister was circumambulating the sacred *tulasi* plant in the central yard and grinned at him mischievously, while her lips were muttering prayers. Jagan retired to his room, asking himself, 'Is no one interested in my opinion of the girl? No one is prepared to inquire whether I like her or not. Does it mean that they are all opposed to the idea?' Nor did his brother pause to enlighten anyone, but proceeded to the backyard in order to help his father at the well.

But somehow the information leaked out and his sister was the first to come to his room when he was about to leave for the college, her eyes glittering with mischief. 'Aye! Hai . . .' she cried and clicked her tongue provocatively. 'Someone is getting married soon . . .' The house was in great excitement. His brother's wife had been summoned from her parents' house in order to help with the arrangements for the wedding. Stage by stage the tempo increased. His father wrote numerous postcards every day between noon and three and carried them to the railway station in order to make sure that they went by the mail train. He had many relatives whom he highly respected, elders without whose sanction he never proceeded in any matter. Every day the postman's arrival was awaited by him at ten o'clock. In those days a postcard cost only three paise, but one could cram on its face and back as many hundred words as one pleased. After receiving the approvals from his elders, Jagan's father carried on several consultations with his wife in whispers in a far-off corner of the second courtyard. Jagan, as became a junior, was careful not to show too much personal interest in his marriage, but he was anxious to know what was going on. He would have been snubbed if he had inquired. He had to depend upon his younger sister, who stood about casually while the elders talked, eavesdropped, and brought him news. She would seek him out as he sat at his desk apparently studying, and then whisper to him, 'Grand-uncle has approved.' 'Father is writing to the bride's people tomorrow; they are waiting for an auspicious time.' 'Father wants a dowry of five thousand rupees,' which really worried Jagan. Suppose the other refused? Then what? 'They want to have the marriage celebrated in September.' Only three months! Jagan felt scared at the thought of becoming a married man in three months. It was all right as long as one dreamed of a girl and theoretically speculated about marriage, but to become a positive and concrete husband, it was a terrifying reality. 'Why do they want to have the marriage so soon?' he asked.

Father's letter of approval went to Kuppam village. Many, many letters passed between the parties. A voluminous correspondence grew, which Jagan's father harpooned methodically on to a long iron spike with a circular wooden stop at one end, by which system they had preserved their family correspondence from time immemorial. One evening the bride's party arrived with huge brass trays covered with betel leaves, fruits, saffron, new clothes, a silver bowl of fragrant sandal paste, a huge heap of sugar crystals on a silver plate and a pair of silver lamps. A dozen priests were assembled in the hall. A few neighbours and relatives had been invited and Jagan was given a new *dhoti* and made to sit in the centre of the assembly. They then unfolded a sheet of paper, on which they had previously spent a considerable time drafting the exact wedding notice, getting the names down correctly. The senior priest of the house, a gaunt old man, stood up and read the notice aloud, his voice quivering with nervousness. It announced that Jagannath, son of so and so, was to marry Ambika, daughter of so and so, on the tenth of September, etc., etc. The father of the bride handed this important document ceremoniously to Jagan's father, together with an envelope in which he had put currency notes, half the dowry in advance, and gently suggested, 'Please ask your elder son to count the cash.' Jagan's father made some deprecating sounds, but passed the envelope on to his elder son for counting, who lost no time in performing the task and confirming, 'Two thousand five hundred.' 'It was not necessary to count,' said Jagan's father gracefully, 'but since you insisted on it . . .' 'In money matters it is best to be assured. How could I be sure that my counting was perfect? I always like to get cash counted again and again,' said Jagan's father-in-law, at which everyone laughed as if it were a brilliant piece of humour. Then they all adjourned for a grand feast prepared by a company of expert cooks. Huge plantain leaves were spread out in the second court, with silver tumblers and bowls for each guest and a dozen delicacies and side dishes in addition to heaps of softly-cooked ivory-like rice. A pipe-and-drum party seated in the front part of the house created enough din to make it known to the whole town that a marriage was being settled. The house had been brilliantly lit with numerous brass lamps as well as gas lamps, which shed an enormous amount of greenish illumination everywhere. Jagan felt overwhelmed by the celebrations. He kept thinking, 'All this for my marriage! How seriously they have taken it; no backing out now.' By the midnight train the bride's party were seen off. When they were gone, Jagan's mother and her relations went in and lost no time in assessing the value of the clothes and silver left by them as presents. They were satisfied with the weight and design of the silverware. Mother expressed her utmost approval by telling Jagan, 'Your father-in-law is not a mean sort; see how solid all the presents are!' Jagan, identifying himself with them, felt personally complimented.

The house wore an appearance of extraordinary activity as September approached. Jagan lost count of time. His end-of-term examinations were over and his father had permitted him to take time off from college and assist the people at home. Mother went about saying, 'Although we are the bridegroom's party, we cannot spare ourselves; there are things to do.' Clothes had to be chosen for the bride and others, for which purpose Mother and her relations went to the Universal Sari Emporium and spent eight hours at a stretch examining gold borders, fabrics and hundreds of *saris*. Jagan spent much time at his tailor's shop measuring himself for silk shirts and a dark suit; his mother and the others seemed keen that the bridegroom should appear in a suit during the wedding procession. Jagan would have preferred to be clad in his *dhoti* and *jibba*, but he was forced by everyone to accept a tweed suit. His elder brother was very vehement on the subject, having himself gone through it all some years ago. He also took charge of the printing of invitation cards and ran between Truth Printing and their home and prepared an elaborate list of addresses. Father harassed everyone about the list, asking if so and so had been included, and, if not, to do it at once. He woke them up at midnight to suggest a name just occurring to him. He did not want any friend or relation remotely connected with Jagan to be overlooked. No one had ever suspected that Father would be such a keen sender-out of invitations or could collect or recollect so many names, although he was never sure whether the name or initials were correct (sometimes he knew a person only by a pet name), whether so and so was living at that address or even whether he was alive at all.

They sent out three thousand invitations. The result was that an enormous crowd turned up by every bus, train and vehicle, at the wedding in Kuppam village. Jagan's whole time was spent in greeting the guests or prostrating himself at their feet if they were older relatives. The priests compelled him to sit before the holy fire performing complicated rites and reciting sacred *mantras*; his consolation was that during most of these he had to be clasping his wife's hand; he felt enormously responsible as he glanced at the sacred *thali* he had knotted around her neck at the most auspicious moment of the ceremonies. He was overwhelmed by the scent of flowers and jasmine garlands and holy smoke, the feel of expensive silks and lace on his person and the crackling new *saris* in which his wife appeared from time to time draped as in a vision. Her voice was not so gruff as it had sounded in the company of the harmonium; she had an enchanting smile, voice and laugh and she spoke to him with shy reserve whenever he was able to corner her and snatch a little privacy in the house which was crowded every inch with guests and visitors. He found the company of so many a bother and distraction. Whenever he found a moment to talk to his wife someone or other would butt in with the remark, 'Come on, come on, enough; don't get attached to the apron strings yet; you have a whole life to sit and admire your wife, whereas you will lose sight of us after the marriage.' These were routine jokes and interruptions in any marriage party, but Jagan felt particularly martyred, and felt he would have been happier with fewer relatives and friends around. The noise, the music of drums and pipes, the jokes and feasting went on for three days and ended with a photographer organizing a huge group with the bride and the bridegroom seated in the centre. The celebrations, on the whole, concluded peacefully, although at one stage a certain bitterness arose over the quality of the coffee supplied to the bridegroom's house by their hosts, and one of Jagan's uncles, a very elderly man, threatened to leave the marriage party.

There was one other embarrassment on the night of the wedding feast. Someone who held the highest precedence in the family hierarchy (Jagan's father's cousin, a seventy-five-year-old man who had come all the way from Berhampore for the marriage) was given a half-torn banana leaf to dine on and was seated in the company of children instead of in the top row. This threatened to develop into a first-class crisis, but the girl's father openly apologized for the slip and all was forgotten. Something that upset all the womenfolk of the bridegroom's party was that the bride was not provided with the gold waist-belt that had been promised when the original list of jewellery was drawn up, the goldsmith in the town had delayed and finally, when the piece was delivered, it was found to be made not of one gold-sheet, but a number of little gold bars intertwined with silk cords. The women felt that this was downright cheating. 'They are saving the gold!' they commented angrily. They would have even gone to the extent of stopping the marriage, but for the fact that Jagan did not approve of all this hullabaloo over a gold belt, explaining to his mother, 'This is the latest fashion; nowadays the girls do not want to be weighed down with all that massive gold.' At which they became very critical of him, saying that he had already become hen-pecked, and was already an unpaid advocate for his wife's family. Even his brother managed to take him aside during this crisis and say, 'Don't make a fool of yourself so soon. Why don't you leave these problems for womenfolk to discuss in the way they want?' Jagan had the temerity to reply, 'It is because they are criticizing my wife, poor girl!' At this demonstration of loyalty his brother left him with a wry smile, saying, 'You are obsessed, it is no use talking to you.'

Jagan was given a room in the middle block. When he and his wife shut the door, they were in a world of their own within the confines of the heavy four-poster. At the performance of the consummation ceremony, Jagan's father had insisted on the nuptial suite being furnished properly at the expense of the bride's party. In one corner of the room Jagan was supposed to have his study (he still had his examinations to face). When they were alone, Jagan spent all his time in love-making. He lost count of time. He found his education a big nuisance, cut his classes, and came back home and sneaked into his room and failed in every examination, forcing his father to comment that Ambika should be sent back to her parents' house at least for six months if Jagan was ever to take his degree. At home Jagan spent very little time with his sister, mother or brother, as he used to, but shut himself in and awaited his wife's arrival. But she had her own duties in a large joint household; she had to do her share of work in the kitchen, helping her mother-in law in cooking, serving, scrubbing and sweeping the house, washing vessels and finally awaiting her mother-in-law's company for every meal. It would be unseemly for a daughter-in-law to seek her husband's company when the others were busy in the house in various ways; the elder daughter-in-law set the model for these codes of conduct, modelling herself on Jagan's mother, who had had her training early in life when she entered the family as a daughter-in-law. Ambika often enough reminded Jagan of her obligations as a daughter-in-law, but he was blind to everything except his own inclinations. When he came home and waited in his room for his wife's company and she was busy elsewhere, he sulked and quarrelled with her or pretended to be absorbed in his studies when she came. His wife always liked to have him in a pleasant mood and sooner or later would yield to his inordinate demands. His father severely reprimanded him when he found him indifferent to his studies. His mother often commented, 'A son is a son until the wife comes,' feeling sore that he could spare so little time for the others at home. His younger sister said, 'Who may you be, stranger? We have forgotten your face.' And his wife herself often said, 'Please don't create all this embarrassment for me. At least pretend that you are interested in the others.' His elder brother took him into the garden and advised, 'I know how you feel about things. I have passed through it all myself. If you spend four hours in your bedroom, at least give the others an hour now and then; otherwise you make yourself unpopular at home.' With one thing and another Jagan's stock was pretty low at home, but he did not care, as he lived in a perfect intoxication of husbandhood. Later, when his wife failed to have a baby and there were whispers and rumours, Jagan told his wife, 'I wish people could see us now on this side of the door, and then they would stop talking.'

Despite all his bragging there was no outside proof of his manhood. They had been married for almost ten years now; he had failed repeatedly in the Intermediate and was now failing in the B.A. class and still there was no sign of a child in the house. His brother had moved off to Vinayak Street with his entire family, which had become quite a crowd now. His sister was married and had gone to her husband's house. The big house had become silent and people began to notice how empty it was. Jagan's mother began to grumble that there were no children at home; it was one more stick to beat the daughter-in-law with. When she was tired with housework, such as washing and scrubbing the floor of the entire house, she went about muttering, 'All one asks of a girl is that she at least bring some children into a house as a normal person should; no one is asking for gold and silver; one may get cheated with regard to a gold belt even. Why can't a girl bear children as a million others in the world do?' All this was heard by the daughter-in-law scrubbing another part of the floor; she went on with her work without replying and took it out of Jagan when the door shut on them for the night. Sometimes she treated it as a joke as they sat, he with his B.A. text before him and she on the edge of the table with her legs swinging: 'I dread the monthly periods nowadays. They will start commenting . . .'

'Why don't you pretend, as some modern girls do, that you are not in the month?' But that was a frivolous suggestion. In an orthodox household with all the pujas and the gods, a menstruating woman had to isolate herself, as the emanations from her person were supposed to create a sort of magnetic defilement, and for three days she was fed in a far-off corner of the house, and was unable to move about freely. Jagan was very irritated and cried 'Are they not satiated with children? My brother has provided enough children for several houses and my sister has begun in the true tradition with three children in four years. Why can't they be satisfied with affairs as they are now?'

'Because your mother would have nothing to comment on if we had a child,' Ambika suggested, then mumbled, 'As far as our family is concerned, all my sisters have many children, and your mother's insinuation that I am infertile . . .'

Jagan at once rushed to the defence of his own family. 'On our side too there can be no misgiving. Do you know there is a group photo of my grandmother at the centre of all her children and grandchildren and do you know how many heads you can count?'

'Forty? Fifty?' asked Ambika. 'We also have a group photo in our house with our grandmother; do you know how many children and grandchildren and great-grandchildren there are?'

'One hundred and twenty?' asked Jagan mischievously.

His wife replied, 'No, don't try to joke about it; one hundred and three; and the photographer, it seems, charged four times his usual price.' She was reddening under her skin, her temper was slightly rising as she said, 'We are not an impotent family.'

Jagan was irked by her suggestion and looked up from his book with consternation. He had no answer to give. His devotion to bed had unconsciously diminished lately. Thinking it over, he recollected how often he rolled up a carpet, took a pillow and went out to sleep on the verandah, grumbling about the heat. 'It is getting to be very hot here; shall I sleep on the verandah? Would you be afraid?' 'Afraid of what?' Ambika would ask jokingly at first, but gradually, as time went by, with irritation. He hardly noticed her mood and went out and slept. This had become a more or less permanent arrangement except for when she returned, after a long absence, from her father's house, when he would give her passionate attention for a week running, hardly worrying about whether he was adequate; it was a question that he never at any time asked himself or his wife. He felt fatigued by all the apparatus of sex, its promises and its futility, the sadness and the sweat at the end of it all, and he assumed that his wife shared his outlook. Moreover, he had read in a book that Nature had never meant sex to be anything more than a means of propagation of the species, that one drop of white blood was equal to forty drops of red blood, and that seminal waste and nervous exhaustion reduced one's longevity, the essence of all achievement being celibacy and conservation.

It had become imperative for him to produce a child, and he

didn't know what more he could do about it. Ambika herself was beginning to crave one. He had to do something about it. She sulked and blamed him with her looks. When she saw him rolling up his carpet, she said rather bitterly, 'Why don't you go and sleep at the foot of Lawley Statue? It must be much cooler there.' When she taunted him thus, he felt extremely confused and attempted to joke it off with, 'That statue was not built for us to sleep on,' which even as he was uttering it sounded extremely silly in his own ears. When she taunted him further, he would put out the light, and pull her to the bed, and roll about, imagining himself to be the 'Sheik' in the Hollywood film in which Rudolph Valentino demonstrated the art of ravishing women.

His father suddenly said one morning, 'Next Tuesday we are going to the temple on Badri Hill. You had better apply for two days' leave from your college. Your wife will also come.' When Father said anything so specific there could be no discussion of the subject. Jagan was about to leave for his college. His father, who generally spent his time in the back garden, had come up to the middle part of the house to tell him this, which itself indicated the seriousness of the situation. Still, Jagan had the hardihood to ask, 'Why are we going to that temple?'

His father said, 'The temple is known as Santana Krishna; a visit to it is the only known remedy for barrenness in women.'

Jagan blushed. He wanted to assure his father of his wife's fecundity and describe to him the group photo in their house with her grandmother and the one hundred and three others, but he felt tongue-tied; one didn't discuss these things with one's father – nor with one's mother. He was a determined student this year, having made up his mind to pass his B.A. in order to prove that husbandhood was quite compatible with scholarship; that would at least prevent people from blaming his wife for his failure. Whenever the results came out and he had failed, there were pointed references within Ambika's hearing, so that the moment the bedroom door was shut she would say, 'Why don't you pick up your books and go away to a hostel? Your mother seems to think I am always lying on your lap, preventing you from touching your books.'

She looked so outraged that he felt like mitigating the seriousness with a joke of his own brand: 'If I have been failing it is because I don't believe education is important, that is all.'

'Your mother remarked that, being uneducated myself, I want to drag you down to my own level.'

'Why don't you put your fingers into your ears whenever Mother talks in that strain?'

'Why don't you use your intelligence and pass your examination?'

He said, 'Yes, that is also a good idea,' and applied himself to the task with all his might. He never arrived late for his class, never missed a lesson, and drew up a general chart of subjects and a working timetable. He sat at his desk and studied far into the night. Into this nicely readjusted life his father came crashing with his plan for visiting the temple.

Jagan pleaded, 'Can't we go after the examinations?'

His father glared at him and said, 'We have waited long enough,' and then, feeling that he sounded too commanding, added, 'This is the only month when we can go up the hill; if the rains start we shan't be able to get there. Full of leeches and such things. Ten months in the year it is raining up there.'

The base of the hill had to be reached by bus. The party consisted of Jagan and his wife, his father and mother. He felt touched by his father's solicitude in offering to climb the hill at his age. His mother looked extraordinarily pleased at reaching a solution at last for the barrenness of her daughter-in-law. She kept on saying, 'Good things only come with time. Otherwise, why would I not have thought of all this earlier, last year for instance?' She was bawling over the noise of the bus as they occupied a long seat, clutching their little bundles. Ambika felt a little shy. Some other woman in the bus asked across the aisle, 'Where are you going?'

'To the temple on Badri Hill . . .'

'Ah, the right time to go, and you will be blessed with children.'

'Not me,' said Jagan's mother. 'I have enough.' And they all laughed.

A man sitting beside the woman leaned forward to say, 'If the god blesses you, you may have twins. I know from experience!' And they all laughed again.

'One does not ask for twins; they are difficult to tend. We once had twins in the house of a distant relative, and the parents just went mad, both the babies demanding feed at the same moment or rejecting it at the same moment. I shall be happy if my daughter-in-law has a child, the next following in the normal way,' said Jagan's mother.

'How many sons have you?' asked the woman and they went into details of their family arrangements. Someone on the back seat was sick and the bus had to be stopped every now and then for him to lean out and relieve himself. Ambika, as became the daughter-in-law of the house, sat beside Jagan's mother, and Jagan sat beside his father, who had the businesslike aspect of someone going out to negotiate a contract.

Jagan would have enjoyed his wife's company rather than his father's, but it would be unthinkable for women to sit with men, and Ambika had to keep her mother-in-law company out of courtesy, so that Jagan was forced to sit by his father. It was a long seat running end to end below the windows. On Jagan's other side, there was a man from the forest with a string of beads around his neck, holding on his lap a small wooden cage containing a mottled bird, which occasionally let out a cry, sounding like doors moving on ancient, unoiled hinges. When it made this noise, it drowned the conversation of the passengers (quite fifty of them in a vehicle expected to accommodate half that number legally, some with tickets, some without, for the conductor pocketed the cash and adjusted the records accordingly, for which purpose he was constantly pulling out a pad and making entries). Remarks, inquiries, advice, announcements, the babble of men's talk, women's shrill voices and children crying or laughing, formed a perfect jumble and medley of sounds constantly overwhelmed by the shriek let out by the mottled bird. Jagan's father was engaged in a prolonged conversation with a peasant on his right, who was cracking groundnuts and littering the floor with shells, on the subject of manures and the technique of well-digging. Jagan glanced up at his wife and noticed that she was tired, the noise and the rattle were wearing her out. He wished he had her at his side. He would have pointed out and said, 'See those trees, and those hills? Aren't they beautiful? Are you aware that this trip is for your benefit?' and she would probably have retorted, 'For yours, let us say. I don't need a miracle to conceive. Remember the group photo in our house.' And then he would have teased her, pinched her back and so forth, which would have ended in a quarrel or in her laughing over it all. One couldn't say definitely. After all these years of married life, he could not really anticipate her reactions. Sometimes she took things easily, with the greatest cheer, sometimes she stung him and glared at him for the same remark. She was a model of goodness and courtesy and cheerfulness generally, but she could lash with her tongue when her temper was roused.

A few weeks before, Father had complained that something was wrong with the sauce; it turned out that it was over-salted. An on-the-spot inquiry was held. The mother-in-law demanded, 'Ambika, did you add salt to the sauce?' Ambika said, 'Yes, of course, Mother,' in a polite tone from inside the kitchen. Mother was serving the men in the dining hall. At her daughter-in-law's admission, she dropped the plate in her hand and went in, demanding an explanation. 'Who asked you to put salt into it?' The girl replied haughtily, 'I don't know,' at which they heard the elder lady saying, 'Should not anyone have the sense to ask whether a thing is already salted or not? What's to happen when several hands add salt? The stuff is fit only for the street gutter, not for eating; this is how everything gets wasted and ruined in this house, I know. I know how it all happens . . .' 'Bring some more rice,' said Jagan's father from the dining hall. Ambika took the rice and served, leaving her mother-in-law to continue: 'One doesn't ask for extraordinary things; they are not for us, we are not destined to enjoy the spectacle of a gold waist-band, like hundreds of others, but one wants at least a sensible . . .' She did not finish her sentence. Ambika was heard to cry, 'I don't care,' and dropping the dish, retired from the scene. She shut herself in her room and refused all food, throwing the whole house into a turmoil. She complained that she was not feeling like eating, that was all. Later in the week, when the situation had calmed down, she explained to Jagan, 'Do you know what I said to your mother? "Why are you so obsessed with the gold belt? What has it to do with salt or sugar? Have you never seen a gold belt in all your life?" ' Since that day, his mother had been very sparing in her remarks, particularly with reference to the gold belt. They had all along under-estimated Ambika's temper.

The bus deposited them in a village at the foot of the hill. It was probably the smallest village on any map, consisting of two rows of huts and a couple of wooden stands made of packing cases on which a little merchandise was displayed, mainly for the convenience of pilgrims going uphill – coconuts, bananas, betel leaves and flowers.

Mother was evidently tired after the journey and sat on a boulder to rest herself, while Father carried on interminable negotiations with the coconut-sellers over the price, trying to beat them down. Finally he yielded, grumbling that these villagers were spoilt nowadays and had become exploiters of the worst kind, and flourished his fists in anger. 'We have come from twenty miles away. Should we not expect some consideration for our trouble? If I had known the price of things here, I'd have brought all the stuff from home,' he cried irascibly.

Mother interposed from where she sat, 'That is not permitted. Custom requires . . .'

'Yes, yes, it was written in the *Vedas* ten thousand years ago that you must be exploited on this spot of earth by this particular coconut-woman. True, true,' he said cynically, glaring at his son and daughter-in-law sitting on another boulder, hinting that if only people displayed normal fecundity, one would not have to buy coconuts at an exorbitant price. Jagan squirmed at the look his father gave him and felt more impotent than ever, but Ambika, at whom he glanced, looked defiant, as if ready to bring out the group photo of a hundred and three.

But for the fact that he was a coward, Jagan would have asked his parents, 'Haven't you enough grandchildren? Why do you want more? Why don't you leave me alone?' Meanwhile the coconut-woman was saying, 'Don't grudge a little extra expense; the grandson will bring you a lot of good fortune when he arrives.' At which the old gentleman softened and asked, 'How are you sure it'll be a son, not a daughter?' 'No one who prays at that temple is ever disappointed with a daughter,' she replied.

As if in fulfilment of the coconut-seller's prophecy, Mali was born. The very minute he was delivered (in the village home of his mother) he was weighed on a scale-pan, even before the midwife could clean him up properly, and an equivalent weight in gold, silver and corn was made up to be delivered to the god on Badri Hill, according to the solemn vow made during their visit.

When she came home, bringing the three-months-old baby, Ambika's parents had sent with her an enormous load of gifts, as prescribed in the social code for the first-born.

A huge feast was held to which a hundred guests were invited; they had to cover the floor of all three segments of the house with dining leaves. Mali still looked puny and hardly able to bear all the gold and jewellery the fond grandparents had heaped on him. After dinner, chewing betel leaves with great contentment, Jagan's father looked very happy. The house was filled with the babble of guests and laughter. Women in groups simultaneously carried on conversations at several pitches. The baby, passed from hand to hand, cried, unable to bear the disturbance around him. A smell of incense, flowers and sandalwood filled the air, as on any auspicious occasion. The two grandfathers retired to a corner for a moment, leaving the other guests. 'Mali,' said one, 'will have a deposit of a thousand rupees, earmarked, to which we will add a hundred on each birthday. This has been the practice in our family for generations whenever a child is born.'

'So is it with us,' said the other. 'After all, we must provide for the new one and give him a good start in life.'

'A new son in the house is a true treasure in this life and beyond life.'

'I was dreading Jagan would be without issue,' said Jagan's father.

'I was in no doubt at any time. Barrenness is unknown in our house.'

A look of triumph glowed on Jagan's face as he went from guest to guest, prostrated at their feet, and received blessings. Ambika followed him, prostrated, and was also blessed by everyone. She held herself up proudly, having now attained the proper status in the family. She looked especially gratified that she had enabled them to add, if it could somehow be done, one more figure to the group photographs on the walls of both the houses.

Chapter Thirteen

Brooding on the past, Jagan must have dozed off at the foot of the statue. He was awakened by the clamour of birds alighting on the head of Sir F. Lawley. Jagan bestirred himself and looked at his house, now touched by the morning light, its heavy cornices emerging into view. 'A little brighter now than at night,' he said to himself, 'but it has an unhappy look; it will never get back the light and laughter of other days. Who's there to brighten it? Not my son, nor his so-called – what do we call her, really? What name shall I give her? Anyway, where are they? Lost sight of. They don't come home. Where do they go? Never tell me. They are both alike. They are not the sort to make a home bright, unlike my mother or even Ambika when she was well. On the contrary, they blacken their surroundings. Probably they will be happier without me there.'

Jagan felt it would be impossible for him to get back to that house. 'It's tainted, but it is not my house that's tainted. It is his. Who am I to grumble and fret? I am sixty, and I may live for only ten or fifteen years more, whereas Mali, with or without his story-machine, will have to go on for sixty or more years in that house. May he be blessed with longevity!' Jagan revelled for a moment in visions of Mali at eighty, and that profoundly moved his heart. But the immediate thought was: 'Where will Grace be when Mali is eighty? Still in the same situation?' Perhaps Mali would succeed in sending her back. It was the best possible solution – if they still spurned his suggestion for a quick solemnization in the hills.

He felt hurt at the recollection as if a needle had probed a wound. 'I have probably outlived my purpose in this house. If I live for ten or fifteen years more, it will have to be on a different plane. At sixty, one is reborn and enters a new *janma*.' That was the reason why people celebrated their sixtieth birthdays. He remembered his father and mother, his uncle and aunt and a score of other couples celebrated a man's sixtieth year like a wedding, with pipe, drum and feasting. People loved to celebrate one thing or another all the time. He had had his fill of them, and had nothing to complain of. Mali had proved that there was no need for ceremonials, not even the business of knotting the *thali* around the bride's neck. Nothing, no bonds or links or responsibility. Come together, live together, and kick away each other when it suited them. Whoever kicked harder got away first. Kick? Where was the kick? They sat in the green car with their legs intertwined in spite of what they had said of each other. Puzzling over things was ennervating. Reading a sense into Mali's actions was fatiguing like the attempt to spell out a message in a half-familiar script. He had no need to learn anything more. No more unravelling of conundrums just as there was not going to be any more feast or music in that shuttered house before him. When his sixtieth birthday came, it would pass unnoticed. A widower had no right to celebrate anything. He was fit only for retirement. What a magic word! If one had to shake off things, one did it unmistakably, completely, without leaving any loophole or a path back.

He still had to pay his visit to his house, to collect a few things he needed, though he would prefer to walk off, just walk, as the Buddha did when he got enlightenment. It was five o'clock, his usual hour for the bath for half a century.

An hour later, after his morning ablutions and nourishment, he came out of his house, carrying a little bundle, in which among other things was included his *charka*. 'It's a duty I owe Mahatma Gandhi. I made a vow before him that I would spin every day of my life. I've to do it, whether I'm at home or in a forest.'

The sunlight, the cold bath and the gruel he had had, mitigated somewhat the ardour of his renunciation. He still had the key in his hand. 'Must leave it somewhere,' he thought, 'with someone. I can't take it with me . . . But why not, after all, it is the back-door key. The main key must be with Mali. If he never opens the door again, well, it's his business: it's his house that is going to become haunted with evil spirits, which might throw things about with a clatter.' Jagan did not fully believe in it, but he knew instances of deserted houses where such things happened. After all, evil spirits too needed accommodation somewhere. He chuckled at the thought of his inquiring, inquisitive neighbour. 'Let him ask all the questions he likes of the ghost storming my house.'

He still felt bothered about the key. 'Why can't I leave it with my brother? It will be a good excuse to visit him.' He toyed with the idea. Engage Gaffur's taxi, run to Vinayak Street and leave the house key with his brother. Years ago, when he was chosen to take part in the National Struggle, he took elaborate leave of everyone before volunteering for arrest. How his brother had tears in his eyes. The entire family were moved by his self-abnegation, accompanied him in a body half-way down the street, although they disapproved generally of his patriotic acts. He sighed for those warm and crowded days, and longed for a similar send-off now. When they could show such intense feelings for a jail-going man, they could as well display a little of it to one retreating from life – even more so since this was going to be a kind of death actually, although he'd breathe, watch, and occasionally keep in touch, but the withdrawal would not be different from death. He longed for a nice, crowded send-off now. But only his brother was left of an entire generation. He felt a longing for a glimpse of him. He had lost all his teeth according to the cousin and Jagan felt curious to know what he looked like now. He felt nostalgic for his brother's gruff voice uttering clipped sentences; ever a positive man and a born leader of younger brothers. The whole street was likely to crowd around Gaffur's taxi to look at one who was reputed to have become the father-in-law of a girl of outlandish origin. His brother would probably keep him standing in the street and tell him to throw him the key from a distance since Jagan's shadow was likely to taint the threshold. He might have to shout his explanation across, 'I am off to a retreat. I'm sixty and in a new *janma*.' He might have to speak about Mali too. 'It's not only his marriage, but you must know the latest truth that they are not married at all, but carry tales against each other, although they sit close in a motor car.' And his brother might shout back, 'Get away, you polluter of family reputations.' And that crowd surrounding his taxi might jeer and laugh, obstruct his taxi, and force him to miss his bus at the Market Gate. Thus he would get caught again in the day's routine, and another day's and another day's. Impossible thought. 'Better carry away the key. After all, it's the back door.'

When passing Sir Frederick Lawley, he saw his cousin riding down clumsily on a bicycle, his tuft flying in the wind, his wheels zig-zagging perilously on to the edge of the storm drain and retracting miraculously to the centre of the road. Jagan stood arrested by the spectacle as he had never seen the cousin on a bicycle before. The wheels seemed to come straight for him. Shouting incoherent inquiries, Jagan stepped aside. The cousin helplessly dashed past him a dozen yards, and fell off the saddle, leaving the bicycle to bolt away by itself to a ditch. He picked himself up as Jagan got over his wonderment and demanded, 'What is this circus-feat so early in the day? At your age! You may kill yourself.'

'Don't I know?' panted the cousin, dusting off the mud on the scratches at his elbow. 'I was in a hurry to meet you and so borrowed the bicycle from my neighbour. If you don't mind, I'll leave it in your house. I dare not ride it back.'

Jagan said, 'I have locked my house and am not going back.' The unmistakable firmness of his tone made the cousin proceed straight to business. 'Come with me. Our lawyer is waiting. Mali needs immediate help.'

'Ah! What has happened?'

'Mali is in prison since last evening . . .' Jagan came to a dead stop on the road and screamed, 'Oh God! Why?'

'He was found with half a bottle of alcohol in his car.'

'Siva!' cried Jagan. 'That's why I discouraged his idea of buying that horrible car!' He vented his rage against the green automobile until the cousin interrupted, 'A bottle could be sneaked in anywhere . . .'

'You don't understand. It's the motor car that creates all sorts of notions in a young fellow,' said Jagan and found an agreeable escape into this theme. 'Everything would have been well if he hadn't bought that car.'

'Don't interrupt me, listen,' said the cousin. 'You must get him out of the police lock-up at once. It's not a good place to be in. We could have got him out last night, if you had not disappeared. Where were you?'

'I was only sleeping on the statue,' Jagan said and remembered his wife's taunts whenever he proposed to sleep out.

'Fine time you chose to give the statue company while I was searching for you everywhere!' exclaimed the cousin, 'We could have got Mali out last night.'

'Oh, what can we do now? Poor boy! In the lock-up! He won't feel comfortable: he has always slept on a spring mattress, since he was seven. How can I get him out?' Tears blurred his sight, until the cousin looked distorted, corrugated and dwarfish. The cousin watched him calmly and said, 'Come, come. Don't let that vagrant see the tears in your eyes.' The cousin was extremely practical and knew exactly what should be done. No wonder he was in such demand, thought Jagan, all over the town. Any crisis in any house, a funeral, marriage, accident or a litigation, brought to the surface the best in the cousin. Jagan asked, 'Which lock-up?'

'In the sub-jail, until the trial begins. Get up, get up. Let us go and see if . . .'

Jagan felt giddy. He pressed his temples with his palms: 'Don't pile on so much. I can't stand it.' He felt faint and stretched himself flat at the foot of the statue.

The cousin said, 'Let us go back to your house.'

'No,' said Jagan resolutely.

'You need·rest. Don't worry. I will manage everything for you . . .' The cousin patted his shoulder tenderly and said, 'Don't lose your nerve, what is all your philosophy worth if you cannot bear this little trial?'

'In the sub-jail . . .' Jagan wailed. 'I know the place; it is very dirty, prisoners urinate in a corner of the lock-up, or have they improved the conditions since my days?' he asked, blowing his nose.

'Naturally, it is all different now.'

'Oh, yes, it must be different, I know, though so awful in those British days.'

The cousin went on, 'The first thing I did was to go out to the sub-jail and plead with the warders there. I saw the boy and spoke to him. I managed to get him a cup of coffee also.'

'Did you give him anything to eat? He must have been hungry.'

'They'll treat him specially. I know the District Collector, and so we can get things done. I got the news at six o'clock. I was returning from the house of the Superintending Engineer where I had gone to fix up a home-tutor for their son. At the turning near the General Post Office an orderly from the Superintendent's house gave me the news. The green car was halted at the Mempi outpost where they generally check for prohibition offences, as they find a lot of illicit distilling and traffic in the jungles high up. A policeman seems to have stopped Mali's car and found hidden in it half a bottle of some alcoholic drink, and you know how it is . . . The police immediately seized the car, sealed the bottle before witnesses, and have charged the inmates of the car under the Prohibition Act.'

'Who else was there?'

'Two of his friends.'

'Oh, his friends have been his ruin. Where is the car now?'

'They drove it down. It will be kept at the police station till the case is finished.'

Jagan sat up, shut his eyes and remained silent, his lips moving in a prayer. 'I . . . I didn't know the boy drank,' he said, coming on a fresh discovery about his son.

'One doesn't have to drink to be caught by the Prohibition. It is enough if one's breath smells of alcohol. There are some fever mixtures which have an alcoholic flavour. A doctor has to certify that he had administered two doses of a fever mixture earlier in the day, that is all.'

'Who would be that doctor?'

'Oh, you are wasting time. Come on, let us go,' the cousin cried impatiently. 'The lawyer will manage all that. Trust him and leave it in his hands . . .'

'What was the green car's business in the hills?'

'That's beside the point . . . Anyway, Mali had gone up to confer with some parties on his business, undisturbed at the Peak House. He was expecting someone representing his foreign collaborators.'

Jagan recovered his composure. 'Ah, foreign collaborators! Impressive words. No one in India knows about business. Always foreign! Well, accepted, sir. But the bottle? How did it get in?'

'Some one left it there. A stranger stopped the car on the mountain road, asked for a lift, got off on the way, and perhaps left the bottle behind.' Jagan felt partly relieved at such possibilities. He studied his cousin's face to judge the quantum of truth in his explanations, but that man avoided his eyes, and said generally, 'Anything is possible these days. You can't trust people, especially strangers. When I didn't find you in, I went in search of Ganesh Rau, our lawyer, the best in our district. Though he is up to his neck in work, he has accepted our case; he knows Mali and admires his plans. He seems to have promised to buy shares in Mali's company when the time comes.'

'Does he believe Mali's machine can write stories?'

'I'd no time to discuss all that, but he said, "Why not?" when I mentioned it.'

Jagan became reflective. The cousin said, 'All that apart, the case is very strongly in our favour. We sat discussing all the possibilities until two o'clock in the morning. I could find no time for sleep at all. At five o'clock I borrowed the bicycle and fell off it four times before reaching you.'

'Don't go on a bicycle again. You may kill yourself,' said Jagan pontifically.

The cousin said, 'He is also looking into the antecedents of the policeman who checked Mali's car at the outpost. That stranger who accosted them could have been the policeman's accomplice. They must have had a grudge against you.'

'Why?' asked Jagan, 'Why should any policeman bear a grudge against me?'

'For a hundred reasons,' said the cousin. 'People are generally bad. He might have been demanding free packets of sweets from your shop; after all, poor fellows, they are so ill-paid that they do seek favours from shop-men. You might not remember it now; but you will have to try and recollect how you threatened to report him to his officers.'

'I have never seen a policeman in my shop . . .'

'Or he might have marked you in those days when you violated the laws . . .' Jagan laughed at this idea.

'If a grudge was to be borne, we had greater cause than the police.'

'Very well, it could be so . . .'

'But Mahatma Gandhi trained us not to nurse any resentment . . . Anyway, the policeman of our days must all be senile or dead now.'

'Or he might have had a brush with Mali some time. Policemen are generally prejudiced against young people driving scooters or cars, you know. This is all just casual talk, that's all; the lawyer will instruct you what to say. We should depend upon his guidance. One thing is certain. Just answer his cross-examination as he directs you. The whole issue will turn on your evidence.'

Jagan said briefly, 'If what you say is true, well, truth will win. If it is not true, there is nothing I can do.'

*

'No, no, don't say so. We must do our best to get Mali out. They could sentence him up to two years under this Act.'

'Who are we to get him out or to put him in?' asked Jagan philosophically. He had recovered from the first shock totally, and spoke even impishly now, although his voice was still a little thick with grief. 'Truth ought to get him out, if what you say is true,' he repeated.

'But the lawyer will have to build it up and establish it,' said the cousin, 'with proper evidence. He is thinking of ways and means. If he is able to establish the malafides of the policeman, we may even file a counter-case in order to strengthen ours.'

Jagan's mind had attained extraordinary clarity now. He threw a look at his bag, lightly lifted it and said, 'I wish you all luck; you and your lawyer and his distinguished client and also that poor soul – the policeman who had the misfortune to stop the green car; but don't expect me to take any part in it. Leave me out of it completely; forget me and I'll go away without asking too many questions.'

'Where, where are you going?' asked the cousin anxiously.

'I will seek a new interest – different from the set of repetitions performed for sixty years. I am going somewhere, not carrying more than what my shoulder can bear. All that I need is in that bag . . .'

'Including the bank book, I suppose,' asked the cousin, 'which is a compact way of carrying things. How far are you going?'

Jagan described the retreat across the river. The cousin was aghast: 'I know that place near the cremation ground. Has that hair-dyer been trying to sell it to you? Forgive me if I say "Keep away from him." He is a sorcerer: knows black magic and offers to transmute base metals into gold . . .'

'I don't care what he does. I am going to watch a goddess come out of a stone. If I don't like the place, I will go away somewhere else. I am a free man. I've never felt more determined in my life. I'm happy to have met you now, but I'd have gone away in any case. Everything can go with or without me. The world doesn't collapse even when a great figure is assassinated or dies of heart failure. Think that my heart has failed, that's all.'

He gave the cousin a bunch of keys and said, 'Open the shop at the usual hour and run it. Mali will take charge of it eventually. Keep Sivaraman and the rest happy; don't throw them out. You can always come over to the retreat if there is anything urgent, or to render an account. I'll tell you what to do. At the Market Gate buses leave for Mempi every four hours starting from eight-thirty in the morning. You are a busy man, but please help me now.'

'Yes, I'll do anything you say,' said the cousin, rather intimidated by Jagan's tone. 'The lawyer wanted two thousand rupees for preliminary expenses. He will arrange the bail. Mali should be out before this evening.'

'A dose of prison life is not a bad thing. It may be just what he needs now,' said Jagan, opening his bag and taking out his cheque-book. Resting it on his knee, he wrote out a cheque and handed it to the cousin.

'If there are further charges?' asked the cousin.

'We'll pay them, that is all. You can ask me whenever you like. I am not flying away to another planet.' The cousin was amazed at the transformation in Jagan, who kept repeating, his eyes still wet, 'A little prison life won't harm anyone. I must not miss the bus at Market Gate at eight-thirty. I don't want to ask questions, but tell me where is she?' he asked, rising and shouldering his bag.

'She has friends who have found a job for her in a women's hostel,' began the cousin, but Jagan dismissed the subject halfway through the other's explanation and said, 'If you meet her, tell her that if she ever wants to go back to her country, I will buy her a ticket. It's a duty we owe her. She was a good girl.'

MORE ABOUT PENGUINS
AND PELICANS

For further information about books available from Penguins please write to Dept EP, Penguin Books Ltd, Harmondsworth, Middlesex UB7 0DA.

In the U.S.A.: For a complete list of books available from Penguins in the United States write to Dept CS, Penguin Books, 625 Madison Avenue, New York, New York 10022.

In Canada: For a complete list of books available from Penguins in Canada write to Penguin Books Canada Ltd, 2801 John Street, Markham, Ontario L3R 1B4.

In Australia: For a complete list of books available from Penguins in Australia write to the Marketing Department, Penguin Books Australia Ltd, P.O. Box 257, Ringwood, Victoria 3134.

In New Zealand: For a complete list of books available from Penguins in New Zealand write to the Marketing Department, Penguin Books (N.Z.) Ltd, P.O. Box 4019, Auckland 10.